THE LIPTON STORY

ERRATA

Under BY THE SAME AUTHOR for *That American Woman* read *So Lovers Dream;* for *The Sugar Islands* read *The Sunlit Caribbean.* On page 1 four lines from foot should read 'earning twenty-five shillings a week'

SIR THOMAS LIPTON

THE
LIPTON STORY

A Centennial Biography

By

ALEC WAUGH

CASSELL AND COMPANY LIMITED
LONDON, TORONTO, MELBOURNE, SYDNEY AND
WELLINGTON

First published March 1951
Reprinted May 1951

Printed in Great Britain by
Lowe and Brydone Printers Limited, London, N.W.10

THE LIPTON STORY

IN THE late autumn of 1849 an Irish-born working-woman on the brink of middle age, who had crossed to Glasgow with her husband a few years earlier, recognised that she was pregnant. Of the five children she had already borne, two only were still alive, and they, a boy and a girl, were in weak health. As autumn turned into winter, the long grey winter of the Clyde, her hopes and dreams for the child she carried were centred upon its health. She prayed for it to be strong in limb and artery. She had no other ambitions for it.

There was small reason why she should. As far back as any record told, her forebears and her husband's—the Johnstones and the Liptons—had lived in Monaghan, near Clones. They were Protestant farmers, concerned with duty and survival, sound solid people, contented with their lot. It was not ambition but the lack of work, the need to eat, that had driven her husband and herself, as it had driven so many other Irish families, to emigrate during the potato famine. She was a practical God-fearing woman with little leisure. She indulged no pipe dreams of sons who built palaces, of daughters who married princes. Her husband was industrious, broad-shouldered, honest, earning at the moment six dollars a week as timekeeper in a paper mill but planning as soon as he had saved enough to open a small grocery. If the child to be born in May should be a daughter, her mother would be proud and happy if she married as good a man; if a boy, should he support a home so honourably.

No child could have been born of a more solid stock; no child could have been destined to fit into a more simple pattern. There was no background of rebel blood, of alien ancestry, of erratic conduct to account for the releasing of an energy so dynamic that before the century had closed the signature of Thomas Lipton on a seven-figure cheque would be honoured in any bank, that the colours of Thomas Lipton would be challenging the wealth and skill of America in one of the greatest sporting adventures of all time, that the hand of Thomas Lipton should have shaken the hands of royalty not only as a guest but as a host. Heredity offers no explanation for the phenomenon of Thomas Lipton.

Nor does sociology, even though Britain in 1850 was entering, in the wake of the industrial revolution, a period of prosperous expansion; which meant in terms of the nineteenth century that a number of opportunists became millionaires, that a vast number of middlemen grew affluent and very many thousands lived in penury, with Glasgow as much as any city in Great Britain exemplifying those changes and those contrasts. A lift was going up, and Glasgow was well placed in it; the discovery of the value of blackband ironstone, up till then regarded as useless "wild coal," and Neilson's invention of the hot-air blast were turning the control of the Scottish iron trade into the hands of the local iron masters. The spreading tentacles of the empire, the expanding frontiers of the United States were demanding carrier services. Steam was supplanting sail, and the Clyde contained the finest shipbuilding yards in Britain. At the turn of the century the population of the city had stood below eighty thousand. It doubled that figure within the next twenty years. It had redoubled and was on its way to trebling it by the time Lipton reached his teens. The law of supply and demand as the nineteenth century understood it was in full operation.

But even though his father was a man whose weekly wage never touched thirty shillings, Thomas Lipton was never to feel himself the victim of unequal circumstances. On the contrary, he was to maintain that he had been given a good start in life. There were slums in plenty then in certain districts. But though his parents were poor his home was very far from squalid. The Scots are thrifty. "A thick 'un," as the gold sovereign was then called in contrast to the smaller half-sovereign piece, purchased a good deal. The yearly rent of the Lipton home was a bare twelve pounds, but that rent provided a four-room flat on the top floor of a four-storeyed house.

The street still stands—a long straight stretch on the south side of the river of flat-faced, flat-roofed houses. Most of the ground-floor storeys have been converted into shops, but here and there the original tenement pattern, built on the French model, can be discerned—no front doors opening on the street, but every fifteen yards or so a low and narrow entrance with main doors opening off it and at the end a stone stairway curving to the upper storeys. The group of houses linked by this common entrance is called a close. A succession of back yards runs behind. There is little to distinguish Crown Street from a hundred others, except that it stands near the "Blazes," the great blast furnaces of Dixon's factories that stain the sky night after night with smoke and fire.

It was a sombre, dingy thoroughfare; but it was the home then, as it is now, of quiet, self-respecting families who took a pride in their few possessions. A door mat was intended to be used. When Lipton's father came back from work a warm substantial meal was waiting him. There would be Scotch broth or potato soup, home-baked scones and oatcakes. In the morning he would start off to his paper mill, nourished by a bowl of porridge.

Young Lipton's boyhood provides none of those passages of thwarted impulse and ingrown jealousy that spur and direct so much ambition. He never smarted under a feeling of injustice, never itched with a sense of inferiority, never felt the need to justify himself, to set himself right with people, to even out a score. His childhood was extremely happy.

He was proud of his home and of his family; of his brother, a quiet pale young man who was studying to be a doctor; of his sister, a thin dark-haired girl with very large dark brown eyes who embroidered with exquisite needlework his mother's scarves and handkerchiefs. He was proud of his family, particularly on Sundays when they set out, the five of them, for church, his brother looking very youthful in a white bow tie, wide-ended and wide-knotted, somewhat like a Christmas cracker; his mother and sister in wide black crinolines, with tight-fitting bodices and white lace at the wrist and throat; his father with black gloves and a black high-buttoned coat that fell away above the heavy links of a gold watch chain, his thick grey beard concealing the black four-in-hand tie that filled the entire gap between his coat and collar. He was proud, too, of the provision shop that his father was to open later, at No. 11, in the house next door. It was small; very small. But it was their own. He enjoyed the going and the coming, the exchange of gossip. He enjoyed the drama of it all, the wondering what each customer would buy and in what quantity. He enjoyed watching his father dress the window. Sometimes he was allowed to help. He had few toys at home. His parents could not afford them. But he did not miss toys once the shop was opened. The shop became his nursery; he would think out new ways of arranging the hams and butter as the child of richer parents thinks out new patterns for his bricks and soldiers. Once when his father was serving eggs he said, "Why not let Mother serve them? Her hands are smaller. They would make the eggs look larger."

Most of the provisions the small shop stocked, the eggs, the butter, and the hams, were shipped from Ireland by a peasant farmer, a friend of Mrs. Lipton. Young Tommy would go down to the docks to meet the Irish packet. It was a proud day when he first wheeled his barrow along the Broomielaw. He received from his mother a weekly wage—of fourpence.

From the age of seven, the year his brother died, he was sent to school. In those days education was not compulsory, but schools were cheap and the standard of elementary education has always been high in Scotland. In the St. Andrew's parish school, facing Parish Green, for a weekly fee of sixpence paid personally to the headmaster, he learned to read and write, to add and subtract and multiply. The headmaster was a man of character, to whom Lipton in later years was to pay high tribute. But the Broomielaw was more fascinating than the schoolroom. Young Tommy had none of the studious instincts of his brother. He wanted to be about, to be doing things, seeing people, listening to their talk. As his tenth year passed he grew restless when he heard his parents discussing ways and means: the pile of savings was not growing as rapidly as it should. He felt guilty to be sitting at a desk, before a blackboard, having money spent on him when his parents were in difficulties. He was strong and broad and healthy. He ought to be earning money.

On a grey November morning in 1860 he set out as usual across the river with his satchel, but not, however, to turn right out of Saltmarket into Parish Green. He went straight on to Trongate. Then he turned left, looking at window after window till at last in Glassford Street he saw outside a stationer's—A. W. Kennedy—a notice: *Boy wanted. Apply within.*

His eyes were bright that night as he hurried back through Crown Street, with the satchel he was carrying for the last time banging against his hip. He was a worker now; every Saturday he would receive a bright half crown. His eagerness, his excitement overcame his parents' opposition. There was no school-leaving age; there were no inspectors of education then.

The next months were among his happiest. His work was varied. He was always being sent on errands to this or the other section of the town. He learned to know Glasgow as he knew his pocket. Glasgow is not an obvious city. Its skies are grey and its mists keep breaking into rain. It is built out of a cream-coloured local granite that soot and smoke have darkened. In spite of its medieval clock towers with their gilt hands and numerals, it is not a tourist's city. For a schoolboy, though, it is "a finger beckoning to adventure." At the ends of its streets are masts and funnels. There is the sense always of the sea, and the sense that the sea brings of things being about to happen. It would have been strange if young Lipton had not learned to love it.

He loved, too, the independence of the wage earner. He was half free of discipline. He attended night school for a little, but his new headmaster was uninspiring. He soon broke off his studies. He was happier in the streets and round the docks. He was big for his age, and strong. He had none of the organic weakness that had killed his brother and kept his sister pale. He gave and received blows easily in the rough-and-tumble of the gutters. He was soon one of the chief figures in the "Crown Street Clan," leading and planning raids upon the other streets, fighting and being beaten by the area bully, but giving so nearly as good as he was given that the bully kept away from Crown Street in the future.

In what is known now as Glasgow Green, but then was called Low and High Green, levelling operations had left a number of large holes which had filled up with muddy water. On these ponds in the evenings the Crown Street Clan would sail wooden boats that they cut out of the lids of boxes with their pocket clasp knives. They formed a yacht club of which young Tommy was the commodore. Because of his Irish ancestry, he christened his yacht the *Shamrock*. "I doubt," he was to comment later, "if the sons of the rich ever have quite such free-hearted happiness as the children of poor people do."

He was happy with the Crown Street Clan, he was happy sailing his wooden yacht, but his happiest times were on the docks; and indeed those were exciting times along the Broomielaw. The Anchor Line had only just been founded, but its progress during its first years was rapid. Within a few months of the sailing of its first liner, the *Tempest*, to Bombay, a Lisbon service was started, another began to South America, and a fourth to Quebec and Montreal. With excited eyes he would match the traffic of the quay, would watch the *Vasco da Gama* and the *Ignez de Castro* being loaded for the Mediterranean ports with pig iron and manufactured goods, to return a few weeks later with oranges, lemons, dried fruit, and oil. On a September afternoon in his eleventh year he was to watch the launching of the *United States*. Three-masted, carrying sail, and single-funnelled, riding low in the water and with no high superstructure, she seems now in pictures more like a yacht than a transatlantic liner; indeed her tonnage was a bare twelve hundred tons. Yet she was able to maintain with the *John Bell* and the *United Kingdom* a regular fortnightly service to New York. To the eyes of a ten-year-old boy in 1860 she was as much the symbol of romance and glamour as ever the "Queens" were to be in the 1940s.

The days were few when he did not spend at least a few minutes on the docks. He would watch the sailors at work upon the decks; he would gossip with the stevedores and longshoremen; he learned more geography from their stories of far places than ever he had learned at school. He would repeat over to himself as though they were magic charms the names that kept punctuating the sailors' talk— New Orleans, Valparaiso, Philadelphia. He bought himself an atlas so that he could trace their journeys.

He was happy, but he was at the same time restless. A half-crown piece a week was not enough. He looked for a better job and found it, with a hosier's, Tillit and Henderson, now of Prince's Square, then of Miller Street, to cut out cloth patterns and gum them into sample books for travelling salesmen. Before he had been in this employ a month he asked by letter for a raise of salary. He was answered by the cashier with a pencilled note: "You are getting as much as you are worth and you are in a devil of a hurry asking for a rise." More than forty years were to pass before he was to receive another note under the firm's letter heading and then under a very different circumstance.

He accepted the cashier's rebuff; there was nothing else for him to do, but his heart was not in his work. He counted the hours till he could escape to the Crown Street Clan. He had no use for the drudgery of routine work at a desk, but his Scottish training would not allow him to throw up the five shillings a week. He held down this job till a better one came his way, as a cabin boy on one of the Burns steamers that plied nightly between Glasgow and Belfast. He was paid eight shillings a week and all found. He had not believed that any boy of thirteen could be so rich. It was a hard life that entitled him to such riches, but it was not too rough for him. He loved the sea; he loved the life of ships; he loved the constantly recurring dramas of arrival and departure: the sailings at night, the anchorings at dawn, the ghostly look of the Clyde on summer mornings as the ship steamed up from Gourock, the sun already mounting but scarcely a sign of life along the roads.

He loved the companionship of the crew, the talk of sailors, the occasional glimpses of the passengers as they paced the deck in their heavy ulsters; as they sat after dinner in the saloon over their brandies and water and cigars. They were business men for the most part, salesmen and representatives of firms, with a fair sprinkling

B

of sportsmen and tourists. As he hurried about the ship upon his duties he would always pause as he passed their quarters, catching a glimpse through an open doorway and a haze of smoke of bearded, bewhiskered faces. He was impressed by their patrician manner; their stiff-starched linen had a polish, their black braided coats a gloss that he had never seen on Sunday in the church at Hutchestown. He would ask the stewards who they were. It was the first glimpse he had had of the world of prominence and wealth. On his returns to Crown Street he would excitedly describe their habits, recounting the gossip of the lower decks. Three quarters of the thrill that any adventure, any chance conversation brought him was the telling of it to his mother afterwards.

Between son and mother there was a strong and strengthening bond. Here at last was the son that she had longed for, that she had despaired of having. Instinct warned her that the thin dark girl who was so skilful with her needle would never bear her grandchildren. There had been times, many times during her later thirties, when she had wondered whether she and her husband should not have had the courage, as so many of their countrymen had had, to sail west instead of east, to America instead of Scotland, to the wider opportunities, the fresher, cleaner air of a new continent. She had wondered, often wondered. She knew now that she need not have. Tommy was strong and healthy, vigorous and vital, always full of schemes. Here at last was the son that she had dreamed of, the son who would justify her womanhood.

As she sewed and ironed—she was never idle for an instant—she would listen proudly when he told her of all that he had seen and heard and done. His blue eyes glistened in a way that warmed her, in a way that frightened her as well. As she watched him leaning above his atlas, noting how his voice glowed, how it seemed to linger over the syllables of those magic words—Chicago, San Francisco, Charleston—as though he were sipping a rich wine, she knew that he would not be content for long to sail across a narrow channel.

His love of the sea frightened her, yet the same instinct which had warned her of her elder son's short tenure assured her that she would not lose her younger one. He would always come back to her in the end. When the moment came for him to go he must have his head.

It came, that moment, sooner than she had expected and in a way that she had not expected. Trouble had been raised upon the steamer. One of the cabin lamps had smoked, discolouring the ceiling. A scapegoat was demanded. In those days cabin boys were not protected by a seaman's union. Young Lipton was held to be responsible. He was given a week's wages and told to go. He was not despondent, though. He was thrifty and he had saved. He strolled down the Broomielaw. An Anchor Line steamer was taking cargo. Where was she bound? he asked. New York, they told him. Were they taking on steerage passengers? Of course they were. In those days there was no need for passports, for visas, for quota numbers. The road of private enterprise ran broad. A steerage ticket cost eighteen dollars. Young Lipton was not yet fifteen. Ninety-nine parents in a hundred would have exercised or threatened to exercise their legal rights. His mother had been reconciled to maybe a year-long journey, but not to this. So many of her countrymen had crossed the Atlantic.

They had talked, nearly all of them, of coming back, but so few had. Each month, each year, the hold of the home country had grown weaker. They had formed new ties. The odds against Tommy's coming back were high. She knew, though, that she must not cross him. She set about his packing as though he were going to Edinburgh for a week-end visit.

§ 2

He sailed in the early spring of 1865. In later life he was to say that he had crossed on the *Devonia*. His memory, however, played him false. The *Devonia* was not built till 1878. It was in one of five other ships that he must have travelled. Nearly a quarter of a million emigrants, mainly Irish and German, were now crossing the Atlantic every year. Successful settlers were buying prepaid tickets and sending them back home. The recent decision of the Anchor Line's directorate to abandon their Montreal service—which had been impeded by the closed winter season of the St. Lawrence—in favour of a direct New York service had been amply justified. In the very year that young Lipton sailed it had started a regular weekly service with a fleet of five ships—*John Bell, Hibernia, Brittania I, United Kingdom, Caledonia II*—and a gross tonnage of just under 7000. The *Caledonia II* was over 2000 tons, with a sea speed of 10½ knots and accommodation for 60 saloon and 550 third-class passengers.

In any of these he may have travelled. But though we do not know the actual ship, we can guess how he travelled, and in what company. We can picture the crowded quarters, the litter of trunks and bundles, the packages of food—steerage passengers fed themselves—the babble of foreign tongues, the despair on certain faces, the hope on others. It is all of it in *Martin Chuzzlewit*.

In later years, when he raced across the Atlantic in six days, he would compare the setting of that first journey—the bare tables, the backless benches, the clustered mattresses, the ill-cooked stews—with the wide verandahs, the thick carpets, the deep upholstering, the specially ordered menus of the *Leviathan* and *Celtic*. He would compare the company of these later voyages—the bankers and the politicians, the socialites and artists—with the uncouth emigrants of that first crossing, the inarticulate, uneducated adventurers, to some of whom he endeared himself by writing their letters home.

Nor was the New York which was to welcome him in those days any less different externally from the New York that he was to see for the first time on that late April morning. No Statue of Liberty was lifting its torch of freedom. No sky line of jagged battlements came within sight as the steamer swung round past quarantine. The meadows of Hoboken ran green along the west bank of the Hudson. The spire of Trinity Church was the highest landmark of downtown Manhattan. Externally it was an altogether different city; yet not at heart. There was the same tonic quality to the air, the same atmosphere of speed and hurry, of confidence and competition, the same sense of a new world opening.

When the ship drew to its moorings young Lipton had less than eight dollars in his pocket. In the whole continent of North America he did not possess a single friend. He felt no qualms, however. He would make his way all right. As he leaned against the taffrail he could see on the docks below a number of hotel touts offering their custom. An idea struck him, and he dashed down the gangplank. He sought the canvassers till he saw a face that he could trust, till he heard an Irish voice. "I've friends aboard," he said. "What are you offering if I bring you a dozen lodgers?" "Free lodgings for a week," he was informed. He hurried back on board. He canvassed among the passengers whose home letters he had written. Within half an hour he was back with his dozen lodgers.

The house to which he took them, Mike McCalligan's at 27A Washington, no longer stands. The entire lower section of the street has been torn up. But from the scattered sections of it that still remain it is possible to recreate its appearance in the '60s. A succession of red brick four-storey houses with iron balconies, running parallel with the Hudson, it may well have reminded young Lipton of the Broomielaw, with the tall chimneys of Babbitt's soap factory to recall Dixon's "Blazes."

In later years he made a point, on every visit to New York, of driving through the section of the city that he had known in boyhood. The sections that were familiar grew yearly fewer. The population had been under a million then and there were no skyscrapers. The Battery had only just ceased to be a fashionable promenade where bustled ladies could saunter under the trees to catch the fresh sea air. Only a few weeks before had the Commissioner of Emigration taken over Castle Garden. Yorkville was a village. Bloomingdale Church stood on a rocky promontory opposite a farm, with a sloping roof stretched over a kind of gallery like a Swiss or German house. The Old

Tavern, the winter rendezvous of sleighing parties, still stood, but with its fences down and its path hidden by weeds. Central Park had recently been opened, with the Crystal Palace bringing the city as far north as Forty-second Street. Union Square was still a fashionable residential centre with a fountain playing in its garden. Broadway and Fifth Avenue were the only arteries of traffic down which horse-buses were not drawn on rails. The side streets were dirty and uneven, full of holes and ruts. Fifth Avenue, from Washington Square to the reservoir on Forty-first Street, was a sombre if imposing succession of private houses. At night, with the curtains drawn across its windows and the pavements silent, it was to seem to a French visitor accustomed to the *opéra bouffe* atmosphere of Napoleon III's Paris a street of tombs, like Cairo's city of the dead. The colour, the noise, the animation, all that is symbolised by the two words New York, were concentrated upon Broadway, that "grand succession of commercial palaces" with its "gaily coloured brick, its brownstone and granite giving way here and there to white marble, pure and brilliant without speck or flaw," its sidewalks lined with elms, the broad thoroughfare swarming with white two-horse-drawn omnibuses whose high-perched driver you paid through the roof.

The New Yorker of the 1940s would not know where he was could he be transported backwards through time to the New York of the 1860s. Yet just as Martin Chuzzlewit's bewilderment is recognisably akin to that of many present-day Englishmen on their first evening in Manhattan, so are Lipton's early experiences in 1865 being reproduced to-day. The crowded lodging-house, the eight beds crammed into one small room, the polyglot attempts at conversation, the sudden quarrels after drink over some imagined insult, the tramping of strange streets in search of work, the diminishing store of savings, the fear of what will happen when the last cent is spent, all these the displaced person of the 1940s knows; these were the lot of the young Lipton in the 1860s.

In one sense he arrived in America at an unlucky, in another sense at a lucky, period. The Civil War had just ended. War industries were closing down; demobilised soldiers were flooding back. Prices were high. There was a lack of work. For days young Lipton harassed the labour agencies in vain. But though the labour markets of the North were crowded, in the ruined, devastated South there was a desperate need for labour. There was a job in Virginia in the tobacco fields. Would he care to take on that? the agent asked him. He would say he would.

Taking a long view, he was lucky to have arrived in America when he did. At almost any other time a young man of his drive and vigour would have found work in New York. If he had, he would never have got that knowledge of, that feeling for, the country which later was to prove invaluable.

For the next forty months he was to travel up and down the country, between the eastern seaboard and the Mississippi. He worked in South Carolina in the rice fields, as a carman outside New Orleans, as a fireman in Charleston, as a plantation bookkeeper. His life had the picaresque quality of a Smollett novel, a constant variety of scene, a constant succession of brisk, sharp incidents. Once in the Carolinas he was chased by an enraged Spaniard who imagined that he had betrayed a confidence. For months his cheek showed a knife slash. Once he stowed away on a coastal steamer. Once he worked his passage. On his arrival at Charleston he welcomed the outbreak of a fire since it gave him an opportunity to earn two shillings an hour. Three days later, with the fire extinguished, he was out of work and penniless. Twice he returned to New York in search of better pay: each time to find the markets crowded, to be forced back to the rice and the tobacco fields. The only period when he was immobile was in Virginia when a hatchet slipped, cutting his foot severely, and the proprietor of the plantation took him into his own home to be nursed by his wife and family.

Those forty months would provide the material for a roisterous Roderick Random novel. But we know of them only what he has himself chosen to tell in interviews and in the early chapters of his autobiography. There is no means now of re-creating them.

No record remains; no record ever does remain of the early years of those who are born obscurely and who do not emerge from their obscurity before their thirties. The upper and the middle classes set their activities on record from their earliest years. There are school magazines, there are college groups, there are guest books, there are snapshot albums. There are holiday and week-end visits with people who keep diaries, write letters, publish autobiographies. Throughout their lives, members of these worlds keep in touch with the acquaintances, the friends, the relatives whom they knew in childhood. The industrious biographer can find innumerable cross references to the subject of his studies.

Lipton's biographer cannot do that. During the first twenty-seven years of his life Lipton did not meet a single person who made any mark on the world whatsoever. He was not a member of any club, nor any cultural or athletic group whose activities have been recorded. Moreover, by the time he was forty he had stepped completely out of the atmosphere he knew in boyhood. Though he was always extremely quick to welcome any old friend or the relative of any old friend, there was no one in the last half of his life with whom he could swop boyhood memories. He was a poor correspondent. He was without literary or artistic interests. His intimate friends were not the kind of men who write their reminiscences. His appearances in the indices of contemporary books are few and casual. He never kept a diary. In that sense the task of his biographer is hard. He did, however, keep his press clippings. Eighty-four large volumes of them repose in Glasgow, in the Mitchell Library. They provide a voluminous record of his activities and make the task of his biographer, though arduous, direct. They do not begin, however, till the year 1877.

. For the first twenty-seven years of his life we have to rely upon what he has himself told us, and his memory on occasions played him false. He liked in later life to embroider his conversation with references to his early struggles, but he was a man who lived in the present and in the future. He did not brood. Those early days are gone now like the cigar smoke which floated over the conversations which recalled them. Of two things only we can be certain—that every week he sent a proportion of his pay cheque back to Crown Street, and all the time the magnet of Manhattan was in operation.

On those first evenings in New York, on those two brief returns, he had watched with shining eyes the smart carriages sweeping up Fifth Avenue, the fashionable men and women sauntering across Central Park, the men in their shining hats, the women in the shadow of their parasols. He had felt no envy looking at the bright interiors, the gilded ceilings, the heavy candelabra that he had glimpsed through half-drawn curtains. One day he would own such a house. One day he would drive beside his mother in such a carriage. New York, with its noise and hurry, its clear, cold air, its sense of unfrontiered possibilities, was the great shop-window of a store in which he would one day have earned the right to buy. New York—it was always in the background of his thoughts, the fountainhead, the springboard. He would not consider that he had made good till he found work here.

Three years were to pass before he did. Then, for the first time since he had landed, it was in work for which by taste and training he was fitted—in the grocery section of a department store.

To Lipton, who remembered the tiny shop in Crown Street which could barely hold six customers at a time, the contrast of a bustling New York store was an unceasing fascination. He studied the difference in methods, the different way in which the goods were displayed, the different relation between the customer and salesmen. The wares might not be any better than the Scottish wares, but they were better shown; the assistants took a more personal interest in the customers. There was an atmosphere in this New York store that encouraged you to buy. He looked each morning at the high piles of merchandise, at the gleaming counters, at the advertisements, the smart assistants. As he watched the bustle and animation of the scene he kept thinking of the ways in which the shop in Crown Street could be improved.

He loved his work and, because he loved it, he worked hard at it. Promotion came quickly. At last, after four years of struggle, he had found his feet. He had fought his way out of the rough crowd of emigrants with whom he had shared steerage quarters on the Anchor liner, who had dossed down with him in Mike McCalligan's, with whom he had trudged through the Virginian tobacco fields. The days of being a stowaway were over. He had served his apprenticeship. Success was on its way. He was adapted to the American pattern, to the American way of life. He had fitted himself into the American scheme. He had found his niche: a niche that he could enlarge indefinitely. There were no limits set.

He had every qualification for a first-generation citizen. He came of solid stock. He was well bred; he had been well trained in manners and in self-respect: religiously but not overstrictly. He had been taught thrift. He was healthy; he was a good mixer. He was tough, but he was temperate. He had given and taken punches in the rough-and-tumble of the streets. He was a natural leader; he had captained the Crown Street Clan; been commodore of the Crown Street "yacht club." He was an opportunist. He had earned his first week's lodging in a foreign country. He had a natural gift for salesmanship. Had he not told his father that the eggs would look larger in his mother's hands? His first nineteen years read like the first chapter of a magazine success story—"Irish Boy Makes Good."

And that, ninety-nine times in a hundred, is what they would have been. This was the hundredth time, however. Though he had been in America three years before he got

this job, he had crossed the Atlantic in his fifteenth year.
He was still in his teens when he was at last established in
New York. He was not old enough to have formed serious ties; no tie at least that held more strongly than his
mother's. She needed him. And he was missing her. As
soon as he had saved five hundred dollars he went back
to Scotland, reversing the normal process, the poor man
seeking his fortune, not in America but Scotland.

It is from this point that his story becomes exceptional.
Had he stayed longer in New York he would very certainly, with his gifts, have been successful. In all human
probability he would have married an American. There is
no reason why he should not have been happy. But had
he stayed, successful though he must have been, happier
though he might have been, he would have been one of
many; he would not have been unique.

It is very unlikely that he would have been the subject
of a centennial biography to-day.

§ 3

HE RETURNED to Glasgow in the spring of 1869.
He had been away four years. He had grown and he
had broadened. He had gone away a boy; he returned a
man. Photographs show him as a tall, spruce fellow with
a thick drooping moustache, with curling hair worn full
above the ears, parted in the centre and brushed slightly
forward over a high forehead.

He arrived early on a Saturday. His instinct after so
long an absence was to hurry home, but his sense of show-

manship counselled him to delay. His return after fifty months away was not just anyone's return. It had to be a triumph. He waited till noon, then when most of his old friends were returning from their work he hired a cab. He had brought back as a present for his mother a barrel of flour and a rocking chair. Placing these on the top of the cab, he told the driver to hurry to the end of Crown Street, then drive to No. 13 as slowly as he could.

The arrival of a cab was in itself something of an occurrence in a threadbare thoroughfare; the spectacle of a cab surmounted by a barrel of flour and a rocking chair was without parallel, and there, as a climax, leaning out of the window, waving and shouting greetings, was young Tommy Lipton, whom everyone had half forgotten, brown and broadened and with a great moustache. It was the talk of the neighbourhood for months.

On the Monday morning he was back at work as an assistant in his father's shop. It all seemed very small after New York. For four years he had lived in an atmosphere of growth. In Glasgow, too, there had been expansion. He had noticed that on the Saturday morning as he had steamed up the Clyde. On the south side of the river there was the Kingston dock. It covered an area of five acres. Yet already, so they told him, it was beginning to prove inadequate. During his two-hour wait before his dramatic drive he had noticed as he had strolled along the docks how much more shipping there was now. He had gossiped with one of the stewards on the *California*, the Anchor Line's newest vessel, whose sister ship, the *Victoria*, he had seen once on the Hudson, gliding to her piers. She could carry two hundred first-class passengers, so the steward told him. There were sixteen ships now on the New York run. Sometimes there were two sailings in a week. Scandinavians were beginning to emigrate in quantities. The Anchor Line had established a North Sea service, landing them in Granton, bringing them by rail to Glasgow.

No, there was no lack of scope in Scotland. It was only that Crown Street seemed the same. Whole-heartedly though he flung himself into his work, into the rearrangement of the stock, into getting to know his customers and the wholesalers who supplied him, he felt half employed. He could do twice as much work as this. The profits rose, but they rose slowly. They were proceeding at a glacier's pace.

He became impatient. He had brought back with him as spoil after his four years away not only a few hundred dollars, a barrel of flour, and a rocking chair. He had other, far richer merchandise on which no customs officer could charge him duty. Enterprise and independence, a quick eye for an opportunity, those he had had at birth, those he had taken with him. But now, added to those, he had a sense of distance, a sense of oneness too. He knew how big the world was, yet at the same time how small. You could cross the Atlantic. You could go south to the Mississippi and you could still get back. He was deprovincialised.

He was rid, too, if he had ever had it, of class consciousness. One man was as good as any other, or at least stood as good a chance. Every man was your equal, yet every man was your rival too. The race was to the swift. That, for his general merchandise.

He had other more specialised commodities. America and Americans had sharpened him. He had seen how they ran their businesses, how they treated their customers, how they displayed their goods; he had seen how they advertised, noted the big sky signs, the big hoardings, the full-page spreads. Advertisement was a power that the British had scarcely touched as yet. "Good wine needs no bush." That was the English motto. But he knew better now. "Quality tells," yes, but quality told slowly. You had to shake the public, to startle and cajole, bully and flatter it. What he had learned in America he started to put into practice.

He worked upon new schemes to attract custom. One morning there clattered up the street a smart newly painted van with the word "Lipton" painted along each side. A small pony was between the shafts. His father looked at it distrustfully. What was this? he asked.

"Your new horse and van."

"Who ordered it?"

"Your son."

"Then you can take it right back to where it came from."

The father refused to discuss it further, and later in the day the neophyte of transatlantic methods had the humiliating task of calling upon the saddlers and cancelling the order. "It won't be long, though, before I order a horse and van upon my own account," he told them. For that was another of his ideas, to open a second shop. He had time and energy enough to run two places. The profits would be doubled.

His parents were outraged at the proposal. Had the boy gone mad! The business was going nicely. One day he would inherit it. It could support a home, give his children a good start. What more could a young man want? Two shops indeed!

Young Lipton listened, shrugged, and made his plans. He always carried a few pounds in his pocket to meet emergencies. He believed in the effect of cash down payments. He waited for an opportunity. Soon it came. A ship from Philadelphia was five days late. To speed the turn, its owners sold off their cargo on the quay. It was the chance for which he had been looking. He invested every penny of his savings in a consignment of hams and bacons, then sold it in the town at a profit of eighteen pounds. The deal confirmed his confidence. If he could make eighteen pounds on one consignment, he could make two thousand on a hundred. Could anyone who had trekked from Charleston to New Orleans think in terms of one shop, one street, one city? It was a question, surely, of a bigger turnover. The more you sold, the more you made. It was as simple as all that. But to sell a lot, you had to have a number of different places in which to sell. You could only sell a limited amount to the inhabitants of a single street.

"On that one deal," he repeated, "I made eighteen pounds."

His parents shook their heads. At least his father did. The mother was less uncertain of the son who had brought her back right across the Atlantic the most comfortable chair that she had ever sat in. It was to his mother rather than his father that he talked. If one shop made a weekly profit of five pounds, why should not two shops make ten, why should not twenty make a hundred? "Why should we not have a dozen Lipton shops? Why should we not have a Lipton shop in every city in West

c

Scotland?" That was his line of argument. Already he had planned a start. Already he had his eye upon convenient premises—on the north side of the river, in a better buying district.

In all his life he was only to covet one thing in vain. On his twenty-first birthday, on May 10, 1871, he opened his first shop at 101 Stobcross Street.

§ 4

THE story of the next few years—of the next thirty years, for that matter—can be told in a single phrase: ceaseless hard work backed by advertising.

It has been often said that the first thousand pounds are the hardest earned. In Lipton's case this certainly was true. His first hundred had already taken four years' earning. It has also been said that no man in the space of a single life has time to amass a fortune unless he takes a short cut somewhere, unless he does something fraudulent or runs an outrageous risk. In Lipton's case that did not happen. His record is unsmirched by scandal. He was never to be accused of anything even vaguely tricky. He never gambled on anything except his own energy and powers. He never borrowed. He paid cash. The only short cut he took was sheer hard work, backed by abstemiousness. He lived for his work and in it. He put back into his business every penny that his business earned. He had no private life outside of his devotion as a son. All his time, all his energy were poured into his work.

"I worked late and early," he said in his autobiography. "I was manager, shopman, buyer, cashier, and messenger boy all rolled in one. If I had provisions to collect off the Irish boat, I went down to the quay myself with a hand-cart early in the mornings; if the customers wanted anything sent to their homes, I shut up the shop temporarily and delivered them in person."

When there were no customers to serve he stood outside polishing the window, gossiping to the housewives as they went by. He was young and smart and handsome in his white overalls and apron; he had a quick tongue and an attractive brogue. He was naturally gregarious, a trait that America had developed in him. Every now and again he would call a passer-by's attention to some particular article that he could recommend. His cheery manner increased his custom. In the evenings, returned to Crown Street, he would work on his accounts, think out new ideas. Occasionally, when hard pressed, he would sleep under the counter in Stobcross Street.

He never wasted time. That was his secret, or one of his secrets. He had several of them. One was his ability to sell goods that were of the same quality as his neighbours' at a lower price. In part he could do this because his needs were small, because he underpaid himself, but mainly he did it by cutting out the middleman. His mother had received her supplies from a friend in Ireland. Lipton followed on her plan, enlarging it. He paid personal visits to the Irish farmers; he saw the crofters in their own homes. Buy on the spot: he followed that practice all his life.

Industry, ambition, a sense of showmanship—these would have brought him success in any enterprise. But the dimensions of that success were to be measured by his flair for advertising. He had genius there.

Even now, seventy-five years later, when for three quarters of a century the most astute minds in commerce have been at work in this arena, Lipton's devices seem original. He started, it must be remembered, in the smallest way, with no spare capital. He could not afford lavish newspaper displays. Nor in those early days would they have served much purpose. Large tracts of the city lay outside his province. Announcements in the Glasgow *Evening Citizen* about a shop in Stobcross Street would have interested only a small section of the paper's clientele. He was working from a narrow base and he concentrated upon his immediate neighbourhood.

He started with the street. He made his shop attractive. His own white overalls were always starched and spotless. Gas jets lit the interior by night. From a pole above the door he suspended a large wooden ham. Swinging in the wind, it caught the eye like a sign over a village inn. On hot days the sun melted the paint and the wood shone so greasily that children refused to believe that it was not real and clustered underneath, looking up at it with envious eyes. He placarded his windows with comic pictures. He engaged Willie Lockhart, one of the foremost cartoonists in the country, to produce a weekly poster. In 1871 large crowds gathered before the picture of a pig slung over the shoulder of an Irishman, to chuckle at the sight of tears pouring from the pig's eyes while its owner explains to the silk-hatted enquirer that the poor pig is an orphan, that all the rest of his family have gone to Lipton's and out of pity he is taking him along there too.

From the street Lipton widened his attack upon the neighbourhood. He bought two of the largest and fattest porkers in the livestock market. He scrubbed and polished them. He tied pink and blue ribbons round their tails and had them driven through the streets under a large banner emblazoned with "Lipton's Orphans." Day after day he drove those same two pigs to Stobcross Street, but always by a different route. He developed the idea. Sometimes instead of using a banner he would have them driven by a typical Irishman in knee breeches, cutaway coat, billycock hat. On the pigs' sides would be painted: "I'm going to Lipton's, the best shop in town for Irish bacon." One of his cartoons showed an Irishman being tugged along the street by a pig. It was captioned "Lipton's Leading Article."

Within a few weeks his custom had increased to such an extent that he needed an assistant. The boy he hired was so shabby that Lipton, out of respect for his shop, bought him a new suit. On the fourth morning the boy did not appear. Nor did he on the fifth or sixth. That afternoon Lipton went round to the boy's house to ask if he was ill. "Oh no," his mother said, "he's doing splendidly, and all thanks to you. With that new suit to recommend him, he's got himself a better-paying job with another firm."

Lipton could be impatient where inefficiency and disloyalty were concerned, but on this occasion he kept his temper.

"Madam," he said, "your son will get on in life but not, I'm afraid, very far. He's not long-sighted. He doesn't know when he's got in onto a good thing on the ground floor."

He hired his next assistant on a six months' contract.

He needn't have. Before the contract had expired the business had so prospered that Lipton was able to open a second shop. The assistant became an assistant manager. He was to remain on the Lipton pay roll for forty years.

That was the beginning. As he began, so did he continue. The new shop was in a better district. It was larger and he had greater scope there. He exploited the same methods, making full use of Lockhart's talents. His windows were decorated not only with the weekly poster but with pictorial price cards. Hens were displayed on strike "because of the low price of eggs." A picture of an old woman with a broomstick belabouring a fallen man was headed "Butter Down Again." Models of hens and dairymaids, "statuary in butter," stood between the high mounds of cheese.

"Lipton's orphans" soon became a catch phrase in the neighbourhood. When a local Unitarian preacher wished to insult the Catholics he described a group of priests as "shaven, shorn, and shovel-hatted as though they were bound for Lipton's." An obese old woman waddling slowly along Argyll Street failed to understand why her progress was exciting so much derisive interest, until it was charitably pointed out to her that on her back street urchins had pinned a placard, "Bound for Lipton's."

As his capital increased his stunts became more elaborate. "Funny mirrors" was one of his most successful. He set a pair outside his shop, one concave, the other convex. The concave mirror, which elongated the body, making the face look haggard, was headed "Going to Lipton's." The other, showing an enormous paunch and a broad grinning face, was headed "Coming from Lipton's." Distorting mirrors have been for many years now a favourite "Fun Fair" feature, but then they were a novelty, particularly for children. Lipton's shops provided a popular form of inexpensive entertainment for the young.

He exploited the association of plump good health with

Lipton's. Slenderness was not then valued highly, and a procession of twelve "buxom ladies" bearing baskets inscribed "We shop at Lipton's" did not inspire the ribaldry which they might to-day. Down one side of the street he paraded a line of cadaverous males, each of them bearing the placard, "Going to Lipton's"; on the other pavement was a line of fat, red, jovial men ticketed "Coming from Lipton's." To the Victorians as to the Arabs, a sleek, well-fed appearance was something to be proud of, a proof of prosperity and success. It was assumed that any man who could afford to would "do himself well." A thin man was either unhealthy or poor—both of which were crimes in the 1870s.

Another of his stunts—this came in 1877—was the issue of the Lipton notes. They were in size and feel exact reproductions of the one-pound notes that were then issued by a leading Scottish bank. They carried the royal coat of arms. They had the £1 sign engraved in the top right-hand corner. The word *One* ran across the centre. In the lower left-hand corner was the date and the name Glasgow. In the lower right-hand corner was a cashier's signature. At a first superficial glance it was an ordinary one-pound note. But closer scrutiny revealed a number of small differences. The word "Lipton's" was boldly set under the crest. Above the cashier's signature was that of Lipton, followed by the word "proprietor." Round the margin ran the slogans: "Try Lipton's Cap Hams—199-201 Paisley Road—Try Lipton's Fresh Eggs—21, 23, 25, 27 High St."—and in the centre under the word *One* was printed "GREAT IRISH HAM BUTTER and EGG markets. I promise to give on demand in any of my establishments

HAM, BUTTER and EGGS as given elsewhere to the value of one pound for fifteen shillings"—it being one of his favourite slogans that in Lipton's you could buy a pound's worth of goods for fifteen shillings.

It was an ingenious advertisement, its possessor being bound to feel sufficient curiosity to read it carefully, spotting all the differences between it and an ordinary pound. It led to a great deal of talk; several amusing stories were going round the town of people having their pockets picked of wallets that contained only Lipton's notes. There were newspaper references to "who steals my purse steals trash."

It was, at the same time, a dangerously two-edged joke. Many people in those days could not read, and the notes were so similar that there was inevitably much confusion. Many genuine mistakes were made, and in a number of cases there were attempts at fraud. A labourer was sentenced to twenty days imprisonment for trying to pass a Lipton note in an eating house, while a similar case against a girl was only brought in "not proven" because it seemed possible that the girl might have been deceived. Finally an action was brought against Lipton himself in the small-debt court for the sum of one pound, being the loss sustained by the plaintiff through "inadvertently taking in change handed to him at a bookstall one of Lipton's notes." Judgment was given for the defendant, but Lipton came in for censure from the bench, his act being stigmatised as "most impudent and reprehensible," a criticism which was amplified by a leader in the Glasgow *Evening Citizen*. "Mr. Lipton was amply warned by the sheriff as to the serious mistakes and troubles—not to say actual loss to individuals—certain to result from the issue of such imitation notes, the imitation being so close as either to be passed off as genuine among people unable to read or carelessly accepted by others in the frequent hurry of business."

Lipton had no objection to being a public nuisance where his own interests were concerned. He would boast, for instance, of how he had trained his "orphans" to lie down in the middle of the road and create a traffic block. But there were limits to being a nuisance. He recognised that, though he was being talked about, it might not be in the way he wanted. Very sensibly he withdrew the notes.

It was his first big-scale "stunt" and it was his only one that was not a complete success. Only on two other occasions were his devices criticised, but they had achieved their purpose first. There were no other breaks in a long unbroken succession of successes. As early as 1878 the local press was remarking that "the name Lipton is in a fair way to becoming a household word in Glasgow."

And not in Glasgow only. Slowly at first but with rapidly gathering speed the business was enlarging. The postal street directory and the register of electors recount the story. By 1873 the Crown Street shop had been abandoned. His parents, now over sixty, were in retirement in Radnor Terrace; another two years and there is a fresh address, in Franklin Terrace. Before the seventies are past they are in the suburbs, in a semi-detached house in Cambuslang—Johnstone Villa, which is known now as the Lipton Memorial Nurses' Home. Simultaneously in the business section of the directory the entries become more numerous and more impressive. Soon there is an establishment in High Street, then one in Paisley Road. By 1878, No. 101 Stobcross Street is no longer listed. A grocer called Cochrane is installed there; 57-59 Jamaica Street is added, then the big warehouses in Lancefield Street. Greenock appears, and then Dundee. It is a story of steady progress, of progress conducted always on a pattern: the small shop catering to the poorer classes. The poor woman's twenty shillings was as good, he would insist, as the rich man's pound. A child of the people, he served the people. He saw every transaction in terms of the people whom he had known in boyhood. That was his strength. He multiplied his units, but the unit remained unchanged. He never got things out of focus. He never outreached himself.

He had found a formula and he stuck to it. He put back into his business every penny that his business earned. As soon as he had saved enough he opened a new shop. His Irish sense of independence resented the idea of taking in a partner. His Scottish thrift would not let him borrow. To begin with, his rate of progress was inevitably slow. It takes a long time for two shops to make sufficient profit to finance the opening of a third shop, but fifteen shops can swiftly supply the capital for a sixteenth. By 1880 he owned more than twenty. When interviewers asked him about his politics he would answer with a smile, "My politics are to open a new shop every week."

In the opening of these shops he followed the same technique. For a week in advance he would publicise his visit with street parades, with posters, with newspaper advertisements. Because he advertised in their columns and because his parades were news, his openings were publicised in the local press.

"For several days past," wrote the *Leeds Mercury*, "advertisements in the newspapers and posters on the walls of the town have informed the public that 'Lipton's coming.' Many readers no doubt supposed that Lipton would prove to be a new theatrical star, but at last the secret is disclosed by the opening at No. 18 Kirkgate of an extensive ham and bacon establishment."

A Greenock paper broke into verse:

> Good news, good news to one and all
> Good news has come at last
> For orders to our boatyards now are coming thick and fast.
> But better news than that I'll tell
> For Lipton, Scotland's pride
> Has opened a new Irish Branch
> At Greenock on the Clyde.
> We'll hae' a ham of Lipton's cure
> And eggs and butter fine
> They're half the price and better
> Than those we bought lang syne.

while a Belfast leader, headed "Lipton's Come," began: "For several days past, the word Lipton has been in the mouth of every citizen in Belfast. Fancy and attractive designs on the dead walls, a band of attractively attired sandwich men whose movements were regulated by an admirably mounted courier heralded the advent of some leviathan."

For every opening Lipton was there himself, in his white apron and his overalls, offering a prize to the first purchaser. The shops were built upon a pattern. There would be a wide horseshoe counter. There would be smart assistants. The ceiling would be hung with hams, the counters piled with butter. At night there would be the glitter of gas jets within opal globes. "His shops," said a contemporary correspondent, "looked like a fairy cave." On one point in particular he insisted—there must always be something to attract the children. He loved children. He knew also that mothers would deal with a shop where their children could be kept out of mischief. In one shop he had a large American clock that changed its picture every thirty seconds. The pictures were, of course, advertisements. In Glasgow he had a magic lantern. Years later Keir Hardie, one of the first Socialist M.P.s, wrote in the *Labour Leader* on the occasion of Lipton's knighthood—an occasion that he might well have exploited as an attack on the capitalist regime—"I have always had a soft spot for Thomas Lipton. As a small boy in Glasgow doing the shopping for my mother, I was ready to walk an extra two miles to see his pictures."

By the start of the 1880s people in a dozen cities were wondering "what Lipton's would be doing next."

His next "stunt" was one of his most famous—the import, display, and sale for the Christmas of 1881 of the largest cheese that had ever been made.

He ordered it from America, and every detail in connection with it was amply advertised. For six days, so Glasgow was informed, eight hundred cows had given their entire milk. For six days two hundred dairymaids were employed. The world's greatest experts were called into consultation. Not only the largest but the best cheese that had ever been made was being prepared for Lipton's customers.

Such intense curiosity was aroused that when the steamer carrying it docked, hundreds were waiting on the quay and the streets were lined to cheer as it was borne triumphantly by traction engine to the store in High Street. All through December crowds gathered outside the shop to see the vast mountain of cheese that by now had been nicknamed "Jumbo."

But Lipton's ingenuity was not yet exhausted. Another idea had struck him. Why not treat the cheese as the housewife treats a Christmas pudding? Are not the sixpences in the pudding one of the chief excitements of a Christmas dinner? Why not, then, insert golden coins—sovereigns and half sovereigns—into Jumbo? It was one of his happiest ideas. A long metal butter taster was driven into the cheese, turned round, and then drawn out. Into the long circular strip thus extracted sovereigns and half sovereigns were inserted and the strip replaced. Hundreds watched the operation. When the cheese was finally cut up on Christmas Eve the anxiety to secure a slice was so intense that a special squad of police was requisitioned to control the crowd. The squad was not on duty long. Within two hours every ounce was sold.

Monster cheeses became henceforth a fixed feature of the Lipton Christmas. He installed special machinery for them in America. Not only Glasgow but every town with a Lipton market had its cheese. The arrival of each cheese was news. There was little need to buy advertising space. He received inches of free publicity in the editorial columns.

Occasionally local authorities would raise objections. The Sunderland police argued that the presence of sovereigns in the cheese constituted a lottery. Lipton had his answer ready. His lawyers told him that he would not be breaking the law if he warned the public that any money found within the cheese must be returned to the store. He did so in a frivolous advertisement. Very naturally not a gold coin came back to him.

Objections were also made in Newcastle. But here the cause of complaint was different. The police were afraid that the public might throttle themselves by swallowing coins in error. Lipton adapted himself to this new attack. He advertised a "police warning" to the effect that anybody buying a portion of Lipton's Giant Cheese stood in danger of being choked by one of the many sovereigns that were concealed in it. Once again there was a record rush.

Lipton was by now as much identified in the public mind with "Jumbos" as he had been ten years earlier with his "orphans," and he caused no surprise in 1893 at the Chicago fair when he bought the Canadian exhibit of a twelve-ton cheese.

His purchase, as usual, was paragraphed throughout the country. Every detail of its journey to Montreal was publicised. It was welcomed at the Broomielaw by crowds as large as those that twelve years earlier had honoured the first Jumbo. At that point, however, the flow of paragraphs ceased mysteriously. The explanation is to be found in a modest technical journal devoted to dairy problems. Fourteen months, it pointed out, was a mature age for a cheese, and this particular cheese had been sitting in a tent in the Middle West at a mean summer temperature of 90°. The holds of a modern liner may be waterproof; they are not always dampproof. There it left the matter. No doubt the cheese had been·insured; it had supplied immense publicity. Lipton did not regret his purchase. But the amateur of culinary sensations cannot help wondering with an almost prurient curiosity as to the kind of shock that would have been administered to his olfactory senses by a twelve-ton cheese that had gone bad.

And all the time his business was increasing. Soon the Irish farmers and crofters were unable to keep his shops supplied. He was forced to look farther afield, to Scandinavia and to Russia. Russia was to prove disappointing. "The red-tapism was awful. And the uncertainty of being allowed to continue the enterprise when the government saw that you were making a profit was too terrible to contemplate," was his verdict. Scandinavia was to prove a more satisfactory source. Before long, however, even this supply proved inadequate. His thoughts turned westward. Why not America? Why not his own stockyards in Chicago? In 1869 he had left America with five hundred dollars in his pocket. Twelve years later he was to return a buyer, with ample credit at his back.

The late seventies, the early eighties. They were years of unceasing, of unsparing effort. Each day, each hour, in its passing, was crowded with dramatic incident, with schemes and plans and triumphs, a constant, varying eventfulness. Yet to the biographer seeing it in retrospect it is all like a journey down a long French road between a line of poplars. He was always doing the same kind of thing. His hobby was his work. He had no other. He never gambled, never played cards. He never went to a theatre or a music hall. He had no friends, or rather he had only business friends, and those he only saw in business hours. There were no other hours.

He had no hobbies, no forms of relaxation. He did not drink. When he was offered a cigarette he would shake his head. "I'm one of the biggest smokers in the city, but not cigarettes." "What do you smoke, then? A pipe? Cigars?" He would shake his head again and laugh. "Neither. I smoke bacon." He had no prejudice against alcohol or nicotine, though he recommended temperance. "Corkscrews have sunk more people than cork jackets have ever saved." But he always served wine at his own table. It was just that as regards himself alcohol and nicotine took up time that could be better occupied with business; they interfered with what he really cared about.

In his first months in Stobcross Street he often worked so late that he preferred to sleep under the counter rather than walk back across the river. Later, when his parents lived in the suburbs, it was usually the last train home he caught, and that at the last moment. He was fond of telling reporters of an occasion when the cab went so slowly that he jumped out and ran, so that when the driver reached the station he was to find that for some while he had been driving an empty cab with a pile of pennies on the seat.

Lipton was always on the move, opening a new shop, visiting a manager or agent, catching the night boat to Ireland, hurrying over to Chicago. He had no private life. He had no time for a private life.

An episode of which the public was not to learn for many years throws an illuminating light on that.

§ 5

On a warm March morning in 1885, in a small village between Gorrock and Ashton on the northeast shore of Scotland, a girl in her nineteenth year was keeping watch over the tollhouse. Her name was Catherine McLeod: she was the second of four children. There was a momentary slump in the shipbuilding trade in Glasgow, and her father Donald had leased the tollhouse as an extra means of support for his growing family. The four children and their mother took turns collecting the toll. There was no gate across the road and they had to be on their guard lest a shepherd driving his flocks from his hills or a resort visitor in his carriage should pass without paying his fee.

On this particular day Catherine had cut her foot upon a stone earlier in the morning. The foot was hurting, and she was sitting barefooted in the doorway of the tollhouse when she heard the clatter of horses' hooves. She had barely time to pull the sandal over the bandage and hobble out into the road.

At her signal a pair of horses, black and sleekly groomed, were halted. They were spirited and well matched. They were driven by a man who seemed to be in his early thirties. He had very bright blue eyes and dark curly hair that waved back from his forehead. His face was lined and rather rugged, yet it struck her as being sensitive. He was broad-shouldered and strong, and though he wore a neat dark suit, his small cap was set at a jaunty angle. He stared at her very straight. It did not surprise her that he should; a good many men had stared at her since she had watched the tollhouse. Her figure was trim and supple; her hair, which she wore in pigtails, was thick and wavy; she had long-lashed hazel eyes. She knew that she was pretty. But there was something different in the way this man stared at her.

"You've hurt your foot," he said.

He was the first traveller who had noticed that her foot

D

was bandaged. There was friendliness and sympathy in his voice.

"You shouldn't be walking about on it," he said. "You should be at home with a doctor to dress it for you."

His friendliness touched her, yet at the same time, to her surprise, it made her feel shy and awkward.

"That's a fine pair of horses you've got there," she said.

"And it's lonely sitting up here driving them. Jump up beside me and we'll take a drive."

His voice had a warm Irish brogue, but she shook her head. She was too busy, she said. Besides, she didn't know him. He laughed. And when he laughed the lines of his face were cut up into amusing wrinkles. He gathered up his reins and drove away. It was not till he was out of sight that she realised she had forgotten to collect the toll.

Next morning she set off to watch the road again. Her mother checked her. "Not to-day, Catherine. It's one of the boys' turn."

"I know, but I'd be glad to. I've nothing else to do."

"That's very kind. But I want you to go down into the village for me."

Ordinarily Catherine was glad of an opportunity to gossip with the younger people. Usually she hurried down into the village to have as long a time there as possible. This morning, however, she loitered on the road. Every time she heard the clatter of horses' hooves she turned her head. When she reached the village the shopkeeper's daughter Anne had exciting news for her. A Buffalo Bill show had opened on the edge of the town. Anne had seen one of the performers in the village wearing furred breeches and a great tan hat. It was exciting news. Such shows were rare in Scotland. For a moment Catherine forgot about the wagonette and the two black horses. But only for a moment. There was the clatter of horses' hooves in the village street; swinging round from the counter, she caught a glimpse through the open door of a small cap set jauntily above dark wavy hair.

"Look," cried Anne, "there goes Tommy Lipton."

That afternoon Catherine sat by the tollhouse pensively, though it was still not her turn to watch the road. She knew now all about the blue-eyed driver with the warm Irish brogue and the grocery stores that bore his name. No doubt he was visiting on the west coast of Scotland in search of a likely business to buy. Would he open a store near Gorrock? she was wondering. He was a bustler, a man who made quick decisions. Already, most likely, he was on his way back to Glasgow, his business done here.

Next morning, however, when she was in the kitchen she heard a voice in the road raised in greeting, a familiar Irish voice. She glanced at her mother, saw that she was busy, then hurried through. Her father was on duty, and and there at the toll beside him was young Lipton.

"This is my daughter Catherine," her father said.

The young man chuckled.

"I've met her already these two days ago," he said. "I asked her to go for a drive with me and she refused because she didn't know me. Perhaps she'll consider now that we've been properly introduced."

That evening she sat beside him on his driving seat in a white dress, with her hair braided and her head held high as she drove down the village street, past the row of low-roofed stone houses, waving proudly to her friends. She had forgotten about the Wild West show and her date with Anne.

It was the first of many drives: drives back into the hills which rose behind the village; drives through the fields that would soon be bright with heather; drives that invariably finished on the shore, where they could sit among the pebbles, looking out over the sea, watching the sailing boats and the fishing boats and the occasional steamers far out on the horizon. He loved the sea, he said. He felt lost if he was away from it long. He told her how as a boy he had loitered along the docks, watching the big ships come in, how he had listened to the sailors' talk and repeated over to himself as though they were charms names like Valparaiso and New Orleans. He talked of his first voyage out, of those long journeys south through Virginia and the Carolinas. He told her about his first shop in Stobcross Street, of his pound notes and of his orphans, till it was time to clamber back into the wagonette and drive in the twilight to the tollhouse.

For a month, for six weeks, it went on like that, then one April afternoon he told her that he was going away next morning. He had brought her a photograph, a tintype as a keepsake. He had written something on the back.

They never met again. Conditions in the shipbuilding trade improved. At the end of the summer Catherine's father gave up the tollhouse and went back with his family to Glasgow. Catherine found work there as a milliner's apprentice. Sometimes she would see a photograph of Lipton in the Glasgow papers. Had he ever gone back to the tollhouse and asked for her? she wondered. He was very busy: so busy that even during that spring at Gorrock he had never given up a whole day to her. He had always arrived in the late afternoon. His work came first. He had talked about his work half the time.

Then there was his mother. He always carried her picture with him. His proudest moment had been his gift to her of her own coach and horses. Her praise was his richest reward. He had told Catherine one particularly revealing incident. One morning he had had a slight difference of opinion with his mother just as he was about to set off to his day's work, and they did not part on their usual affectionate terms. He worried about it all the way to his office, and at his desk could not concentrate upon his work. At first he thought of telegraphing, then decided it would not do, that he must go straight back home and put things straight.

His mother was quietly awaiting his return. "I know well enough what you've come back for, Tom," she said. He returned to his office with his mind at peace.

His mother and his work—they were powerful rivals. Had the man who was so absorbed in them any spare place in his heart for anything but the most casual encounter? Had he ever gone back and asked for her at the tollhouse? If he had, and had found her gone, he could have written. The new tenants had her address; they could have forwarded a letter. If he had cared at all, surely he could have written? Though even as she thought that, she knew that he was the kind of man who never did write letters. "I suppose I could write myself," she thought, but knew even as she thought it that that was something which her pride would never let her do. She shrugged. It was no use worrying. Besides, she had her own life now. She was young and gay and pretty. Soon she found herself in love. His name was Robert Stewart. He was a railroad engineer.

He was young, industrious, already launched in life. There was no reason why they should not marry.

At first they made their home in Scotland, in Dumbarton, but her husband had a brother who had crossed to America, made good, and settled in Duluth. He urged his brother to come out and join him. Finally, when her youngest child was five years old, Catherine let herself be persuaded.

The experiment succeeded. She felt at home in Minnesota. The lake reminded her of the bays and firths of Scotland. She never regretted either her marriage or her change of country. She did not cease, however, to follow the career of Thomas Lipton. Once after the death of her husband she went back to Scotland and saw her old friend, the daughter of the shopkeeper. They talked together of the drives that she had taken along the coast in the spring when she had missed seeing the Wild West show. "Why don't you go and see him while you're here?" Anne asked. Catherine shook her head. He might have forgotten her; she might have to remind him who she was. That was a thing she could not face. She went back to Duluth to live with her married daughter, to remain silent when neighbours discussed the *Shamrock's* chances.

§ 6

IT WAS in '85 that he met Catherine. The years were hurrying by.

Eighteen eighty-seven, the year of the Queen's Golden Jubilee. It was an occasion that Lipton could not miss. He addressed a letter to Her Majesty.

I take the liberty of writing to inquire whether your most gracious Majesty would be pleased to accept of the largest cheese ever made. The cheese which I purpose presenting to Your Majesty as a Jubilee offering would weigh about 11,200 lbs. or not less than 5 tons and be made from one day's milk of 8,500 cows.

The cheese will be of the finest quality that can be manufactured. Your Majesty will readily understand that in order to make a cheese of this size, special machinery and plant are required; so that should your Majesty be pleased to signify your gracious approval the necessary preparations will be happily and speedily gone on with.

I may mention that the cheese will be made in Canada; and I am sure your Majesty's subjects there would be delighted with the additional opportunity thereby given them of showing their loyalty to your most gracious Majesty, while at the same time marking an event which has few parallels in the history of this or any other nation. The cheese will be ready about September next.

Trusting sincerely that your Majesty will accept what would be the most marvellous product of dairy enterprise of all ages, I have the honour to be your Majesty's most humble servant . . .

He received in reply a courteous letter from Sir Henry Ponsonby, pointing out that the Queen could not accept presents from private individuals to whom she was not personally known.

Undeterred and unabashed, Lipton handed over the correspondence to the press. It was one of his two advertising acts, apart from the Lipton note, when his judgment and taste were criticised. The *Birmingham Daily Times* had a leader headed "Respectfully Declined," opening: "Of all the suggestions that have been made for suitable offerings in connection with the Queen's Jubilee, we cannot imagine anything more malapropos than the presentation to her Majesty of a cheese weighing five tons"; while

The *Pioneer* published a rhythmical composition that concluded with the lines:

> Snubbed by a Queen!
> Go, think of it in silence and shame
> And weigh against a piece of cheese
> The glories of a throne.

But though his taste was criticised, the consequent advertisement was considerable. His letter and Sir Henry Ponsonby's reply were widely published in the provincial press, and in a number of papers a correspondence started as to the various charitable causes to which Lipton's offer might be diverted. He did not regret his offer.

1887–89. They were the years that were making him a millionaire. Every month his business grew. But in his success he could no longer take the full enjoyment he once had. His mother was now close on eighty. Every month her strength diminished. Every month his anxiety increased. He scarcely dared to go abroad for fear of what might happen in his absence. Finally, in the autumn of 1889, the greatest personal sorrow of his life befell him. On a warm October afternoon he drove away beside his father from the grave in the Southern Necropolis in Glasgow into which his mother's coffin had been lowered beside his two brothers' and three sisters'. In silence he recrossed the river. He could not believe that it was true. To have lost one's mother—it was something that happened to other people, not oneself. His whole life had been built round her. He had worked to save her work, worked to buy her presents, to make her life full and happy. His pleasure in his successes had been measured by her pride in them. What focus would he have now for his ambition?

That night after his father had gone to bed, he took down his collection of press cuttings. He had three volumes now. One by one he turned the pages. They brought her very close to him. His every plan had been first discussed with her: those old pictures of Willie Lockhart's, how they had laughed together over them. That giant cheese. It was she who had said, "It must not only be the biggest cheese, it must be the best as well. The quality mustn't suffer." Those puns in Mr. Quiz's columns:

Shakespearean—Lipton's are shortly to produce Ham-let.
Appropriate advertisements—Lipton's hams illustrated by cuts.
Going the Whole Hog—Lipton, an egg-selling master in the philosophy of Bacon.
Oh, horrors. "Home for little boys at Farmingham" is advertising in all the Yorkshire dailies. "Farming*ham*." A light breaks in on Mr. Quiz—"Can this be Lipton's orphanage and have we all this time been eating——?" But the idea is too horrible to entertain.

Silly enough puns, no doubt, but how proud they had been of them at the time. They were the proof of his popularity. That music-hall sketch of Jimmie Willison's, *Soosie Spareribs, or Lipton and His Hams*.[1] This article about the opening of the new shop in Greenock, how excitedly he had shown it to her.

Stage by stage the story of his life over the last twenty years was told in these three albums.

That second trip of his to America, not this time as an emigrant but as a buyer. How well he remembered the night when he had come back to tell her that he was to sail next morning. She had shown no surprise. "That's a

[1] See Appendix II.

very good idea, Tommy," and had set about the packing of his trunks.

She had always fallen in with his ideas. They were all of them, after all, her own; an amplification of her own. What she had done on a small scale he had done upon a large. She had cut out the middleman, and so had he. She had bought her dairy produce direct from Ireland; he had owned his stockyards in Chicago. "It's all been your plan," he had said to her.

As he turned the pages of his albums he felt he was reliving the years and dreams that he had shared with her. What would he do without her? "I'll have to work harder still," he told himself.

He did. The next ten years were the hardest of his life. In the following spring his father died. He was now completely on his own. He had nothing to live for but his work. He worked unsparingly.

In the summer of 1890 he booked a passage to Australia. He needed a rest, he said. Perhaps he did. But he had other plans. At Ceylon he was met by a representative, Frank Duplock, whom he had sent on ahead.

"Well, and what are the prospects here?" he asked.

"They're pretty good, sir."

"Then I'll break my journey."

It was his first visit to the tropics. The Colombo that met his eyes on that hot June morning was superficially very different from the city with which the modern tourist is familiar. There was then no alternative to the G.O.H.[2] The racecourse was on Galle Face Green. The

[2]Grand Oriental Hotel.

present Colombo Club was its grandstand; its paddock
was to be, in the near future, the site of the Galle Face
Hotel, behind whose garages you can see the old stables
still. Superficially Colombo was very different. Yet in essentials it was much the same: the humid heat, the glare
of sunlight off the tall white buildings, the shaded boule-
vards, the Indian shops; the silks, the curios, the sapphires;
the Tamils with red spots upon their foreheads; the sidewalks stained with betel juice; the brassbound rickshaws,
the sentries outside Queen's House, the lighthouse in the
very centre of the town, the air of bustle and prosperity, of
general hopefulness—they were all there in Lipton's day.
Victorias instead of cars. But that was the only difference
—the only essential difference.

Had Lipton any prescience as he drove that morning to
the G.O.H. that he was on the brink of a whole reorientation of his life, that once again that infallible sense of
timing which those who are born without it dismiss as luck
was bringing the moment and the man together? Subconsciously he may have had, but he was in fact no more than
following out the familiar formula that his mother had
laid down, of buying direct from the producer. He had
recognised the possibility of tea as a new commodity for
his shops, and in terms of his invariable principle he had
decided to examine the proposition on the spot.

He could not have chosen a more propitious moment.
For more than two hundred years tea had been drunk in
England. It had been introduced at the same time as the
other two great temperance drinks, coffee and chocolate,
in the middle of the seventeenth century. Pepys records
himself as drinking it for the first time in 1660; Charles
II's wife, Catherine of Braganza, encouraged its use at

court in place of "the spirits and wines with which English ladies habitually heated and stultified their minds, morning, noon, and night," Edmund Waller including in a birthday ode to her the couplet:

> Venus her myrtle, Phoebus has his bays.
> Tea both excels, which she vouchsafes to praise.

Dr. Johnson was described as "a lover of tea to an excess hardly credible." It was always a popular drink in England, and in America, too, until the 1770s. It was, however, an expensive one; in the first place because of the East India Company's monopoly—a monopoly which was largely responsible for the Boston Tea Party—and secondly because it came from China. The races of the clipper ships with their tea cargoes in the 1860s make a fascinating chapter in the history of sailing, but the cost of transport was so great that in servants' halls in England in the middle of the nineteenth century it was beer, not tea, that was provided to the staff. It was not until the Indian variety came upon the market that tea became a beverage for the masses.

That happened in the last part of the century. When the East India Company lost its monopoly of the China tea trade the governor-general, Lord William Bentinck, appointed a committee to examine the possibilities of tea production in India on a commercial scale. Through the efforts of that committee it was soon discovered that tea could be grown not only on the slopes of hills but in the plains, a discovery that coincided with the substitution of steam for sail and the construction of the Assam-Bengal Railway.

Within the space of a few months tea came within the

means of the poorer household, and the demand grew brisker as the supply increased. By the late 1870s nearly forty million pounds of tea were being shipped each year from India. Within eight years that figure had been doubled. By the close of the century the amount had been redoubled. To-day India produces 560,000,000 pounds of tea a year.

The 1880s marked the real start of the boom. And for several years the brokers of Mincing Lane, recognising that his shops would be an excellent outlet for their wares, had been trying to persuade Lipton to place tea chests beside his hams and cheeses. Lipton was in agreement, but he had no use for middlemen. He decided to prospect himself.

He came at the right time. Nor could he have chosen a better centre from which to operate. Ceylon had entered the market only a few years earlier. Up to the middle of the 1870s her chief produce had been coffee, then blight destroyed the crops. In 1878, when the blight reached its peak, she was producing a bare twenty thousand pounds of tea a year; by 1883, with her half-ruined planters turning in desperation to an alternative crop, she was producing more than a million and a half; by 1888, twenty-four million pounds. A lift was going up and there was plenty of room in it for Thomas Lipton. "You can buy estates here for a song," Frank Duplock told him.

Next day he went up country. Slowly the train climbed out of the hot, humid plain, past paddy fields that curved like rivers between groves of coconuts to paddy that was planted in terraces along the side of hills, their curves following the contours of the ground. Slowly the air cooled and the vegetation changed, coconut palms giving way to stretches of grey-green rubber trees that in their turn were replaced by tea shrubs.

If in essentials the Colombo that Lipton saw on that first June morning is not so very different from the Colombo that confronts the traveller to-day, the upcountry life and landscape are practically identical.

Inevitably during sixty years there have been changes in the actual manufacturing of tea. More was done then by hand and less by engine power, but the essential process was the same, with the fresh-plucked leaves transported from the gardens to the factory, usually by overhead wires across the valleys, with the green leaves laid out for withering for eighteen to twenty hours till they had lost half their weight, acquiring the smell of fresh green apples. In those days they were laid out not on trays in a series of high shelves—the tats—but along the floor, and in consequence less evenly. There was little artificial withering with hot air and fans, and the leaves were sun-dried, often losing their flavour through delays owing to misty weather. In such respects a number of small improvements have been effected, but the rolling to extract the moisture and the sifting over thin meshed trays with a division into the dhools and the big bulk, with the dhools being laid out to ferment before the firing, as a prelude to the grading of the blackened leaf over a series of different meshes and the sorting out of the bulk tea into its separate grades, as Pekoe and Broken Pekoe, Orange and Broken Orange Pekoe— they are all very much as they were then, with the women squatting on their haunches at a long zinc table cleaning the tea by hand, extracting grit and stones. The man who could invent a machine for doing that would make a fortune. With their gold and silver bracelets, their nostrils pierced with jewels, and round their necks the little golden emblem that is the Hindu wedding ring, whose string the husband breaks during a divorce, they look to-day very much as they did to Lipton on that first visit.

The general appearance of an estate, too, is little altered. There are the tall grevilleas—Australian silver oaks —and the small dadap trees to break the wind, to shade and to manure the soil. There are the straight even rows of bushes with the lines of soil running red between them, as though a gigantic comb had been drawn down the hillside and across the valleys. There are the pluckers with their bamboo baskets slung onto their backs, and the rope held on the forehead over the dark blanket—the "clumby" —which protects their shoulders, working quickly with both hands over the matted surface of the close-pruned bushes, plucking the buds and the two top leaves, tossing each handful over their shoulders into the basket. They are paid by the basket, and an overseer moves among them, making sure they do not scamp their work or that they do not overfill their baskets and consequently bruise the leaves. Each field is plucked every ten days. In the other fields there will be men at work stamping in the manure, weeding, pruning, ditching.

Each group has its own factory and its superintendent. Each group is subdivided into three or four divisions, with an assistant superintendent over each. The divisions are like small villages with their schools, their shops, their dispensaries, their temples, and the row of barrack-like coolie lines. Including the young and the old, the babies and the infirm, there may well be as many as twelve hundred in a division. The responsibilities devolving upon the superintendent are very great. He has all the personal problems of

his labour force—illness, advances of pay, marital dis-
agreements, complaints about harsh treatment. There is
always a risk of fire, and insurance companies used to insist
that one European should be on duty all the time. The
planter is nearly always an ex-public-school boy from England or Scotland, chosen for his intelligence and skill at
games, very much as an army or a naval officer would be.
The standard of choice has altered little, and in most ways
the routine of his life is what it was.

Then as now he works for half a year as an apprentice
—"a creeper," he is called, before he is made an assistant
superintendent with a bungalow of his own and the responsibility of a division.

His routine is constant; there is the early rising in the
dark, the careful shaving while he hears the tom-toms
beating—first for the women to prepare the rice for the
men's breakfast and later for the men to rise. After the
muster roll at six he will return to his bungalow for his
own breakfast, but by seven o'clock he will have begun the
long five-hour stretch in the fields, supervising the work,
examining the tea nursery where the shoots are trained,
his eyes skinned for any lapse of discipline, for the weeding
coolie, say, who has not brought a sack with him in which
to collect the weeds. He will return to his bungalow for
lunch to find his mail, with his official correspondence
waiting for him. There may be so much paper work that
he will not be able to leave his desk till the coolies are
dismissed to their lines at four o'clock. It is unlikely that he
will have finished his work till half-past five. It has been a
full twelve-hour day. He will not have his first drink till he
has bathed and changed, till close on half-past six. Most
nights he is asleep by ten.

His social life is limited to one mid-week evening and to the Sunday morning at the club. The club will be an hour or so away, but he will be there on Sunday on the tennis court by nine. Tennis will be followed by pink gins and gimlets, and it is unlikely that he will sit down to his curry tiffin before half-past two. His one mid-week evening, probably on a Wednesday—an upcountry club opens only one night a week—is not dissimilar. It will begin quietly with tennis and tea, but it will be midnight before the planter is back in his own bungalow sitting down to dinner.

That is the planter's life as Lipton saw it at Dambatene in the summer of 1890. That is the world of which he decided to become a part.

Like all his decisions, it was a snap decision, and his entry into the tea trade is as good an example as commerce offers of the big man meeting the big moment and making the most of it. To-day he is known, apart from his yachting, almost exclusively as a tea merchant. Yet he was forty years old and a self-made millionaire before he handled one ounce of tea. And when he did enter the tea trade it was in the interests of his markets that he did so. He can have had no idea of the commitments he was undertaking. He looked on tea as he had looked on ham and eggs, on bacon and butter, as something that would attract more custom to his shops. He adopted his invariable technique. His unit, as always, was the public that he had known as a boy in Crown Street. Tea was selling at that time at three shillings a pound, too high a figure in his opinion for a working-class family living on two pounds a week. By cutting out the middleman he believed that he could reduce that price to one and sevenpence and still make a substantial profit.

E

He prepared his campaign accordingly. A showman first, he concentrated—once he was satisfied about the quality—on the appearance of his wares. At that time tea was stored in chests and weighed out for the customer, who inevitably must have doubted sometimes whether the tea was fresh and whether she was receiving her right weight. Lipton had a better scheme—to sell it in packets, by the pound, half pound, and quarter pound. The tea would be fresher, the brand standardised, the packet easier to handle. He visualised an attractive label of a Tamil girl with a basket on her head. He had his slogan ready: "Direct from the tea gardens to the teapot."

He entered the tea trade in the interests of his markets. The coffee slump had sent down the value of real estate so catastrophically in Ceylon that he needed to spend only half of the £75,000 he had brought out with him to invest; he thought of tea as something to be taken in his stride, but within a few months of his return he had realised that he had underestimated the possibilities of this new venture. The demand for a tea in packets at one and seven the pound was bigger, far bigger than his three hundred shops could satisfy. An immense opportunity lay to hand. He did not hesitate. He seized it. If that was what the small-incomed housewife needed, she should have it. He was going to sell tea wherever there was a demand for it. And that was everywhere. Where there was not an immediate demand, he would create it. It was the kind of challenge that he relished.

He proceeded to advertise tea as fifteen years earlier he had advertised his "orphans" with posters and street parades. Every vacant hoarding was a site for the words

"Lipton's Tea." He advertised in trains and buses; he had sandwich men dressed as Indians parading through the streets. It was the turning point in his career. His shops had made him a millionaire. His tea made him a multi-millionaire. He made money so fast that he lost count of it. Income tax stood at 5 per cent. Supertax had yet to be invented. He ploughed back his profits, spending nothing upon himself. His warehouses in Glasgow became inadequate, so he moved to London, establishing headquarters in the City Road, taking a house for himself at Southgate. The move to London was symptomatic. But it was much more than a mere accretion of wealth that marked at this point the basic change in his career. That change was deeper and more subtle. It lay in the fact that the word Lipton had ceased to be the name of a series of chain stores and become instead the trademark of a national commodity.

Up till now he had concentrated upon the towns and districts where he had a shop. There was no point in his advertising Lipton's hams in Wigan if he had no branch there. Nor, although he had as many as sixteen branches in London, was there any point in his taking space in the *Daily Mail* or *Telegraph*. He had concentrated on the districts where he was represented, in the *Islington Gazette* or in the *Kilburn Mercury*. But now through tea, Lipton's became a household word. The bare word was *ipso facto* an advertisement. "I advertise my business, not myself," he was fond of saying. But from this point on, any advertisement of the name Lipton was also an advertisement for his firm. It was a reorientation whose full significance was to become apparent later.

§ 7

ON A JULY MORNING in 1894 he stood in the doorway of his new home to welcome the five hundred members of his London staff whom he had invited out to spend the day with him. It was his first party here and his guests were to have the freedom of his grounds from ten in the morning until nine at night.

To-day Southgate is a station on the Piccadilly tube; to-day the grounds of Osidge are built round on every side by rows of two-storeyed villas. But then Southgate was a village with its nearest station, Palmers Green, twenty-five minutes' walk away, while Osidge was a sixty-acre estate with a history of seven hundred years—it was called Huyeseg in King John's Charter to the monastery of St. Albans. There was hardly a house along the Pimm's Brook Valley. The fields ran green to Whetstone. The *Daily Argus* was to describe the view from its verandah in terms of "the beautiful stretches of billowy well-wooded rolling country that could hardly have been equalled had they been purposely constructed by a skilful landscape gardener."

Many descriptions of Osidge were to appear during the next forty years, of its long irregular succession of roofs and chimneys; of its French windows and Venetian blinds, its low ceilings, its trelliswork, its endless corridors; of its orangery and orchid house; of the Sinhalese servant with embroidered cap who answered one's ring; of the inside hall with its Indian carvings, Japanese bronzes, South African horns; of the dining room with its portraits of his parents; of the pitch-pine-panelled billiard room with the lions' skins, its elephant head, its porcupine-quill chairs; of its lawns, its cedars, and its rhododendrons; of the summer-houses that had been constructed in the branches of its oak trees and approached by rustic steps that wound about the trunk. It was large and comfortable, with most of its rooms facing the southwest. But it was unpretentious; it was essentially a home. It was a good place for the kind of party that he had planned. And this party was to be as good as he knew how to plan.

His guests on this July morning were met by brakes at Palmers Green. An elaborate programme of sports and entertainments had been arranged for them. There was every kind of "picnic race"—wheelbarrow, sack, three-legged, blindfold, egg-and-spoon, donkey, and transformation. The guests were handed on arrival a facetious sports card on whose cover was designed a steaming cup of tea, "The Lipton Cup, to be run for by the human race." The band of the Scots Guards was to play: the pipers were to dance a sword dance. There would be lunch and tea and supper, ample meals at which no alcohol was served.

No alcohol for the staff guests, that is. Such rules did not apply to journalists, and Lipton was resolved to get the maximum publicity for his party. The *Sporting Illustrated and Dramatic* had sent down both a cartoonist and an interviewer. The *Daily Argus* was represented, so was the *Daily Telegraph*. In the room reserved for the press there were wine and whiskey. Lipton had his special bottle wrapped in a napkin. The liquid that came from it sparkled and was amber-coloured. It might have been a special brand of champagne, but in point of fact it was ginger ale.

Lipton was always at his best with journalists. A Glasgow contemporary has described him at this period as being "a gaunt austere man of military bearing, a commanding presence, in repose awe-inspiring, but when he spoke all this vanished and he became well-mannered, amiable, and jocular." All reports tend to show, however, that he was very rarely in repose. He was tall, handsome, and ruddy-cheeked. He was somewhat vain of his appearance and never lost an opportunity of getting sunburned. He was a man who exuded geniality. He was always laughing, always making jokes, always telling stories. It was very hard to make him serious, to tie him down to anything. Even at a business conference he would behave as though he were at a party.

On this particular day he was in the best of spirits. His guests had come in all manner of attire. The women for the most part made an attempt to copy the "creations" the Princess of Wales had worn at Ascot, tight-bodiced and high-bodiced with wide-spreading skirts containing a recollection of the bustle and wide floppy hats. The men, however, showed no such uniformity. The bicycling craze was just beginning, and many of them wore knee breeches and stockings and Norfolk jackets. Others were dressed as for the seaside, in white flannel trousers, brightly striped blazers, and straw hats; others were in formal city clothes, silk hats, frock coats, and cashmere trousers. One guest was clad in kilt. Lipton, who was particular about his clothes, had selected a costume that was designed, presumably, to put all his guests at ease: light sponge-bag trousers, a dark frock coat worn open to display a lavender-coloured double-breasted waistcoat, a high-winged collar, a loosely knotted polka-dot bow tie, and a wide-brimmed and brightly ribboned "boater" tilted at a jaunty angle over his left eye.

All day long he was in the highest spirits as he judged the races, congratulated the winners, commiserated with the vanquished, conducted the exhausted to the refreshment tables, and sipped his ginger ale and gossiped with the press. "The boys" could not ask him too many questions. He told them about his "orphans," about his pound notes, about his monster cheese. They asked him the secrets of his success. "Secret of it? Make no secret. Advertise. That's the secret of it. Advertise all you can. Never miss a chance of advertising." He said it with a twinkle and a laugh, with a boyish boastfulness that was engaging.

He told them the stories that in the next thirty years he was to retell many hundred times: of how he had scattered leaflets from a balloon at a time when ballooning was a novelty, offering a prize at any of the Lipton's markets to any possessor of a leaflet; of how he had once found a local manager perplexed as to how he was to get a three-ton cheese from the docks to the store. On his way from the station he had noticed that a circus was in town. "Hire an elephant," he promptly answered. His manager acquired the services of the elephant for thirty shillings and a procession jubilant small boys attended the triumphal progress of the monster cheese.

"Never miss a chance to advertise. But make sure that what you've got to advertise is good," he added.

That night after the guests had gone he stood outside on the verandah looking across the valley. Standing there, his hands upon the railing, he had the sense of being on a ship, of being on a journey. It was very quiet now, with the noise of London barely audible. How often had he not stood like this at night upon a liner; leaving Colombo or New York, the decks deserted, the good-byes said, the dark waters round him, a sense of the unknown ahead, of adventure starting. He had that same sense now. They had asked him that afternoon about his plans. He had had his answers ready. He was entering the jam market. He was following the familiar formula, buying on the spot, cutting out the middleman; he had his own fruit farm in Kent. English fruit would be better for jam than continental and tropical fruit, he said. The fruit that ripened slowly developed superior qualities over fast-ripening produce. Scottish strawberries, he said, had a finer flavour than English strawberries.

Those were his plans as he had thought them out that morning, with the interviews in mind. But now, alone in the dark, with the spire of Whetstone Church in silhouette on the horizon, the valley studded with an occasional street lamp or uncurtained window, with the light from the billiard room patterning the lawns, revealing the debris of the party, with his hands resting on the railing of his verandah in the same way that they had rested so many times on the taffrail of a liner, he had a premonition of other, far further plans, of being started now here in London on a journey whose ultimate harbour he could not discern.

Many columns about the staff party were to appear during the weeks that followed in the London press. Lipton's tea was by now as much a household word throughout the country as twenty years earlier Lipton's hams had been in Glasgow. As early as 1891 a full-page cartoon of a New Year's fancy-dress ball in the *Illustrated London News* had included a picture of a sandwich man dressed as an Indian carrying a placard, "Lipton's Tea." It was the smallest picture in the cartoon, but it was the one advertisement. That was three years ago. Now Arthur Roberts, that much-loved music-hall comedian, was starring in a sketch in which a charming young lady stepped from a Lipton's tea pictorial advertisement and sang a duet with him. He called her Miss Lipton, flattered her as though she were a pound of tea, which gave many opportunities for *double-entendre;* then they both stepped back into the hoarding. It was the London 1890 version of Jimmie Willison's *Soosie Spareribs* in the Glasgow of the 1870s.

A few weeks earlier Lipton had made out a cheque for more than thirty-five thousand pounds to the customs officers in payment for his dues on imported tea. He had made the payment in the same week that the Chancellor of the Exchequer had put an extra penny upon the income tax. The cheque was a news story in half the papers in the country. "Windfall for the Exchequer," it was headed. And there were such facetious comments as, "Why all this fuss about an additional penny on income tax? Let good patriots drink more Lipton's tea so that the cheques for duty may increase till taxation is abolished."

"And when I think," Lipton chuckled, "of all the fuss I made when I paid a paltry thirty-five hundred on a consignment of eighty tons. I had those eighty tons drawn through Glasgow in a procession of forty lorries with pipers at their head. Forty lorries, thirty-five hundred pounds. In five years' time I'll be making them out six-figure cheques."

He laughed as he said that; just as he had laughed twenty-five years back when he had promised his mother that soon she would be driving into town in her own carriage. He was the same man at heart, and indeed he looked the same. His personal appearance during that quarter of a century had scarcely changed. There is little difference between a photograph taken in 1876 and one taken in 1897: the hair is still parted in the centre; there is the same thick drooping moustache, the same goatee, the same twinkle in the eyes, the same trim figure. Perhaps the forehead is a little higher, the hair a little thinner and a little curlier about the ears, but the only real change is in his clothes. In 1877 a man's suit was five-buttoned. The bottom four buttons of the jacket were left open so that the coat fell away over the waistcoat. The narrow triangle between the high white collar—they were called chokers— was filled with a four-in-hand that a tiepin held in place. By 1897 the frock coat had come into fashion. It was double-breasted and was worn open except when a man was standing. The waistcoat was cut sufficiently low for two studs to show above it in a stiff white shirt. The collar was winged, like a modern evening one. A loose bow tie was modish. Fashions had changed a lot in twenty years, but the man inside them had not. It was in externals only that he looked different. Just as it was only in externals that the routine of Lipton's life had changed.

In the late 1870s he was living with his parents at Cambuslang, going in by train to Glasgow every morning. Now he was driving into London behind a pair of Kentucky trotters. Except for tourists in Ceylon, such as Clement Scott, the dramatic critic, he had no friendships outside his business. And business friendships in England were at this time confined to offices. He never went to a theatre. He never dined in London. His only entertainment was an electrophone—a telephonic contrivance never popular and now long extinct that could be plugged in to certain London concert halls and theatres. He went straight home as soon as he had finished work. His staff party at Osidge became an annual affair, but it was his only party in the year. Occasionally he would take home two or three of his associates to a dinner that would be in fact a conference. Occasionally, but not very often, a neighbour would drop in for billiards. But that was all. In London, a multi-millionaire in his middle forties, he was leading the same life that he had led in Glasgow in his early twenties as the owner of two small stores, when every now and then he slept under the counter rather than waste time walking home. Of the life that was being lived about him, he was profoundly ignorant. He had no conception that he was coexistent with a period that was to be known in retrospect as the "naughty nineties." It is doubtful if he had ever heard of Aubrey Beardsley: he had certainly never opened a copy of the *Yellow Book;* he must have read of the Wilde scandal, but it is unlikely that he discussed it. No one was less in sympathy with literary or behaviourist eccentricity. Besides, he was extremely busy.

In that he was more typical of his day than might be at first suspected. Because of the Wilde scandal, because Ernest Dowson and Lionel Johnson drank themselves to death, because of *Les Fleurs du Mal* and Beardsley's grotesque gnomes, the nineties are invariably recalled in terms of absinthe and the Café Royal, in the same way that the 1920s are recalled in terms of Scott Fitzgerald. In actual fact a great number of playwrights, novelists, and poets were, during the hectic twenties, laying the basis of solid reputations, and the nineties saw Kipling, Hardy, Meredith, and Bridges at their best, with Henry James, Conrad, Wells, and Bennett at the start of their careers.

The first number of the *Yellow Book* seems indeed, at the distance of more than half a century, a singularly restrained knocking of the younger generation at the gates. It contains in "Stella Maris" a sultry tribute by Arthur Symons to "the chance romances of the streets," a whimsical "defence of cosmetics" by Max Beerbohm which the critics took over seriously, and a relatively suggestive drawing by Aubrey Beardsley, *L'Education Sentimentale*. But the greater part of the book is highly innocuous. The contributors include such venerable names as Edmund Gosse, A. C. Benson, George Saintsbury, and John Oliver Hobbes; a fifth of the book is devoted to a short story by Henry James, while the father of the present writer won his literary spurs there with a twenty-page plea for "reticence in literature." The nineties were very far from being "all bawd and Baudelaire." But because the three most brilliant of *les jeunes* were also the most wayward, the green carnation has been accepted as the symbol of the decade.

The fact that it was, influenced, if indirectly, the course of *The Lipton Story*.

It is one of the features of Lipton's life that he should always have been the right man in the right place at the right moment, like a character in a play, whose entrances are being prepared for him by the action of the plot while he is off the stage, while he is no more to the audience than a name upon a programme. Lipton was apart from the spirit of the decade, but the decade nevertheless helped set the stage for him. In spite of its affectations, in spite of its pose of *fin de siècle* world-weariness, the green carnation was a gesture of revolt, a defiant reaction against the decorum of the long Victorian regime. Everything had gone too smoothly for too long. There was a need now for frivolity and colour; for something new. And though the scandal of the Wilde exposure discredited one particular aspect of that revolt, the first forts of the defences had been taken. Certain barriers had gone down. And the very fact that that particular aspect of the revolt had been discredited made the way easier for Lipton.

Not that the most acute scanning of the horizon could have revealed in the mid-1890s the part that Lipton would be playing within five years' time; no one could have been more unknown. Everyone had heard of Lipton's teas. But no one knew or cared whether there was a real man behind them any more than they knew or cared whether there was a real man behind Dewar's whiskey, an anonymity to which no one could have been more indifferent than Lipton. He was far too busy to worry about anything that did not directly concern his business. He was working with every ounce of energy, not merely to increase his commercial empire, but as an anodyne to deaden his sorrow for his mother.

He had now no relief from work, and the pressure of work was increasing monthly. By 1893 Ceylon was exporting more than eighty million pounds of tea as opposed to twenty-four million pounds in '88, and by '98 the figure had reached one hundred and twenty million. In the expansion of the Ceylon tea trade Lipton's interests were intimately identified. The produce of his five estates could no more meet the demand for his quarter- and half-pound packets than the counters of his three hundred shops, and he was soon buying heavily in the Colombo auctions.

He publicised his Ceylon estates; the labels on his packets illustrated the various stages by which tea was brought from the upcountry estate, by basket, by train, by steamer, to the London table. He gave, or rather did not discourage, the impression that all his teas came from his own gardens, but if every packet bearing a Lipton's label had come from his own property, he would have needed to own half the island. He slashed his slogan, "Direct from the tea garden to the teapot," but in point of fact, and very obviously, that is how all tea reaches the consumer, only—what is not so generally realised—it has to be blended on the way.

The process of tea manufacture after the tea has left the factory is briefly this: It is, in the case of Ceylon, sent first to a broker in Colombo, who distributes samples to the various shippers. The shippers taste it, set their price on it, then bid for it at the auction in accordance with that price and their respective needs. The various kinds of tea, once bought, are then either shipped to England to be blended, or are blended on the spot to be exported to various overseas markets.

Success in tea depends upon skilful blending. The quality and bouquet of good Indian or Ceylon tea are derived from the leaves that are grown in the hills at a height of three or six thousand feet. A straight estate tea is a magnificent drink, but the marketing of it could not be a profitable proposition. Moreover, its taste varies from day to day, month to month, year to year, just as the taste of wine does; it is the blender's job to produce an article that will have the same look and flavour year by year. As many as twenty different teas will go into one packet, the fine up-country teas being blended with the fuller-bodied teas grown at medium elevations. The tea merchant cannot, like the vintner, declare a vintage year. It is not his business to produce a superb tea that he cannot repeat. It is his business to find the best tea whose standard he can steadily maintain. At this time the tea that went into the Lipton packet was a blend of Ceylon and Indian teas in the requisite ratio to give a distinct Ceylon character, the blending for trade in the United Kingdom being done in London.

In actual fact only a small part of the tea that went into Lipton's packets came from his own estates. At the same time the ownership of those estates was of great impor-tance to him, both as publicity and because they provided a good training ground for his staff, because they kept his Colombo staff in touch with the realities of tea production, and because the ownership of estates allowed him to enter samples of his own tea at exhibitions. The Dambatene group produces some of the finest tea that can be tasted. Once he offered a packet of gold-tipped tea for public auc-tion in Mincing Lane that sold at thirty six guineas the pound.

Lipton could not have entered the tea trade at a more propitious moment. Within a few months his sales were accelerating at such a pace that he was planning to enter the American market. "That great republic," William H.

Ukers has remarked, "was born with a prenatal disinclination for tea": a disinclination that was encouraged during the middle of the century by its introduction, through
German and Austrian immigrants, to the excellence of
coffee—a beverage that the English cook has never understood. Tea was scarcely drunk in America in the 1890s,
and Lipton was more than shocked by the cavalier treatment that was extended on the other side of the Atlantic
to "his leading article." In April 1892 he wrote in the *Ceylon Observer:* "I saw last autumn in Chicago, at the door
of one of the leading grocers in State Street, tea exposed
to all kinds of weather as you would rice and barley at
home. When you purchase tea in those shops, they put it
up in a very careless manner and a cheaply got-up bag. I
asked about Ceylon tea and they said they had never
heard of tea from that place. They had Colongs, Japan,
and common sorts of green tea. These teas, if they had
ever been good, were entirely destroyed by the careless
way in which they were treated."

He was convinced, however, that Americans could be
persuaded to like tea once they had learned how it should
be stored and served. He decided to invest heavily in the
project and persuaded Ceylon to take a stall in the
Chicago Exposition of '93.

Ceylon owed and owes a great deal to Lipton. But his
relations with Ceylon were not always cordial. The Ceylon
planters had lost heavily through the failure of the coffee
crop, and they were anxious to recoup as quickly as they
could. They considered that Lipton sold his tea too
cheaply. They wanted, moreover, to publicise Ceylon tea
as a competitor of Indian tea. They distrusted a proprie-

tary brand, while Lipton naturally wanted only the best
and most suitable tea to be packed under the Lipton label.
In early days Ceylon and Lipton were working at cross-
purposes. Lipton, taking a longer view, identified the island's interests with his own, a policy the planters on the
whole resented. It was all very well, they said, for Lipton
to plaster his tea packets with pictures of Dambatene, to
fill his house with great brass gongs and immense ebony
elephants, to have his front door opened by a Sinhalese
servant in a long white dress and long hair held in place
by tortoise-shell combs. It was all very fine publicity for
Lipton to appropriate Ceylon as a private colony, but
where did the rest of Ceylon come in? Even now the Cey-
lonese will say resentfully, "Have the English ever heard
anything about this island apart from Lipton?" And
though at this late day it is impossible to discover whether
he was ever officially proposed, it would appear to be certain that he was never elected to the Colombo Club.

§ 8

TEA during this period was his first preoccupation, but
he did not on that account ignore his markets. His
policy was to open a new shop every week, and in 1892 a
North Country member of Parliament was to say to his
constituents in discussing the Home Rule Bill, "If Ireland
has a parliament of her own, then Wales will have one,
and Scotland will surely have one. The North of England
will be demanding one. Parliaments will be as common as
Lipton's provision stores and I respectfully submit that
they will not be equally as useful."

F

His press-cutting albums for the 1890s read like the stages of a Roman conquest. Ipswich, Derby, Oldham, Nottingham, one by one they were incorporated in the Lipton empire. In paper after local paper appeared a general handout article headed "A Gigantic Business," opening with the words, "Hitherto America has had the reputation of excelling the world in the way of big things . . ."

Every year brought its own special triumph. In 1895 he got a royal warrant to supply the Queen with tea. The War Office gave him a canteen contract in which he showed his old appreciation of the particular need of the poorest purchaser by having made up small penny packets of soap and sauce and blacking. He still thought in terms of the needs of Crown Street. Always, all through his career, that was his strength.

In 1896 he opened his new offices in the City Road. They were the subject of lengthy articles in trade journals.

Everything he touched was prospering, but to the general public he was still an unknown man. In England and in America a lift was going up. The years 1870–1900, before Roosevelt's anti-trust legislation started the first attack upon private enterprise, laid the basis of innumerable transatlantic fortunes. England had not been seriously disturbed by war since Waterloo. The resources of the Empire had multiplied. Lipton had made a fortune, but so had a great many others. He was in the middle nineties just one of several: and one, moreover, who had never publicised himself, who had never been "seen about," never "been anywhere," never given himself a chance of being talked of.

No one could have foreseen, least of all himself, when the New Year's chimes of '97 rang to him across the valley, that before he next heard those bells he would be a public figure.

That spring when he visited Ceylon he travelled on the *Oratava*. When the ship ran ashore in the Red Sea his reaction to the accident was typical. The captain having given orders that some of the cargo was to be jettisoned, Lipton persuaded one of the engineers to cut him out a stencil, and while the other passengers were hurriedly packing such luggage as they could carry by hand into the lifeboats, he was hard at work painting the slogan, "Drink Lipton's Tea," onto such of the abandoned bales as would be likely to float in the shallow water. This was the second of the occasions on which his love of publicity was considered to have exceeded the limits of propriety. He was no more abashed, however, by the captain's rebuke than he had been by Sir Henry Ponsonby's. No sooner was he ashore than he persuaded a cable station to send an "All's well" message back to London. The cable, with its signature "Lipton," was printed in every paper in the country. Though he lost his luggage in the Red Sea, he received ample compensation in publicity.

He arrived in Colombo at the end of March. He had invited there as his guests Lord and Lady Breadalbane, the first members of what was then called "the big world" to become his friends. They were certainly prominent members of it, the Marquis of Breadalbane, in honour of whose first ancestor "The Campbells Are Coming" had been written, a Knight of the Garter, the owner of half a

million acres, husband of the Duke of Montrose's youngest daughter, was in addition one of the foremost Liberal
peers whose services to the party had been recognised by
Gladstone with the Lord Stewardship of the Royal Household. Lipton had met them on a train, and a friendship
that was to prove lasting had arisen quickly. They had attended his staff party in '96 and had agreed that after big-
game shooting in India they would visit him in Ceylon.

He prepared a typical tourist's fortnight for them, a few
days to begin with in Colombo at the G.O.H., a day or
two in Kandy at the Queen's Hotel, and then the tea estate at Dambatene. They did all the tourist things: at
Kandy they drove through the Peradeniya Gardens and
saw the orchid house; they watched the sacred elephants
being bathed; they took off their boots outside the Temple
of the Tooth and saw the great jewelled bell in which the
sacred relic is preserved. The yellow-robed librarian
showed them the holy books, long narrow strips of parchment held together by cord and bound in silver, explaining how the parchment was first inscribed with a long
pointed pen and then rubbed over with black paste, giving them an inch-long section as a souvenir. In the evening, before dinner, they strolled round the lake which the
last King of Kandy had constructed by the flooding of a
paddy field.

Then they went on to Dambatene. The railway now ran
the whole way to Haputale. As they climbed, the air grew
cooler till it was almost cold, Lipton warning them that
the change of altitude very often made the visitor feel faint
for the first few hours. They had their first taste of un-
blended tea, Lipton watching them with a twinkle as they
sipped. Yes, there was as much difference, they assured

him, between this and packet tea as between a château-bottled Lafite of a great year and the *vin ordinaire* of a table d'hôte. After tea he took them out into his garden. Then, as now, though it has been rebuilt since, the estate house at Dambatene stood on a spur of land from which at the foot of the garden the hill fell precipitately two thousand feet towards the valley. In Colombo the press-men had assured Breadalbane that there would be much at Haputale to remind the head of the Perthshire Camp-bells of their home on Loch Tayside. "Those reporters were right," he said. Lipton smiled. "You wait till you see the view from my shooting box."

The shooting box stood on a farther and higher spur of land, a thousand feet or so above Dambatene. At the very edge of the spur Lipton had had built a wide stone seat. He loved looking out over big distances. It gave him a sense of power. Few finer panoramas can be seen. On a clear day you can see the sea sixty miles away. In the mid-dle distance is a sheet of water, one of the old tanks by which, before malaria had driven out its population, that section of the island had been irrigated. There are the winding red paths upon the hillsides, the dull green of the jungle grass, the brilliant green of paddy, the wintering rubber trees, grey and ghostlike, the dark stretch of jungle, the bright gleam of the river, the white spire of a Catholic church, the corrugated iron roofs of coolie lines and fac-tories.

Standing beside his guests, Lipton pointed out the land-marks one by one, then stretched his arm towards the left. "My Oakfield tea estate," he said. He moved his arm over the centre. "Monerakanda, that's mine too." His arm swept across to the extreme right. "My rubber estate, Keenapitya." Sweeping his arm from right to left across the landscape, he gave the impression of owning the entire island.[3]

With curious and speculative eyes his guests observed him. If they were a new type to him, he was very certainly a new type to them. Nothing could have been less like the conventional self-made millionaire, the Sir Gorgius Midas of the Punch cartoons. He may well have presented them with a conundrum. What, they must have asked themselves, was a man such as this doing with that large house in London, these tea estates out here, a multi-millionaire who did not spend a penny on himself, who put back into his business every penny he earned, who never allowed himself any fun, yet who had none of the instincts of a miser, who was generous, who was always giving things away, who had none of the instincts of the recluse, who was on the contrary extremely sociable, who enjoyed company, who met a new acquaintance three quarters of the way? "This can't go on," they must have thought. "He's bound to break out somewhere soon. A man like this can't live forever for his business." At the back of their minds there can have been little doubt of the way in which he would break out. Forty-six. . . . It was the dangerous age.

Well, and they were half right at that.

A few days later their ways for the time divided, the Breadalbanes going on to China on the *Coromandel*, Lip-

[3]They tell a story in Colombo of an occasion when Lipton was rash enough to stage this particular and very favourite act in the presence of an employee who had every reason to believe that his contract was shortly to be ended. "All mine," Lipton said, "all mine." The employee bustled forward. "No, no, sir, you're mistaken. Your Oakfield estate ends there. Your Monerakanda estate doesn't begin till there, and Keenapitya . . ." The employee started on his return trip that afternoon.

ton sailing for London on the *Austral* on the sixteenth of April.

The days and hours that immediately precede a change of fortune have, in retrospect, when that change is unforeseen, a curious quality of dramatic irony. There should have been a last-minute feeling, and there wasn't.

Was it in that spirit that Lipton in later years looked back to those last hours in Ceylon, or had he a premonition, a foreknowledge, that there was awaiting him in London a "date with destiny"?

He reached England at the end of April.

In the following week there appeared in *The Times* a letter addressed by the Princess of Wales to the Lord Mayor of London:

In the midst of all the many schemes and preparations for the commemoration of the Queen's Diamond Jubilee, when everybody comes forward on behalf of some good cause—when schools, hospitals and other charitable institutions have been so wisely and liberally provided for—there seems to me to be one class that has been overlooked—the poorest of the poor in the slums of London. Might I plead for these—that they also should have some share in the festivities of that blessed day, and so remember to the end of their lives that great and good Queen whose glorious reign has by the blessing of God been prolonged for 60 years.

Let us therefore provide these poor beggars and outcasts with a dinner or substantial meal during the week of the 22nd of June. I leave it to your kind and able organisation to arrange that the very poor in all parts of London should be equally cared for.

She enclosed her cheque for one hundred pounds.

It was the kind of appeal to which Lipton invariably responded. For many years he had been in the habit of giving cheese and hams or a consignment of tea to local charities. He had a giving nature, and it was good publicity. It was natural for him to offer for this occasion all the tea and sugar that might be needed for the Princess's Fund.

His gift, as he had expected it to be, was widely publicised, and he was thanked warmly by the Lord Mayor, Sir George Faudel Phillips.

"How's the fund going?" Lipton asked.

"Not too well, I am afraid," the Lord Mayor answered.

There had been a good many recent claims on the public's charity. There had been the Indian Famine Fund and a fund for the Welsh miners, another for wounded Greeks. Sir Edward Lawson was organising a shilling fund in the *Daily Telegraph*. Every family in the country had been involved in additional expenses of one kind and another. The Princess's Fund, as the last arrival, was faring so badly that of the £30,000 that would be required only a sixth had been subscribed. Lipton made his mind up quickly. He took out his chequebook and wrote an order for £25,000.

It was the most important single act in his whole life.

It has been said that with that cheque Lipton bought his knighthood. And in a sense he did. Yet nothing can have been farther from his intention when he signed it. He knew of course that his gift would be a good advertisement. With his eye for the effective slogan, he must have foreseen that it was the kind of gesture that would catch the public's eye. By insisting that his gift should be anonymous he knew, too, that he would excite curiosity and that he would get double publicity when his identity was finally revealed. He can have had no intention of remaining permanently anonymous. He was not the man to do good, or indeed anything, by stealth. He was a man, it must be remembered, who had no private life, who was absorbed in his business, who lived for his work, whose fun, whose hobby was his business. "I advertise my business, not myself," he said. But he had reached the point where any advertisement for himself was also an advertisement for Lipton's. He was no longer the owner of a chain of stores; he was the salesman of a national, of an international commodity. Publicity for "Lipton" was publicity for Lipton's tea. He could never act, he never did act, in a purely personal capacity. He and Lipton's tea were one.

At the same time he had a giving, a generous nature and a great feeling for the poor. He had lived among them. He had been one of them. He was not a man who rationalised his actions. He tried to kill two birds with a single stone and usually he succeeded. He trusted his instincts and he acted swiftly. His actions were subconscious thought. If an inner voice said to him, "Do this," he did it and prepared to exploit the consequences. He was like a boxer who sees an opening, punches, cannot foresee the effect of his punch, but is poised to follow up. If Lipton had thought the matter out before he signed that cheque—and we can be very sure that he did not—his reasoning would have been, "I shall be doing a great service to a great many unhappy people. I shall also be getting many thousand pounds' worth of free, and therefore the best, publicity." That is how his subconscious reasoning counselled him.

He knew what he was doing. But he did not know, he could not have guessed, how much he was doing. As a "stunt" that cheque was to prove more effective than a ten-ton cheese. The press leaped upon the story. Paragraph after paragraph speculated on the identity of the unknown donor. Lipton was not then well known outside the circle of his business interests; his name would not occur automatically to a newspaperman in connection with large-scale charity. He had been connected with the fund through his offer to supply the tea and sugar, and the Press Association laid their bets on him. But the Central News favoured Mr. Astor, while there were those who insisted that it was either Sir Edward Lawson or Sir Ernest Cassel. To an interviewer who asked him whether he was the donor Lipton laughingly replied, "I wish you would tell me where I could borrow twenty-five thousand pounds."

For ten days the paragraphs piled up. Then at the psychological moment, when curiosity was at its height, before it had begun to wane, he allowed the Lord Mayor to reveal the secret—the story being put out that the indiscretion of the bank clerk who had handled the cheque made further concealment of the donor's identity impossible.

The news value of the story was instantly redoubled. Lipton was a new figure in the field. Sir Ernest Cassel and Mr. Astor had signed so many cheques. The interviewers swarmed round the offices in City Road. And Lipton was telling a new audience the story of his early struggles, his "orphans," his leading article, his monster cheeses, his buxom ladies, his pound notes.

The general fanfare of panegyrics was accentuated rather than diminished by the one or two captious criticisms that came from the left-wing press; from the *Daily Chronicle,* who argued that this kind of charity was by no means desirable, that poverty should not be alleviated but the causes of it removed; and from *Reynold's,* at that time a belligerent news-sheet, whose leading article makes strange re-reading now, half a century later, when income tax and death duties, as the legacy of two wars, have liquidated industrial fortunes. "Our rich classes," it said, "have . . . apparently . . . made up their minds that the old Roman policy adopted in Rome's decline of 'Bread and Games' is the policy to play now. There are so many rich people who can afford to buy the masses and who will not hesitate to do so if any large policy or social reform becomes in their opinion dangerous. Our democratic friends who think the problem before them is so simple would do well to give some attention to this aspect of the question."

Lipton's punch had landed and he was swift to follow it. He denied at first that there was any question of his being given any say in the organisation of the dinners. But of course, and very properly, within a few days the control of proceedings was within his hands. Naturally he publicised the dinner with habitual, trained skill. Australia presented twenty thousand carcases, and he supplied exact details of how those carcases would be apportioned. He loved statistics and so, up to a point, he knew it well, does the public. He gave the kinds of statistics that were wanted. To provide four hundred thousand persons with a meal consisting of a one-pound meat pie, a two-pound loaf, a quarter-pound plum pudding, a quarter pound of cheese, and one half pound of cake, seven hundred tons of food would be required. Four hundred Pickford vans would be needed. Since one man could pack thirty parcels in an hour, sixteen thousand men would be required to work an

eight-hour day; nine thousand waiters would be needed
to distribute the packages.

Research has failed to reveal a single reference to
Thomas Lipton in *The Times* up to the end of December 1896. But from May 1897 onwards scarcely a
day passed in which there was not some reference to him
in the London press. By the time the Jubilee Dinner had
been given with spectacular success, he had his second
trump to play. He was busy with another project, the
Alexandra Trust to provide wholesome food for the poor
of London at the price of a few pennies. His contribution
to this trust was to be £100,000, which was the Lipton way of following up a punch. Within three months of
his return from Ceylon he was a public figure.

His inner voice could not have counselled him more
wisely; it might even be credited with powers of prophecy.
Two consequences to that anonymous gift Lipton could
not have conceivably foreseen. He realised, naturally, that
royalty would be grateful. The Princess of Wales had been
faced with the humiliating prospect of having her fund
written off as a failure. She was in a fix, and someone would
have had to extricate her—probably Sir Ernest Cassel. She
must have been worried quite a little. Lipton's cheque was
the more welcome because it was completely unexpected.
It was perfect timing. Twenty-five thousand pounds at
that moment meant more than a million later on. Of
course Lipton realised that. But equally at that time
royalty meant little to him. The court was a world
apart. He can scarcely have realised the full greatness and graciousness of the princess whose gratitude he
was to earn; certainly he cannot have guessed that that
gratitude was going to lead him to the first real friendship

of his life. How could he have foreseen that his first personal friend was to be the future King of England?

Nor could he have foreseen the repercussions that his gift was to have on the other side of the Atlantic, particularly in New York. For fifteen years he had been visiting America. He had stockyards in Chicago and Omaha. A large part of his wealth came from there. But New York was a place that he had hurried through; it was a port, a railway station. He never wasted time. He was not a theatre-goer. He went straight from ship to station and a few weeks later from station back to ship. No one in New York knew anything about him. He had valuable properties in the Middle West, but so had many other men. He had done nothing in England to interest New York. His arrivals and departures were not news. New York in the 1890s was just as much a shop in which one day he would have earned the right to buy as it had been when he was living in Mike McCalligan's.

But now all that was changed. For years he had watched the reporters crowding round this and the other notability. Now they were crowding about him. His gesture had caught the American imagination. He was "Jubilee Lipton," and the cameras were clicking. It was something he could not have foreseen. He was news in New York at last.

It is from this visit indeed that we get our most accurate accounts of him. He was very long and very rawboned, they said. "His legs that moved like scissors when he walked tangled up in front of him on the divan of the Waldorf Hotel like the legs of a great spider." He was "a little robust after the British fashion, with ruddy complexion, a head growing prematurely bald, and the sort of face that anybody would say at once was English if he saw it in the Rocky Mountains or met it at the North Pole. His accent and manner of speech are distinctly British, and London British, with just a touch of the Scottish burr.

"He was dressed," the interviewers continued, "with immaculate neatness. His coat and trousers were of modest black and white striped wool. His vest was of buff linen with conventional pearl buttons. Under his standing collar was a black and white striped silk neck scarf tied in a flowing bowknot. No diamond flashed in the white shirt front. Two drops of gold served in place of the expected gems. A double gold watch chain with large and heavy links crossed his waist. His link cuff buttons were of heavy beaten gold, and a small pigeon-blood ruby gleamed with modest elegance from each set of buttons. He wore no ring. His shoes were of round-toed patent leather."

As every visiting fireman before and since, he was invited to express his opinion of the American woman. He spoke highly of her appearance. It was the period of the bicycling craze. "There are no bloomers and short skirts in England yet," he said; "the women ride in long skirts that catch in wheels and make accidents likely. I like these American short skirts. They seem to go with the bicycle. I shall be glad when London women adopt them." He spoke enthusiastically of the charms, physical, mental, and moral, of the American girl; so enthusiastically, indeed, particularly of the very young ones—they were called "broilers" then—that it seemed hard to understand how anyone who felt so strongly could remain a bachelor.

The story not unnaturally got around that he was looking for a wife, and a Chicago reporter whom Lipton was too busy to see took his revenge by supplying his editor with an imaginary interview. "I have arrived at that age," Lipton was reported to have said, "when I need a wife. I'm forty-seven years old and I've worked so hard that I've had no time to mingle in society and meet young women. I think I'm entitled to a little enjoyment in life. I want a home of my own and a companion who will sit at my table opposite me and pour out the tea at every meal. I've been called a confirmed old bachelor and I suppose it's true, all except the confirmed, but I'm not too old to learn married ways, I suppose, if I find the right sort of woman to teach me. I don't care how much money she has or her position in society . . . all I want is a good wife."

The effect of this "interview" was startling. Sacks of letters arrived by every mail. The lobby and corridors of the Auditorium Hotel were so crowded with waiting females that Lipton dared not leave his suite. It was the one occasion in his life when he had more publicity than he could cope with. It was the one occasion when he lost his temper with the press. "It is outrageous," he said, "that a visitor to your city should be treated in such a manner by the press. There is absolutely no truth in my having matrimonial intentions, and my treatment has been anything but courteous. I really do not know what to do about it, whether to treat the whole thing as a joke or demand a retraction."

On his return to the East the *New York Herald* remarked that there was "a hunted look in his eye and a nervous dread of women." He was an international figure now all right.

§9

O N HIS RETURN to England the pace was to accelerate. At the close of the year his name appeared in the New Year's Honours List as a knight bachelor. It was rumoured that this honour was being paid to him at the personal request of Princess Alexandra. A year before he had been, outside his immediate circle, an unknown man. Now the whole country was delighting in his honour.

"General gratification," wrote the *Daily Telegraph,* "will be felt at the inclusion of Mr. Lipton's name in this list. As a result of his own industry and capacity he has amassed very considerable wealth, which he disburses in the most generous and philanthropic fashion. His contribution to the fund inaugurated by the Princess of Wales for the purpose of supplying the poorest of the population of the metropolis with a dinner on Jubilee Day will be remembered no less because it secured to that generous and charitable object a perfect success than for the spontaneous and modest manner in which it was made."

The note struck by the *Telegraph* was echoed in the other papers. The *Spectator* was, it is true, in a fractious mood and regretted that it "could not entirely condone" Mr. Lipton's appearance in the list "because the honour following so soon on the Princess's ill-advised dinner to the slums makes it look as if the honour had been bought." But the general reception of the press was typified by *Vanity Fair's* comment that he was "an excellent amiable fellow and trade was properly honoured in him."

On January 18, in company with Her Majesty's solicitor, two of Her Majesty's doctors, and three colonial officials who had served Her Majesty's interests overseas, he crossed the Solent in the royal yacht to the house at Osborne that held for the ageing Empress so many memories of the husband who had planned it. Every vista of its grounds and garden, its terraces and winding roads, its long corridors with alcoves painted garter-blue and bordered with plaster sea shells that held bronze busts and statues of the Coburg family, the huge frescoes along the staircase, the symbolic portrayal of Neptune surrounded by a hierarchy of nude gods and goddesses yielding to Britannia the empire of the seas—they all reminded her of Albert.

She received her subjects in the India Room with Princess Victoria Eugénie of Battenberg in attendance and Colonel Lord Edward Pelham Clarke to effect introductions.

The name was announced of "Thomas Johnstone Lipton"; a tall rawboned man knelt upon a tasselled cushion and the Queen, tapping her sword upon the shoulder of the man from whom eleven years earlier she had refused the gift of a mammoth cheese, muttered in guttural accent, "Arise, Sir Thomas."

It was thirty-three years since he had sailed as an emigrant to try his fortune in America. He had travelled very far since then. He was to travel farther still in the thirty-three years of life that still remained to him.

The Queen was old, very old, her sight and senses failing her. The last January drive beside the widowed Duchess of Saxe-Coburg-Gotha was not far distant now. To those nine others, the solicitor, the doctors and the colonial judges, that moment in her presence, that bend-

G

ing of the knee, that tap upon the shoulder, came as the climax to a long career, to many years of service. To Lipton it was a stage of progress. As the yacht ploughed its way back to Portsmouth through the winter dusk he was already planning what was to be seen in retrospect as the high peak of his commercial story—the conversion of the Lipton name and the Lipton interests into a public company.

It was a move that had been long awaited and long prophesied, from the time when he had refused an offer from E. T. Hooley of two million pounds.

On the fifth of March the following paragraph appeared in the London *Statist*:

"If all the paragraphs about the probable conversion of Lipton which have appeared in the newspapers since May 1897 were paid for as advertisements the outlay would be nearly as much as would provide another free meal for the outcasts of London. The alternate assertions and denials of imminent conversion have been used over and over again, according to transatlantic methods, but the thing has been overdone; and, moreover, it is doubtful if the public generally in this country are yet educated up to approval of the 'authorised' statement by almost every newspaper of statements which have more than once been contradicted and reasserted also by express authority. It may be said that this is merely a way of drawing attention to a new company, and that, as it is pretty generally understood, no great harm is done. We do not like it, and we are inclined to think that, in the case of Lipton's, it will not have tended to attract the better class of investors. Of course, after the continuous proclamation about the shares being at a premium (before the prospectus has appeared), there may be a rush to make applications, as there was for the Burma Ruby Mines' issue, and as it was said there was for the Dunlop issues; but it is well to bear in mind that boomed issues have often shown a speedy reaction from an undue market hoist."

A week later the *Statist* was reconsidering its opinion. "The prospectus of this tea and general provisions company," it wrote, "is pretty much in accordance with the widely advertised preliminary announcements. The capital is £1,000,000 in Five per Cent. Cumulative Preference and £1,000,000 in Ordinary Shares of £1, the latter, so far as offered to the public, having the price fixed at £1.5 per share, and dealt in before the prospectus was issued at 15 premium beyond the issue figure of 5s. premium, say £2 for £1 share. There is also an amount of £500,000 of Four per Cent. Debenture stock, redeemable after September 1920 at 115 per cent. One third of each class of shares and Debenture stock will be taken at par by the vendor in part payment of the purchase price.

"The profits of the past have been somewhat less than were generally supposed. Falling from £68,000 in 1890 to £60,935 in 1893, and rising to £121,451 in 1896, the average for the seven years is £93,550. The last year before conversion shows, as usually may be observed in prospectuses of companies of this character, a sudden and remarkable jump. The profit for 1897 is put at £175,984, but the commemoration gift of £25,000 was probably an excellent advertisement of the business, and this, it may be assumed, was not debited to trade expenses. It would not be prudent, therefore, to take last year's profit by itself as a basis of calculation, but if the average for the eight years be reckoned, it comes out at £103,952, and if the goodwill be valued at three years' purchase we have £311,856, giving a total of £1,288,641. The purchase price has been fixed by the vendor at £2,466,666, of which £833,334 is to be in shares and Debentures and £1,633,332 in cash.

"The sensational response to the elaborately worked-up 'boom' in Lipton's conversion seems to us to imply that a vast number of people are ready to take part in a scramble with a chance of picking up premiums. No such rush for shares has been witnessed for many years. As the vendor and his friends together take nearly half of the capital, the Debentures and shares will very likely be kept pretty steadily for a time at a premium, and the vendor in any case will get in cash more than what a business man would consider to be the full value of all the assets of the business, including the goodwill, and he will have his shares and Debentures besides. It is noteworthy that no indication is given in the prospectus of the amount at which the Ceylon tea estates are valued, and a still more important omission is that there is no statement of the expenditure in advertising during each of the eight years. But probably most of the people who have applied for shares did not take the trouble to read the prospectus, and would have applied just the same if there had been nothing but the application forms."

Remarkable scenes took place. "It is only once in a decade," the *Telegraph* reported, "that the city sees an issue attended with so much excitement as that which has characterised the conversion of Sir Thomas Lipton's gigantic business, and it will undoubtedly serve as a landmark by which to estimate the magnitude of similar enterprises in the future."

"At the Lipton offices in the City Road," another paper said, "some hundred extra clerks are engaged, registering the shares, and even they are barely able to keep pace with the work. Sir Thomas Lipton has been besieged with personal applications."

The London representative of the *New York Times* was cabling home about "an extraordinary rush of people who knew nothing about the affairs of the company. But the 'tip' was generally circulated that it was a good 'gamble,' and the craze extended to the West End, where ladies of title, officers, and public men were among the people who besieged Sir Thomas Lipton, imploring him to take their money. At the Bank of Scotland, where the lists were opened, the police had to regulate the crowds."

The *Evening News* printed placards of "The Lipton Scramble," while the *Daily Mail* wrote, "If there had been a terrible panic-stricken run on the bank, people could not have been seized with a more frenzied eagerness to draw their money out than during these four days they had shown to pay their money in."

That was outside the Bank of Scotland.

"In the City Road, however," the article continued, "there was no rush, no hurry, no excitement. The big place was all sheer business. Never in one view had the visitor seen so many clerks as in the great high-windowed office on the ground floor of Lipton's head establishment. There were groves and groves of clerks, vistas of clerks; young clerks with black coats and serious faces; young women clerks with neat hair, all intent upon their paper and accounts. Method and organisation were visible everywhere. The Lipton flotation had the whole city mad, but it had not disorganised Lipton's."

Applications were received for forty million pounds'

worth of shares: almost a pound per head of the entire population of the British Isles. Anyone who thought he had any personal claim on Lipton exploited his power of persuasion.

Herbert Farjeon wrote a lyric once, "I danced with a man who danced with a girl who danced with the Prince of Wales." It was on this system that Lipton was besieged with applications. He chuckled over the situation with a *Daily Mail* reporter. "You have been making a lot of nice new friends lately, Sir Thomas," the reporter said. "You have been surprised, I dare say, to find how many know of you of whom you have never heard."

Lipton laughed. "I received a letter with an application for shares from a gentleman who said that nine years ago he was a passenger on a **P. &. O.** boat in the East, and he endeavoured to recall himself to my memory by the circumstance that he once passed me the mustard."

Lipton himself professed to take the whole thing calmly. He was chiefly concerned, he said, to have the shares issued in record time. "In three days I shall have all the refusals out. After that I don't mind so much. The acceptances can wait a day or two."

It was a big moment for him. Unaided, without a partner, without capital, without gambling, without trickery, he had built up a business that he had sold to the public for two and a half million pounds: of which he still retained the control through a large block of shares.

The *Vegetarian,* of all improbable papers, apostrophised him in the following sonnet:

Lipton! Albeit with affrighted breath
  In sonnet I'd perpetuate your name.
Who in these days of villainy and shame

Days of decrepit creeds and falling faith
Called for two millions and with gnashing teeth
   Men fought that thou should'st fifty million claim
   So great their faith in one whose sounding name
To million hogs's synonymous with Death.

Lo, on thy statue men shall read, "I am
   The man who turned his heav'n-enlightened wit
   On hurling pigs to cold Destruction's pit,
Who, spite of competition quack and sham
   Raised millions from mankind, whose name is writ
In miles of sausage, continents of ham!

How much he himself cleared over the transaction it is
hard to judge. He employed his familiar technique of cutting out the middleman. Brokerage firms got no cut. None
of the issue was underwritten. Only one outside person
seems to have been employed, the eccentric Panmure Gordon. "I'll put two hundred and fifty thousand in your
pocket, Lipton," he had said. "How?" he was asked.
"By charging them a five shilling premium."

One day it is to be hoped that a monograph will be written of Panmure Gordon. He was a type that has vanished
from the world. Educated at Harrow and at Oxford, ga-
zetted to the 10th Hussars, resigning his commission to join
the Stock Exchange, he was the greatest dandy in a day of
dandies, the most wastefully extravagant man in a lavish
period. Asked about his personal budget, he answered that
two thousand a month was required for a gentleman's necessities, carriage, horses, a yacht, a grouse moor.
"Of course if you want luxuries, it'll cost you more."

His bedroom was a sartorial museum. He bought gloves
by the gross; he had thirteen overcoats that he had never

seen, innumerable pairs of boots that he had never worn. A fire in his flat cost him eleven hundred neckties. In his office two shelves were reserved for hatboxes. He lived at Brighton. Every morning after a canter on the downs he rode straight to the station. In a private saloon on the train he changed into his city clothes. He was reputed to have 570 pairs of trousers, one for each day of the year, with a spare pair for rainy days. It is not inappropriate, by the law of contrasts, that such a one should have been the broker for the Lipton scramble. It is pleasant to be able to record that he died solvent.

On the second of June, in the Cannon Street Hotel, Lipton directed his first shareholders' meeting.

It was the first time in thirty years that he had had to answer for his actions. Since the day he had opened his first shop in Stobcross Street he had been beholden to nobody except his mother. It was he who had given orders. Now, when his fortunes were at their peak, there was something ironic, something inappropriate in his having to justify his conduct before a group of strangers.

Perhaps he himself felt that the whole episode was out of character. Certainly his manner at the meeting surprised some of his subordinates. He had memorised his speech, but he had memorised it inaccurately. He made mistakes and needed the prompting of a fellow director. He had not the air of authority to which they were accustomed. Nor did the meeting pass off without dispute, a gentleman of eighty with a blue ribbon in his buttonhole rising to protest against the sale of alcohol in the Lipton markets. If he had known, he said, that the directorate was going to embark on such activities he would never have applied for shares. He was shouted down with offers by the other shareholders to buy his shares from him and the incident was quickly over, but the protest had been made. Nor had it been handled from the chair with wit and ease. Lipton had looked shy and awkward. It was not the anticipated triumph.

Perhaps that was only natural. Lipton was unused to criticism. He was used to having his own way without discussion. Did he, as he watched the shareholders file out, experience foreboding? Did he wonder whether this business he had built up from nothing was still his own? For thirty years now he had lived for it. It had been his life. He had had no hobbies, no interests, no friends apart from it. Strangers were sharing it with him now. Did he suspect as he stammered over that first speech that he would never be able to feel for Thomas J. Lipton, Ltd. in the same personal way that he had for the Lipton markets?

Did he? It is hard to tell. He was a man who kept no diary, who wrote no letters, who was uncommunicative even to his closest friends about his inner feelings. But were he a character in a novel, it is very certain that the practised fiction writer would take that first shareholders' meeting as a crisis date. From that point on the hero of a "Lipton novel" would be made to feel the need for something that was his very own. For thirty years Lipton's had been his life. The stage is set for a concluding section showing how the fortune that had been built up so carefully over so many years was squandered in as many months on pearls and diamonds.

That is the obvious story. And in a way that was the story: it developed, however, along lines that no novelist would have been likely to devise. Lipton did "break out," in an entirely new direction, to serve a passion on which a large part of his fortune was to be spent. It was not, however, a passion that involved musical comedies and tiaras. It was a passion far more improbable, and in the last analysis far more romantic, and it began as grand passions do, light-heartedly. In the summer of 1898 he issued to the New York Yacht Club a challenge for the America's Cup.

§ 10

To appreciate what this challenge involved, it is necessary to put back the clock and review the history and the genesis of these races.

In 1851 the *America,* a yacht specially constructed at the order of six American sportsmen, was sent across the Atlantic as a challenge to British yachtsmen. The social welcome given to the yacht could not have been more expansive, but no one was in any haste to challenge it. Finally Commodore Stevens himself issued a challenge on behalf of the *America.* He offered to match his schooner against any British vessel for any stake from one to ten thousand guineas. Again no one was in a hurry to accept. But at last the *America* got her chance. The Royal Yacht Squadron was holding a race for a hundred-guinea cup. There were no time allowances. All the squadron boats were eligible to sail irrespective of tonnage. The *America* was invited to join the race.

The race was sailed on August 22. Fifteen yachts were entered. The largest was the *Brilliant,* a three-masted 400-ton schooner. The *Aurora,* a 47-ton cutter, was the smallest. The *America* was 170 tons. Within a very short time the *America* was in the lead. At one point she was leading by eight miles. As she passed the Needles she saluted Queen Victoria's yacht. The Queen enquired who was second. Her Majesty's officers peered through the thickening weather and reported that there was no second. Towards evening when the wind fell light—and lack of wind was the one thing dreaded by Commodore Stevens and his crew—the *Aurora* managed to pull down this lead, but even so the *America* crossed the line twenty-four minutes to the good. The third boat did not arrive till an hour later. The majority of the other twelve contestants failed to complete the course. The hundred-guinea cup went home with the *America,* to be handed over by Commodore Stevens to the New York Yacht Club, a permanent challenge trophy in a competition to be known as the America's Cup.

The deed of gift contained a number of stipulations which are of a technical nature and with which the layman does not need to be concerned, the main stipulation being that "the vessels selected to compete for this cup must proceed under sail on their own bottoms to the part where the contest is to take place." The challenger had to repeat the feat of the original *America,* to sail the Atlantic and beat the defender in her own waters.

From 1868 onwards a series of attempts were made to win back the cup. First the British tried through Mr. Ashbury with his *Cambria* and then *Livonia.* Next the Canadians tried with Major Gifford's *Countess of Dufferin* and the Bay of Quinte Yacht Club's *Atalanta.* Sir Richard Sutton made an attempt with the *Genesta,* Lieutenant Henn with the *Galatea,* and the Royal Clyde Yacht Club with the *Thistle*. Finally Lord Dunraven challenged with *Valkyrie* and after a defeat in 1892 challenged again with *Valkyrie III* in 1895.

This second challenge resulted in one of the most unfortunate incidents that have ever disfigured international sport; an incident, or series of incidents, that is best forgotten but that has to be recorded as it constitutes the background to Lipton's challenge. Briefly the facts are these:

The races between *Defender* and *Valkyrie* were sailed at Sandy Hook, and it will hardly be argued that the stewardship of the course was lamentable; innumerable boats packed with excursionists continually got in the way of the two yachts, interfering with the wind and obscuring the view. *Defender* won the first race. During the second race the interference from excursionists was even more exasperating, and shortly after the start the yachts collided, *Valkyrie* carrying away *Defender's* topmast shrouds. The yachts continued on the course and *Valkyrie* won. The committee, however, disallowed the win, considering that *Valkyrie* was responsible for the accident.

Lord Dunraven was not satisfied with this decision; he considered that owing to the interference from the excursion steamers no one could see what was happening; he maintained that he had himself been fouled, and he informed the America's Cup Committee that he would not race again unless the course was kept clear. By this time the relations between Lord Dunraven and the Cup Committee had become highly uncordial, and though a regulation was made that all excursion boats should keep half a mile away from the racing yachts, Dunraven was not satisfied.

On September 12, though *Valkyrie* toed the line beside *Defender*, Lord Dunraven did no more than cross the line; then he sailed away, retiring from the race and leaving the field clear for *Defender*. His action was followed by an outburst of that kind of moral indignation that is specially reserved for athletic contests in which national prestige is involved.

Worse, however, was to follow. On his return to England, Dunraven published in the *Field* an article that was mainly extracted from a report he had sent to the Royal Yacht Squadron. In this article not only did he set out his complaints against the manner in which the course had been encumbered with excursionists, but he charged that "in the first race the *Defender*, after being measured, was surreptitiously loaded so as to sink her four inches deeper in the water, that she sailed in that condition on the first day's race, and that immediately after that race the ballast so loaded was secretly removed so that when measured the next day no discrepancy was found to exist between the two measurements."

This was a serious and shocking charge. Very properly and promptly the New York Yacht Club called for an investigation, which Lord Dunraven was invited to attend. He did so, with Mr. G. K. Askwith (later Lord Askwith) as his counsel. All the evidence tended to show that a visual mistake as to *Defender's* load water line had been made by *Valkyrie's* party. The commission sat for several days. Its investigations were confined to the question of whether *Defender* had or had not been irregularly loaded with ballast, and the examining commission failed to find any justification for Lord Dunraven's charges.

The indignation in America against the preferring of these charges was widespread and intense.

At this late day it is unprofitable to reopen a most unfortunate controversy. There can be no doubt that Lord Dunraven was unwise to make his suspicions the subject of an article in a periodical. It is also clear that the New York Yacht Club did everything within its power to investigate the charges impartially. It was never suggested that the owners of the yacht were themselves guilty of any trickery—it is hardly conceivable that men of such position could have been—and a layman reading the evidence today finds it hard to believe either that extra ballast could have been loaded or that there would have been any point in doing so in view of the fact that the load water line on which *Defender* was measured before and after the race was approximately that under which she had sailed successfully in the trial races.

There are certain points, however, to be remembered: a great deal of money was at stake; a number of unscrupulous persons stood to make large profits; a few years later a not dissimilar case arose in which, unknown to the owner, the ballast of a yacht was found to have been interfered with, and in consequence the winner of some six races was disqualified; finally a certain obscure person who before the races was apparently unpossessed of property retired permanently into conditions of some ease. The last word should be given to Lord Dunraven. Years later in his autobiography, *Past Times and Pastimes*,[1] he was to write:

"I am not sure that I like international contests. In such

---

[1] Quoted by courtesy of Lord Dunraven's executors

matters as yacht racing, polo, golf, and so on, I think they tend to demoralise sport by turning it into a serious business in which national prestige is at stake, and to convert amateurs, playing a game for the game's sake, into professional specialists struggling for their country's sake. Moreover, there are critics in sport, as in everything else, and though rules are in all cases identical, and are equally observed, different people view a game from different angles, and misunderstandings may occur.

"In those days the course was very badly kept. Excursion steamers thronged it and hampered the yachts badly. Not purposely, I dare say, for steamer captains did not understand the effect of their lofty vessels upon the wind and were anxious to give spectators their money's worth. Their unwelcome attentions were probably impartially bestowed, but it would be only human nature if a skipper was meticulously careful not to interfere with his own side. That has all been altered, I believe, and latterly courses have been admirably kept.

"The protest that it was my duty to make against the *Defender* in 1895 created an amount of excitement that could not have been exceeded if someone had deliberately hurled an insult at the American nation. The tide of feeling ran very high. It was a curious, serio-comic experience. The London Stock Exchange cabled New York that they hoped that, when war was declared, excursion steamers would not get in the way of our fleet; and the New York Stock Exchange replied that in the interests of a fair fight they hoped our warships would be better than our yachts. All very funny, but not funny to me, for though I found many very good friends I did not have a pleasant time: and the matter was more serious than comic, for indeed it really looked as though a protest about a yacht race was going to cause serious estrangement between two nations.

"When I went over to attend a very belated enquiry, I was smuggled out of the liner at Sandy Hook. My good friend Maitland Kersey took lodgings for me close to the New York Yacht Club, where the enquiry was held, and I was under close police protection. A protest has nothing to do with motives or responsibilities. It is a mere question of facts—whether so-and-so happened or did not happen, whether this or that was or was not done, whether the protest was frivolous or justified; but when the facts become submerged in a great wave of emotion, they are lost sight of and a protest became absurd. I don't say whether evidence was or was not withheld, but I am very sure that not one of the American crew of the tender in which we lived would have dared to give evidence against the *Defender* had they wished to do so. Well, I am not going to reopen that question even to myself. But I thought at the time, and I think still, that to raise a game or a race to such a pitch is not conducive to real sport."

Such was the background to Lipton's first challenge in the summer of 1898. So bad were the feelings that *Truth* wrote in the course of a long leader, "Not a year goes by without some trouble being threatened in almost every branch of sport. For the sake of peace and quietness such events as races for the America's Cup are rather to be deprecated than otherwise."

In view of what was to happen in the next thirty years, this general background should be kept in mind.

Lipton's challenge came as a surprise to everyone. He had never evinced much interest in yachting. He had, it

is true, as early as 1887, written to William Lynn of Cork,
suggesting that he would like to try for the cup with a boat
designed by an Irishman, built by an Irishman, and
manned by Irishmen. But the suggestion had met with no
encouragement and he had readily abandoned it. In the
many interviews he gave in America as "Jubilee Lipton"
he never mentioned any designs upon the cup. Over and
over again he insisted that his only hobby was his business.
It was suggested at the time, and it has often been stated
since, that he issued his challenge to advertise his teas.
That is true, of course, but only partly true; it is about as
justified as the sneer that he bought his knighthood for
twenty-five thousand pounds. He was a superb showman.
His interests were identified with Lipton's. What was effective publicity for him was also effective publicity for
Lipton's. Now that Lipton's was a public company he was
personally more interested in promoting Sir Thomas Lipton than Thomas J. Lipton, Ltd. It cannot be too often repeated that he was a man of automatic reflexes. Looking
for fresh worlds to conquer, the America's Cup looked to
be as good a bet as any.

The French write of the *coup de foudre*, but as often as
not the grand passion of a man's life starts out of some
quite casual preference, out of a chance invitation to a
cocktail party. That is how it was with Lipton. He had
many irons in the fire, why not the *Shamrock* too? He had
never known failure yet; he did not anticipate failure now.
He knew America and he loved America. He was happy
among Americans. He had no fear of "incidents." "There
is no country in the world," he said, "where a British subject will receive more true kindness or be more certain of
getting better or fairer treatment than at the hands of our

H

American cousins, and whatever the result of the contest may be, I have every confidence that the best boat will win." With a light heart he slipped that extra iron in the fire.

He could afford in that hour to be light-hearted. Not only his own fortunes, but his country's, too, were at their peak. A few Boers might be grumbling in the Transvaal, but who could bother about that? Certainly not Lipton, who was never concerned with anything but the job in hand. Never had he been busier. Never had he been happier. Never had his routine endorsed more fully his motto: "There is no fun like work."

That summer he catered for the Army on manoeuvres. In retrospect it may well seem strange that with war in South Africa only a few months distant the provisioning of an army on the move should have been handed to a civilian firm, and indeed the contract was criticised in certain quarters. But even there it was generally conceded that a difficult assignment had been well fulfilled, and the appointment sent up his stock.

He was busy, too, with the Alexandra Trust. "You can scarcely call it my scheme," he told the *Chronicle*. "It is the Princess of Wales's. She was so impressed by what she saw at our Jubilee Dinner that she now wants to do something for those same people every day and all the year round, not only on occasions."

They were planning, he explained, to serve good, wholesome, well-cooked food at its cost price. There was nothing in the form of charity about the scheme; no person would forfeit the slightest self-respect by using it. Overhead costs were to be reduced. There would be no waiters.

Customers would go to the counters, buy what they chose, and then either sit down and eat it there or take it home with them. A kind of cafeteria, in fact. He hoped to serve a small plate of meat and bread for fourpence, and a full meal of soup, bread, meat, and two vegetables for sixpence.

In the early summer he revisited New York, partly on business, partly to discuss his challenge for the cup. His matrimonial prospects were canvassed eagerly. The *New York World* featured a large cartoon captioned, "Bachelor Millionaire Lipton: Great New York Matrimonial Chances for an American Bride: the Man, the Money, and the Tea."

In the centre of the cartoon, as a framework for Lipton's portrait, was drawn a teapot; on the left were pictures of four young girls, on the right of four aging spinsters. Above the girls was written: "We four New York beauties love you for your success. We love you for your title." Above the four spinsters was written: "We love you for your tea."

The name and address of each candidate were given, and a brief interview was appended in which each lady in her turn admitted that Sir Thomas with his good looks, wealth, and title provided an irresistible combination; Miss Rose McNul, who lived at No. 183 Avenue C, New York, and was described as "a blonde of the Langtry type, and as beautiful as was the Jersey Lily in her girlhood days, with hair of a rich bronze-gold hue, eyes of deepest blue, and a mouth that was irresistible," asserting that she believed firmly in romance, and from looking at Sir Thomas's picture was convinced that she could love him. If that were not the case, his title and money would not "win a single smile from her." She was too young, she insisted, to be mercenary and, being a true American girl, she would not sell herself for a title. If Sir Thomas wooed her he must lay his heart first at her feet.

The other ladies were no less accessible.

But this time there were no awkward incidents, no queues of flower-laded suitors besieging him in the corridors of the Waldorf. He had his answers ready. "I am not looking for a wife," he said. "American girls are bright and charming, but so for that matter are English girls and French girls, so are German and Italian girls—all girls, in fact, except Spanish girls." This final qualification was prompted by the Spanish-American War, his sense of the slogan providing him as usual with a timely answer. So vigorously indeed did he express his loyalty to the Stars and Stripes that when he sailed for England the Empire State Society of the Sons of the American Revolution presented him with a flag.

At Liverpool the press was awaiting him. He was the new thing now, in London, as in New York. Years later, in a reminiscent article, T. P. O'Connor was to write, "One day London awoke and discovered the very remarkable man who had been living in contented obscurity for so many days in its midst. And the modest self-effaced man of business, content with his lot, was dragged willy-nilly into all the giddy stream of London's tumultuous life."

By the following spring the millionaire who two years before was dining every night at home had become a part of international society. The Prince of Wales accepted the presidency of the Alexandra Trust, and Lipton was invited to Sandringham for Whitsun. Everything he did was news.

On the Riviera he was dined by a party of Americans, and in the centre of the table was a flower-built model of the *Shamrock*. The menus—hand-painted seascapes—have each of them a four-leafed shamrock brooch attached to yellow and green streamers, on one of which was printed in letters of gold "The Shamrock." He purchased a steam yacht for three hundred thousand dollars and christened her the *Erin*. At the Prince of Wales Horse Show he bought the Marshall Belle and the Fille du Regiment for $2,750. He took a box at Covent Garden. The American press announced that he had three ambitions for 1899: to found the Alexandra Trust, to win the America's Cup, and to become a peer. His gifts to charity were numerous. He cabled ten thousand dollars to the fund for American wounded in the Spanish-American War. The Prince of Wales refitted his yacht, *Britannia*, for *Shamrock's* trials. When Lipton sailed for America in September he carried the good wishes of the country.

§ 11

HE SAILED at the right time. He could not have arrived more propitiously. The Spanish-American War was over, and New York was preparing to welcome, as only New York can welcome those it honours, the commodore who, sailing into Manila Bay with four cruisers and two gunboats, had utterly destroyed in seven hours a fleet of seven cruisers and five gunboats. Wireless was not then perfected, and with Admiral Dewey's *Olympia* arriving two days before she was expected, Lipton from the bridge of the *Erin* was the first to

spy her. When the *Olympia* had passed Ceylon she had
found there, with Lipton's compliments, a package of tea
for every member of the crew; the *Olympia* was properly
appreciative, and as the launch from the *Erin* drew up
under the *Olympia's* bows, Dewey was standing at the
gangplank. That night Dewey dined on the *Erin*. In all
that followed Lipton was to figure prominently.

Much was to follow. New York has known many proud
pageants during the last fifty years. But it is doubtful if any
has been more spectacular than that which honoured
Dewey in September 1899. The Spanish War was the first
that modern America had fought. It was the last war,
though no one guessed it then, to be waged in terms of
glamour; casualties had not been heavy; spectacular individual feats had been accomplished. It was the kind of
war one read about. And New York was in a mood to
honour in Admiral Dewey one who symbolised in his character and achievements the skill and courage of a nation.

With Van Wyck as the mayor and St. Clair McKelway
as the chairman, a hundred and fifty thousand dollars
were spent upon the celebrations; they were not spent
fruitlessly. First there was the long parade of yachts and
steamboats following the *Olympia* up the bay and through
the Hudson to Grant's Tomb, with J. P. Morgan's *Corsair*
leading the starboard section and *Erin,* with the rainbow
arrangement on her bunting, the American flag at each
truck, and the flag of the Royal Ulster Yacht Club at the
taffrail, leading the port line. The banks were lined with
cheering onlookers; the water was so crowded with river
craft that the surface could only be seen in intermittent
patches.

Then came the long land parade down Riverside Drive

to the triumphal arch built in Madison Square Garden on the model of the Arch of Titus with a touch of the Arc de Triomphe, where Dewey reviewed the troops. Lipton, as the city's guest, rode to take his place beside the saluting base with Mr. Croker, the commander of the *Nixon,* and the Hon. Charles Russell.

It was a tremendous spectacle, with Governor Roosevelt in his silk hat and frock coat heading the New York Troop; with the West Point cadets in their shakos and white trousers, their epaulettes and crossbelts; with the colour company carrying its tattered flag; with the 10th Pennsylvania Regiment fresh from Manila in soiled campaign uniforms; with the admiral's stand glittering with uniforms and the sunlit air full of autumn butterflies that appeared to mistake for flowers the flags and kites and bunting that flew from every window. On that day the old reservoir on Fifth and Forty-first served its last function in the city's life, as the base for a grandstand.

In the evening there was a smoking concert at the Waldorf for the *Olympia's* crew, with Lipton there, to be welcomed with cries of "Good luck, Shamrock!"

That was the last Saturday in September, and with the first race fixed for the following Tuesday, the carnival atmosphere swung over to the races. The races were indeed a continuation of the celebrations, with Lipton now figuring in the title role.

"Never in the history of these races," *Town Topics* wrote, "have there been here so many English men and women and so many noted visitors from abroad to witness them. We have with us, for example, Lord and Lady Charles Beresford; the Earl of Minto, Governor-General of Canada, and the Countess of Minto; the Hon. Charles Russell, Sir Henry Burdett, Mr. and Mrs. Kenneth Wilson and Miss Muriel Wilson, Lady Cunard, the Princess Leopold and Reginald de Croy, of Belgium; Lady Edith Fox-Pitt, Lieutenant-General Sir Andrew Clarke, of Victoria; Sir Horace Tozer, the Hon. W. P. Reeves and the Hon. John Alexander Cockburn, Agents General for New South Wales, New Zealand and South Australia, respectively, and the Princess de Hatzfeldt."

The excitement was intense. Everyone was mad to see the race. Vessels had been rechartered over and over again. British prestige did not at the moment stand particularly high on the other side of the Atlantic. The Transvaal crisis was drifting towards war, and the American press was definitely pro-Boer. Parallels were being drawn with '76. The *New York Times* was calling the whole affair "very sad and very shameful" and was comparing "the high-handed and unscrupulous Chamberlain to Lord North, and Morley and Frederick Harrison to Burke and Chatham." But New York has always accepted the individual for what he is. It had taken Lipton to its heart, and there was a universal resolve that the British boat should be given every chance, that there should be no repetition of the Dunraven episode, that the course should be kept clear.

Every day the excitement mounted. *Shamrock* was proving in her trials a far better yacht than had been expected. She was considered, as she had had to cross the Atlantic, a tougher vessel than *Columbia*, and if hard weather conditions prevailed it was held that she stood a fair chance of winning. Her toast was "reefing tackle and housed top-masts."

In England, too, excitement about the race was grow-ing. At the start interest had been lukewarm, with the *New York Times* correspondent noting a certain apathy, owing to the suspicion that Lipton's challenge had been prompted by purposes of self-advertisement, even suggest-ing that some sections were actually antagonistic to his chances. And perhaps it was only natural that the official yachting world should have been somewhat sceptical. The Royal Yacht Club had come to regard challenges for the America's Cup as its particular prerogative, and Lip-ton's challenge, since he was not a member of the squad-ron, had been made on his behalf by the Royal Ulster Yacht Club. The *Pall Mall Gazette* reported a yachtsman who "preferred to remain anonymous" as stating that Lip-ton's challenge had caused "a mingled feeling of surprise and amusement. For charming though Sir Thomas is, a challenge given by a person who hardly knows the stern of a boat from the bow is not likely to excite much enthusi-asm among yachtsmen."

Lipton had good friends, however, among the press, par-ticularly in the Harmsworth section, and very soon their efforts, coupled with *Shamrock's* good showing in her trials, whipped up excitement. On a plot of land facing the Embankment, behind the *Daily Mail* offices in Car-melite Street, the *Evening News* put up a big hoarding with the Sandy Hook course marked on it and two minia-ture yachts inserted in the back, to be moved through slits in the canvas so that the crowd could watch the progress of the race.

The date of the first race was October 3. That evening

there was jubilation on the *Erin*. *Shamrock* had not won, but on a dead calm day she was in the lead, and a bare half mile from home, when the race had to be abandoned. The betting on the Stock Exchange was even now, and two days later a larger crowd assembled before the *Evening News* cineyachtograph. It was an occasion that was to perplex the organisers of that concern considerably. For though a chill autumn wind was blowing down the Embankment, not a breath of wind disturbed the waters of Sandy Hook. Cable after cable brought the news: "Wind died away, yachts drifting."

As good journalists, however, the staff of the *Evening News* remained undaunted. There might be no race three thousand miles away, but on the banks of the Thames the strangest yacht race in all history was sailed. The *Evening News* ordered the elements. Capricious puffs of wind filled *Shamrock's* sails, leaving *Columbia's* to flap idly. Slowly *Shamrock* drew level and passed ahead amid tumultuous cheers. Then the wind died away, and the yachts, since they had to be kept more or less in their right positions in case of subsequent eventualities, mysteriously drifted back to their former posts. It was a great relief to the organisers when the news finally came through that the race was off and the crowd could disperse, deploring Sir Thomas's ill luck. If only that last gust had held.

For the next race such crowds assembled that the police had to close the cineyachtograph. That was on the seventh. Then fog descended. While it still lay over Manhattan, *The Times* changed its headlines from "Transvaal Crisis" to "The War in South Africa." Thus imperceptibly, like a becalmed and drifting yacht, Imperial Britain moved towards the first of her three Pyrrhic victories. Two days later the fog lifted, and in a smooth sea with a seven- to eight-knot breeze blowing, *Columbia* sailed past the finishing line a mile ahead.

The second race, owing to an accident to *Shamrock's* mast, ended in a walkover victory for *Columbia*. Then three days later, with a biting northerly wind of fifteen to twenty knots driving white horses seaward, under conditions that should have helped *Shamrock, Columbia* proved her superiority in heavy winds as in light, and Lipton's first challenge for the cup was over.

In a sense the actual races were a disappointment. They were too long-drawn. The series dragged on for close upon three weeks. "If the Book of Job were to be written again," said Lipton, "a windless day off Sandy Hook while two yachts are waiting to pit against each other their vast expanse of sail might serve the purposes of an allegory." Race by race, the excursion fleet diminished. But for Lipton the series was not on that account any the less a prolonged personal triumph.

The Times, in a leading article, summed up the general attitude. "The contest has presented one marked feature on which both nations may be equally congratulated, and that has been the complete absence of any of those elements of disagreement by which a former one was unfortunately characterised. The victory will leave no sting behind and will place no difficulty in the way of a renewal of the challenge."

In America, Lipton was hailed as the best sportsman that Britain had sent across. He promised to challenge again as soon as the requisite time had passed. He was seen to the boat by a procession headed by a band, and a loving cup costing a thousand pounds was subscribed for "as a token of goodwill from the American people." The cup was presented at a banquet the following spring by Mr. Choate, the American Ambassador. In his speech of acceptance Sir Thomas said, "I know that to lift the other cup I have got to take to Sandy Hook the best and fastest yacht the world has ever seen. But I am not discouraged. I hope I am not expected to be content with *this* cup."

§ 12

THAT AUTUMN of 1899 Lipton returned from Sandy Hook to find himself as popular as any man in England, and the next ten years were not only to be the best of his life but years as good as any man has been privileged to know upon this planet. He had health, success, and wealth; work he loved and a hobby that absorbed him. He was enjoying the rewards of work, and at no period of history was the stage better set for a man of his tastes and talents. For the first time in his life he was mixing with men and women of the world, and at a time when the prestige of London was unchallenged. The royal houses of Europe were one large interrelated family looking to Queen Victoria as its head. The Emperor of Germany was her grandson. Her granddaughter was Empress of Russia. The thrones of Greece, Rumania, Sweden, Denmark, Norway, and Belgium were all related to her by ties of blood. London was the world's social axis, with the Prince of Wales as the apex of the London scene. And as that august personage was to prove, next to Lipton's mother, the most significant character in the Lipton story, it is necessary at this point to go back in time and give a brief sketch of England's future King as an explanation of how Lipton came to be his friend, and an indication of the kind of world in which Lipton, as his friend, was to play a part.

Between the wars it became the mode to deride the objects of nineteenth-century veneration. The fashion was set by one great writer, followed by several good writers, and aped by a number of less gifted imitators. Biographers, with the connivance of their publishers, sought not for subjects to place upon a pedestal, but for statuary to destroy. And few characters have fared worse than the consort of Queen Victoria. His foibles attracted master marksmanship. He was, of course, fair game. He had all the most tiresome Teutonic virtues. He was conscientious, orderly, temperate, punctilious, serious, indefatigably industrious; his influence on the Queen over the education of their eldest son was lamentable. He had it all planned out: book and study and travel with a purpose, "a meticulous curriculum," so Roger Fulford put it, "appropriate for one who aimed at spending his life in the amply billowing gown of a don, but quite unsuited for one destined by the gods to wear a crown rather than a mortarboard."

No programme less suitable for a boy who enjoyed company, parties, the open air, could have been devised. Yet even so it is scarcely fair to Albert's memory to hold him entirely responsible for the obstinacy with which Queen Victoria implemented his policy after he had died.

That she should have displayed such obstinacy was perhaps inevitable. Her personal experience of the young was, it must be remembered, slight. As a girl she had been kept in strict seclusion in large part because it was believed that her uncle, the Duke of Cumberland, had plans to murder her. Albert was the only contemporary she knew really well. She was not aware that other types of perfection were in existence. Her son must be the replica of her husband. She never forgave Edward for being different.

She saw Edward through her husband's eyes. Because Albert had thought Bertie unintelligent she allowed her son no share in the conduct of the country's business; because Albert had thought him irresponsible she kept him uninformed about affairs of state; because Albert had thought him frivolous she prescribed, as far as lay within her powers, a rigid domestic discipline. When he was a grandfather in his middle fifties she treated him according to a formula that had been laid down thirty-five years earlier for a Cambridge undergraduate and which then would only have been appropriate to a junior-school boy. She never recognised that Edward had grown older and that times had changed. Truth had not changed. The pattern which Albert had approved in 1860 must be conserved in 1895. Max Beerbohm has summed up the situation with a cartoon of a middle-aged, fat, bald-headed man in a morning coat standing in the corner with his face to the wall. The widow sits in the centre of the room on a straight-backed chair, her hands folded in her lap over a tear-stained handkerchief; it is entitled: "The rare, the rather awful visits of Albert Edward, Prince of Wales, to Windsor Castle."

Albert was responsible for that, but Albert was not altogether to blame for it. To appreciate him fully it is necessary to set beside Lytton Strachey's portrait the results of Hector Bolitho's careful investigations. Roger Fulford has spoken of him in terms of "a characteristic which is marked

and constant in the Teutonic race—an infinite capacity
for planning without any power to vary the plan when circumstances demand it." But even so it is very possible that
had he lived he would have realised that there was a difference between the 1890s and the 1850s. He died, however, in 1861, and what he had considered proper then
was still, when the century closed, the basis for his widow's
judgments. He could not have foreseen the blinded adora-
tion with which Victoria would feel herself entrusted with
a sacred legacy to carry out his plans and wishes to the
final detail.

She had, of course, some grounds for her misgivings.
The Prince of Wales was not as a young man particularly
discreet. During the Franco-Prussian War, for instance, he
asked to be kept informed about the progress of events,
and we find the Foreign Secretary, Lord Granville, com-
plaining to the Queen's private secretary that one of his
top-secret notes had been in circulation at a dinner party.
Such an incident confirmed the Queen's suspicions.

His private life, moreover, was a constant worry to her.
She could scarcely be expected to forget that the severe
cold which ultimately proved fatal to her husband had
been exacerbated by the visit he had paid to Cambridge
to remonstrate with his son over an early excursion into
gallantry. So indignant had she felt at the time that when
Albert was dying she did not summon Edward to his
father's bedside, leaving that courtesy to Princess Alice,
while later she admitted to Clarendon that it irritated her
"to see him in the room."

As it began, so did it continue. Nor was the Queen alone
in viewing the Prince of Wales's conduct with disfavour.
Public opinion also was concerned. A young man, certainly

a Prince of Wales, was expected in those days to sow some wild oats. No one seriously objected to the position occupied in his later years by Alice Keppel, and in his youth by Mrs. Langtry—the Jersey Lily who arrived in London in 1879 to seek her fortune with a single dress, no skill as an actress, but a beauty so transcendent that her theatrical ventures never lacked financial backing. He was expected to enjoy himself when he went incognito to Paris. Appearances had, however, to be observed; wild oats had to be sown in private. And twice Edward was involved in a public scandal.

On the first occasion two of his friends were cited as co-respondents in a divorce suit brought by Sir Charles Mordaunt, who further declared in his petition that his wife had admitted to misconduct with the Prince. No proof of any kind was adduced, and the erring wife was at the time of the trial a certified lunatic. But even so the spectacle of their future King being cross-examined in a divorce case was highly unwelcome to the British public. On his next public appearance, at the Epsom Race meeting, he was hissed.

Twenty years later he was to appear in a witness box again, on this occasion in a case that is still discussed, the Tranby Croft baccarat scandal. The two best accounts of it appear in E. F. Benson's *As We Were* and *Youth Is a Blunder* by Elma Napier, the daughter of the chief protagonist.

In brief the case was this: At a private house party, during the St. Leger week, at which the Prince of Wales was present, some of the guests formed the suspicion that Sir William Gordon-Cumming, a baronet and a colonel in the Scots Guards, was cheating at cards by means of a

device known as *la poussette,* which consists of withdrawing part of your stake when your cards are bad and adding
to it when you pick up good ones. They resolved to watch
him more closely on the following night. Their suspicions
were confirmed by what they saw. The Prince, who held
the bank, himself had observed nothing, but when the
matter was reported to him he persuaded Sir William to
sign a document promising never to play cards again for
money. In return for that promise the other members of
the game—there were ten in all—vowed themselves to
secrecy. One of the players, however, did not keep that
vow. Gossip started; there were anonymous letters, and
handshakes refused in clubs. In self-defence Sir William
brought a slander suit against the five persons who claimed
to have seen him cheat.

He defended himself on the grounds that he had signed,
while protesting his innocence, to avoid a scandal in which
the Prince would be involved. Once again the heir apparent had to answer questions in the witness box. He denied
having seen anything irregular, but when a juryman asked
him if he believed in Sir William's guilt, he answered that
he did, in view of the opinion of the five observers. On the
strength of that evidence Sir William lost his case. But
many believed him to be innocent. His counsel, Sir Edward
Clarke, to the end of his life maintained that a mistaken
verdict had been given. Sir William's American fiancée—
the daughter of William Garner, one-time commodore of
the New York Yacht Club—married him on the day after
the trial, while Elma Napier's summing up is this: "It
seems to me now that the strongest thing to be said in
my father's defence is that he had so very much to lose
by cheating, such a trifle to gain."

I

It was certainly not a pretty case. A baronet, a colonel in the Guards, had been accused of cheating; five guests in a private house had plotted to spy upon a fellow guest; a vow to secrecy had been broken. The conduct of the Prince would, however, have appeared to be completely blameless. Yet it was against him that press and pulpit discharged their bombardment of vituperation. "We know no spectacle," wrote Macaulay, "so ridiculous as the British public in one of its periodical fits of morality." He was writing of the fury that attended Byron's separation from his wife. A similar paroxysm of hysteria convulsed the public upon this occasion. Words like baccarat and *la poussette* sounded French and wicked. But the chief cause of complaint was the highly absurd one that the Prince carried his own counters with him. Sermons were preached, leaders printed, questions asked in the House, and W. T. Stead announced a gadget called "The Prayer's Gauge" which would show just how many pious petitions for the Prince's spiritual welfare, in how many churches in the course of fifty years, had been answered with this scandal.

The Queen, in her retirement at Windsor, had had the reports of the case sent to her every evening. She must have shaken her head sadly when she read the leading articles that followed. How right Albert was. He had prophesied this kind of thing. Bertie was frivolous and irresponsible. You thought he was growing more sensible, then something like this happened. He was hopeless, he really was.

Another cause, too, contributed to Victoria's distrust of him. Edward was pro-French. As he was married to a Dane, it was natural, she conceded, that he should have resented the Prussian invasion of Schleswig-Holstein, but during the Franco-Prussian War her sympathies were, at least at the start, with Bismarck. Her favourite daughter was married to the Crown Prince. Albert had always insisted that the French were frivolous and corrupt; it was only because Bertie was himself frivolous and dissipated that he took their side. Sedan fulfilled all Albert's prophecies. How right he was. How right he always was.

Later, when Prussia became Germany with her grandson as its Emperor, she recognised that a dangerous and menacing force was alive in Europe. But even then she was German in her sympathies. Albert had been a German. Moreover, she understood her grandson. She knew his faults—no one knew them better—but, understanding him, she was able through loving him to see beyond them. She was the one person who knew how to handle him. She stood no nonsense from him. "I doubt," she wrote to him, "whether any sovereign wrote in such terms to another sovereign and that sovereign his own grandmother." But when she was dealing with her ministers she half took his side. "William's faults come from impetuousness (as well as conceit), and calmness and firmness are the most powerful weapons in such cases."

The Kaiser behaved outrageously and she knew it. He was at his worst when dealing with the English. He had a chip on his shoulder because of his uncle's greater popularity. "Year after year," E. F. Benson wrote, "he took advantage of the royal domesticity of the Cowes Regatta to make himself domestically disagreeable and of the racing to show himself unsportsmanlike." He would describe his uncle as an "old peacock" and he could not restrain his jubilance when his yacht, *Meteor I,* beat *Britannia.* He was impossible and Victoria knew it; at the same time she was more indulgent towards his failings than her son's, and for a reason that is not hard to seek: he loved her more. He recalled with a sentimental tenderness that Bertie could never feel for his own boyhood his first lessons in navigation on the *Alberta* and those earlier days at Osborne when he had played with old iron cannon. He recalled them as a cool oasis in his fevered life.

His grandmother was the one person in the whole world of whom he stood in awe. It was a relief to his tortured spirit to have that one person to whom he could submit himself, one place where his restless megalomania could be appeased and soothed. He knew it and she knew it and, knowing it, she loved him in the way that many mothers prefer their crippled children. She was not drawn closer to her son because of his quarrels with his nephew. She knew that Willie was outrageous and Bertie was very patient. But her reason was in conflict with her heart. Because her son was Francophile and anti-Prussian she saw yet another reason for keeping his hands out of state affairs.

In consequence, by refusing him responsibilities, by denying him his rights as the heir apparent, she encouraged those very traits in him that she deplored.

Edward enjoyed good company and the pleasures of the table; he loved racing and shooting and the society of pretty women. Deprived of his proper position as a diplomat and an advisor, he concentrated inevitably upon his private and social life. He knew that many of the more conventional families disapproved of him and that a deputation headed by such prominent women as the Duchesses of Leeds and Bedford had protested to the Archbishop of Canterbury against the morals of the "Marlborough House

Set." In self-defence he surrounded himself with the kinds of people who enjoyed the kinds of things that he did. He was easily bored and he had no intention of being bored. He assembled the liveliest elements of the day in terms of vivacity and charm. His set was international. He had always appreciated the wit and vitality of Americans. He refused to accept artificial barriers of class or race. At no time in history has there existed a court society more accessible to a man like Lipton. The Prince's demands of his friends were simple. A woman must be beautiful and amusing; a man must be rich and amusing. Lipton was amusing and very rich. Within a few months of his signing his Jubilee cheque he was on terms of intimate friendship with the Prince.

Several years later the following paragraph was to appear in a social column: "For about the thousandth time, I have heard the complaint, 'What a pity that the King should take up with a grocer like Lipton simply because he has made money.' But the fact is that Lipton is not merely a grocer who has made money. He is a clever man, has travelled much, has seen men and manners in many countries, has a very strong dash of Irish humour, a merry twinkle in his eye, and a very funny way of relating funny things. He is an amusing companion. Moreover, without being pushing, he is perfectly self-possessed. From the very moment when he was presented to the King, he comported himself as one thoroughly accustomed to the presence of royalty. He conducts himself as one sure of his equality with everyone, without ever putting off his respect for the Crown. That is a rare gift and one which is an infallible passport to bored royalties."

It was not surprising that Lipton should have had that gift. He was well bred, of sound Irish stock, nurtured in a Scottish atmosphere. The Scots and Irish are not class-conscious in the way that the English are; they are not fretted by the survivals of a feudal system. During his late teens Lipton had enjoyed the freedom and independence of America. He had been his own master from the day he had opened his first shop; he had never had to cringe, he had never had to be servile; he had never owed money, he had never been under obligations. He had worked his way up the hard way, but he had worked his way up a clean way. He had no chip on his shoulder. He was not in consequence, as are so many self-made men, on the defensive, quick to take offence.

He was the right man for King Edward. The King had two types of crony, the buffoon and the man who could treat him as an equal. Exhausted by court formality and ceremonial protocol, he needed to relax. The age had a taste for horseplay, for apple-pie beds, sliding downstairs on trays, jugs of water precariously perched in the canopies of four-poster beds. For the practical joke H.R.H. had a particular partiality. Christopher Sykes, in *Four Loyalties,* has humorously and pathetically described the indignities to which his uncle was submitted. In this case the Prince's favourite joke was to pour a glass of brandy over his victim's head. Sykes—"Your Royal Highness's obedient, loyal, and most tried servant"—would make no movement whatsoever; he would say, "As Your Royal Highness pleases," and let the brandy drip slowly down his face and through his beard. It was one of the Prince's favourite pleasantries at the Marlborough Club.

Edward needed that type of crony, but he also liked a

man like Lipton who would stand no nonsense; a man who was ready with a wisecrack, who when the King, referring to the K.C.V.O., remarked, "Lipton, I think I shall give you an order shortly," jocularly retorted, "That is exceedingly kind of Your Majesty. It will do me a lot of good in my business. I shall have a price list sent to Your Majesty at once." On another occasion, when the King's nose was bleeding, Lipton dropped a bunch of keys down his neck with the remark, "This'll cure Your Majesty," which it did.

Lipton was, moreover, not so much a conversationalist as a raconteur, which was precisely what Edward wanted. Conversation is often a matter of difficulty to royal persons, particularly to monarchs, whose subjects may not speak to them until they are themselves addressed. George VI confessed once to a privileged and venerable person that he never knew how to start a conversation. "That is a less serious problem than your father's, sir. He never knew how to end one," the answer came. Edward VII suffered from a similar disability. He could not converse. Attractive and intelligent feminine society was essential for him, and it has been suggested that his gallantries were largely enforced by the absence of such companionship at home. Several biographers have referred to the strain placed upon a punctilious man by his wife's extreme unpunctuality. But the little correspondence between Alexandra's intellect and beauty has been barely hinted. He was forced to seek that particular stimulus elsewhere.

Since, however, he was not a conversationalist the effort, the attack had to come from the other side. He was happiest indeed when seated between two beautiful and witty women who talked across him in a conversation of which he was the axis. And in his men friends he valued the same capacity to talk; the fact that Lipton was a raconteur rather than a conversationalist was one of the reasons for the enjoyment his company gave Edward.

It has been sometimes asked how it came about that a man like Lipton, sprung from nowhere, could within so short a time have found himself moving in such exalted circles. The answer is that it is just because he had sprung from nowhere. A European of no particular consequence in his own country, arriving in New York with well-cut clothes, pleasant manners, and one good letter of introduction, can enter a social set inaccessible to an American of considerably higher standing. Michael Arlen said, "An Armenian arriving in England only knows two kinds of persons, duchesses and headwaiters. I've never had a chance of meeting the kinds of people who live in Surbiton."

Lipton arrived in London society very much as though he had been a foreigner. In the spring of 1897 no one had heard of him. By the spring of 1898 everybody had. He came as a South African millionaire might have come, unknown but supplied with the best possible credentials, an engaging manner and great wealth.

He was, too, the type of man that the moment was likeliest to approve. It has been suggested earlier that the era of the *Yellow Book* and the discrediting of the green carnation was not without its influence on the Lipton story. Because of that scandal people who had sneeringly shrugged their shoulders with a "You see where art and all that flimflam lead you" were ready to welcome the straightforward, self-made, "no-such-nonsense-about-him" millionaire.

Finally, and this was a very important factor in his social success, he arrived unencumbered. Nine times in ten the self-made man is handicapped by an early marriage, by a wife who does not fit into the new world to which success and wealth have introduced him, a wife who does not "go down" with his new friends. In the case of nearly all self-made men there is a "little woman" in the background; or else there is a divorce, which in England, even in Edwardian days, would have involved the closing of certain circles. Practically always there are family ties to be considered: daughters to have husbands found for them, sons to be placed in business, old friends to be dropped or schemed for. It is not altogether surprising that members of the established classes are a little cautious, not upon snobbish grounds, of entering into close friendship with the self-made man. They do not quite know what they will be letting themselves in for. There are apt to be so many strings attached.

But in Lipton's case there were no strings. He had no wife, no relatives, no friends. He was rich, he was friendly, he was good company, he was generous. He wanted to give a good time and be given a good time. He was the person, so they put it, for whom they had all been waiting. His timing once again was perfect. Never had England been gay in quite that way before; never was she to be gay in quite that way again. Once again Lipton's career was to be a window opening upon a vanished world. His boyhood had shown the struggles of the poor on both sides of the Atlantic in the middle sixties; his youth had shown the scope that lay open in the seventies to the adventurous; his thirties and forties had shown the immense potentialities of private enterprise; his maturity, at the start of the twentieth century, was now to show the luxury, the extravagance, and the ease of the last decade of Europe's greatness.

It was a full, rich sunset. The prestige of royalty and the inherited wealth of the great families were alike unimpaired. The discoveries of modern science had smoothed the wheels, had heightened the speed of living. The motorcar had stimulated the week-end habit. Dining in restaurants had loosened the exclusiveness of social barriers. An invitation to the Ritz had not the same implications as dinner "in a man's own house." Yet there was not any less ceremony on that account, any less pageantry, any less parade. In many ways Edward VII was extremely formal, exceedingly punctilious. He strongly disapproved of divorce, for instance. In Paris he would never race on Sundays. He was a stickler for etiquette. No one was quicker to notice a misplaced decoration. There was nothing slovenly about his court.

Never, in fact, has there been more display. It was the day of elaborate evening dresses, of stomachers and tiaras. Money went a long way. A bachelor was well off on a thousand a year. And money was being spent with a novel recklessness. Emerson, when he visited England in the middle of the century, had been astonished by the wealth of its feudal families. This wealth had, however, been unostentatiously maintained within the boundaries of family existence. But now the big houses were opening their gates and purses. In 1894 the first attack upon their power had been made by Sir William Harcourt's land taxes. Perhaps some power of divination warned them that within half a century income tax and death duties would ruin them and that their wide acres and big houses would be up for sale. Nevertheless, they were living up to, when not beyond, their incomes.

Money was being spent, too, by a new type of person. South African gold and diamond mines enriched many overnight. The industrial revolution had produced great fortunes in banking, commerce, and manufacture, whose owners—men of modest origin—had preferred to retain their way of living but whose university-trained descendants were now anxious to enjoy the rewards of their grandfathers' enterprise, while many men of rank who had joined the boards of public companies were introducing their fellow directors into their clubs and homes.

Those whose parents have made money easily are ready to spend it easily, and now the heirs of long-established fortunes felt that their turn had come to be extravagant. A week end at Halton, Alfred de Rothschild's house, would suggest, if shown today upon the screen, that Cecil de Mille was overdoing it. A special train was run from Baker Street to Wendover. A private orchestra played during the appropriate periods. A speciality on the dinner menu was *poussins haltonais*—young out-of-season pheasants that had had their necks wrung. There was a private circus in which Rothschild acted as ringmaster in an elegant blue frock coat, lavender kid gloves, and whip. On Sunday afternoons tiny carriages drawn by little ponies with minute grooms in blue livery would drive the guests out to a chalet to inspect a pack of blue-and-white King Charles spaniels, to survey a superb panorama and consume a sumptuous tea.

The amount the Edwardians ate is appalling by modern standards. "No age since that of Nero," wrote Harold Nicolson, "can show such unlimited addiction to food."

In an essay, "The Edwardian Week-end," which appeared in *Small Talk,* he described the cavalcade of dishes that proceeded almost without interruption from the moment a guest was called with "a neat brass tray of tea, toast, and Marie biscuits" till he retired after a midnight supper of devilled chicken to a covered dish of sandwiches upon his night table. At breakfast "rows of little spirit lamps warmed rows of large silver dishes. On a table to the right between the windows were grouped hams, tongues, galantines, cold grouse, ditto pheasant, ditto partridge, ditto ptarmigan. . . . Edwardian breakfasts were in no sense a hurried proceeding. The porridge was disposed of negligently, people walking about and watching the rain descend upon the Italian Garden. Then would come whiting and omelette and devilled kidneys and little fishy messes in shells. . . ."*That was only a part of what there was. All day it went on like that. Food. Food. Food. It was not surprising that the Edwardians used Marienbad as an equivalent of the Roman *vomitorium.*

Such was the world to which Lipton as the King's friend found himself admitted. He was a frequent guest first at Marlborough House and Sandringham, and after the accession at Buckingham Palace and Balmoral. At Cowes he was entertained on the *Victoria* and *Albert*. In return he arranged Mediterranean cruises on the *Erin.* He attended a number of important public functions. The friend of royalty rather than of the aristocracy, he saw the best of the Edwardian Era. He was spared its snobbery. The caste system had by no means broken down. And the members of the House of Lords recognised and revered the degrees of grandeur that placed them in relation to one another

* *Small Talk* by Harold Nicolson.. Constable

higher and lower on the social ladder. Royal persons, however, were unable to detect any social difference between the various categories of fleas that existed outside the vast family circle of their innumerable relations. A baron, a viscount, an earl, a marquis, they were all one to King Edward. So, for that matter, were they to Lipton. Looking from the other end of the scale, he, too, saw an indiscriminate conglomeration of coronets. He would have been astonished had anyone informed him that he was not "in society."

In that he was extremely fortunate. He enjoyed the pomp and missed the pomposity of the period.

He had no lack of pomp. He was the friend not only of Edward and Alexandra, but of Princess Henry of Battenberg, the ex-Empress Eugénie, the King of Italy, Alfonso of Spain—whose proposal to Princess Ena is reported to have taken place on board the *Erin*. Mrs. Keppel was a frequent guest on the *Erin*. Lipton found a place in the American side of his business for her husband. "The handsome appointment which Sir Thomas Lipton has given Mr. George Keppel is very agreeable to the Prince, who is much interested in the family," was the naïve comment of the *Philadelphia Times*. It was with Mrs. Keppel that the King went down to the Solent to see the trial of *Shamrock II* when a sudden gust of wind brought the mast crashing across the deck, missing His Majesty by inches; the King, in terms of the still fashionable pun, remarked on learning that the boom had not been damaged, "If his boom did not suffer, how are we to account for the collapse of his sales?"

The guest book of the *Erin* is starred with famous

names. But only a film with its capacity to show quickly a succession of contrasting backgrounds could give a picture of those next ten years—the royal parties at Sandringham, Ascot, and Balmoral; the Christmases on the Riviera; the Cowes regattas, the cruises upon the *Erin,* the visits to Ceylon and to America; the celebrations for Alfonso's wedding, Alfonso driving down to Southampton in Lipton's car, the royal breakfast on the *Victoria* and *Albert,* the farewell dinner at Osborne Cottage; the opening of Kingsway, the most impressive London thoroughfare to be built since Regent Street, with the King dressed as a field marshal, and Lipton as one of three thousand guests under a scarlet and white pavilion watching while the King turned the key in a gilt globe set on a black pedestal, and fifty yards away the great gilded gates that stood between Aldwych and Kingsway rolled back as though by magic.

Yes, they were great years for the man who once had slept beneath his counter because he had not the time to walk back home.

Not that he neglected his business during this crowded period. Lipton, Ltd. continued to pay its yearly 12 per cent to 15 per cent dividends. Nor that he was any less prominent a figure on the other side of the Atlantic.

His popularity there increased with every visit. In the autumn of 1900 he made a corner in pork on the Chicago market. He denied at first that he had done so. He objected, he said, on principle to corners; it was just that he happened to need pork to supply his shops and to fulfil his army contracts. Gradually, however, it became clear that in point of fact there were only thirty-five thousand barrels to be delivered and that Lipton owned them all, in addition to twice that number which had been bought by people who did not possess a barrel. The ridiculous situation arose of men who had contracted to deliver pork to Sir Thomas at the price of eleven dollars a barrel having to buy it from him at the price of eighteen to twenty dollars in order to keep their commitments. To-day such traffic would be described as "frenzied finance" and there would be indignant articles on "profiteering with the people's food," but in those ampler days it was all held to be shrewd business. "This beats a yacht race," was the cry that greeted the first jump in pork. Lipton's treatment of the situation indeed earned him as much credit as the *Shamrock*. "The driver of fat oxen need not himself be fat, and the man who has cornered the pig market need not be hoggish," wrote the *Chicago Post*.

Sir Thomas wasn't. He could have sold his pork at one hundred dollars a barrel. But he had "no wish to squeeze anybody or to force up the price of pork." He made a number of private settlements "so that while bearish speculators received some painful private injuries, the wounds were not mortal." The *Toledo Times* headed its leader, "Sir Thomas Is Not a Hog." The *Philadelphia Record* headed its article, "Gallantry to His Foes." "Sir Thomas, you're a bird," wrote a New York paper. "You don't roar when we beat your sailboat, so we won't chew the rag when you get even in a commercial way." He was reputed to have cleared three hundred thousand dollars on the deal, which would go a long way, as a number of journalists pointed out, to financing a second *Shamrock*. Only the Chicago meatmen were not altogether happy. And the *Pall Mall Gazette* had its name for them. "Pork butchers in Chicago are cynical creatures. They will scowl and smile the white smile of contempt, but they will not admire. There must be something in the trade that warrants this. Yet those who deal so largely in crackling ought to be merry and wise and not lean and envious."

That autumn saw his second challenge for the cup. In the spring Lady Dufferin launched *Shamrock II,* and in September at Sandy Hook the *Erin's* guest book was once again black with entries. McKinley's death postponed the races but did not diminish the excitement. Mrs. Keppel was there as hostess, with Alice Meynell writing back to her husband Wilfrid, "We have spent two really delightful afternoons on board the *Erin* and have been over the *Shamrock*—a real angel. There is a photograph of Lipton with the splendid Mrs. Dana Gibson on one side of him and me on the other, and Celia[4] standing by. . . . Charles Russell has been very kind. He and Lipton are getting quite morbid about the race. They dream of it. . . ." And later, "We shall hear at Great Salt Lake, I hope, about the third yacht race today. I took a real fancy to Lipton. He is so good-natured and such a boy."

At the same time an English cricket side under the captaincy of B. J. T. Bosanquet was touring in America. The standard of play, particularly in Philadelphia, was high. J. B. King, the first right-handed exponent of the inswerve, which he varied with the outswerve, was considered by many English batsmen to be the best quick bowler of his day; there was also P. H. Clark. Though the visiting side contained several All-England players, the Philadelphians shared the honours in the two test matches that were played. The whole of the English side as well as the

[4]Celia Tobin, sister of Agnes Tobin.

whole of the Oxford and Cambridge athletic team, which had just had their match with Harvard and Yale at the Berkeley Oval, were invited to the *Erin*.

E. R. Wilson has thus described the visit.

Some of the athletes were rather under the weather, as they had been sumptuously entertained at dinner at Sherry's Restaurant after the match—Mr. Chauncey Depew in the chair. We had to make an early start to reach Sandy Hook (7 A.M.) and by the time we got on board the *Erin,* 1500 tons (like the "mountainlike *San Philip*") the enormous excursion steamers caused a good swell and several of us, especially those who had had no breakfast, were defeated before the race began.

I was not one of the worst, but felt far from happy. We had a lovely day, but there was not enough breeze and the result was "no race," with *Columbia* well ahead.

There were very good drinks and table doings. Sir Thomas's immediate entourage were all sporting green ties with a shamrock on them.

In many ways the 1901 series was the most exciting of all those in which Lipton challenged. *Shamrock II* did not, it is true, win a single race, but in the ninety miles of racing there was in actual time only three minutes and twenty-seven seconds difference between the yachts. There was little to choose between the two, and Charlie Barr's handling of the defender was the chief factor in *Columbia's* victory. W. P. Stephens wrote of him that "he knew the rules and his rights under them. Handling *Columbia* as a man would a bicycle, turning her as on a pivot, he took chances that would have been dangerous in the extreme for an average good skipper."

Lipton lost, but his confidence was undiminished. He reminded his friends that the shamrock had three leaves.

K

At a dinner in Chicago he mocked the idea of a Belfast syndicate preparing a new challenge. "No, no," he said, "if the owners try to lay out the total cost of building and racing a challenger before they start on the job, they'll never get her completed. It is impossible to figure on the cost at the beginning, and anyway, a syndicate-built challenger wouldn't be worth a second thought. I believe that a bit of sentiment should enter into a thing of this sort. It isn't the money that I've spent on my boat that made me want so much to win. It's the constant care and time and thought, the planning, the figuring, and the days and weeks and months. Then when you see her out on the water in her white sails, she means something to a man. She's not the product of a combine or the mixture of a dozen different ideas. She's mine—every spar of her."

When he returned to Osidge his carriage was stopped at Palmers Green and the horses taken from the shafts. Flags were waving and a band was playing. A torchlight procession was headed with a model of the *Shamrock*. In November, Lord Tweedsmouth was presiding at the Hotel Cecil at a banquet in his honour, numbering four hundred guests; Lord Rosebery was telling the press that the country needed a business cabinet made up of men like Lipton and Carnegie. When Charles M. Schwab visited the country, it was Lipton who arranged his audience at the Palace.

There was talk that autumn that he was to be made a peer. He denied the rumour, insisting that even if he were offered a peerage he would refuse it. He would not want to be set so far apart from his old friends. The story was repeated in America and made good publicity.

There was talk, also in American papers, that he had been proposed for the Royal Yacht Club and had been blackballed. A year earlier it had been reported that the King, when still Prince of Wales, was unable to attend the meeting at which Lipton's candidature was discussed and had been so irritated that his friend had been passed over that he had refused to go near the clubhouse. The incident was recalled of Cecil Rhodes's blackballing from the Travellers and Edward's resignation as a protest; the *New York Herald* reported the Prince as saying, "It is enough for me to put someone up to have him blackballed," continuing that the Prince was so annoyed over the highhanded behaviour of the more conservative members of the squadron that he was prepared to insist on his friend's election. In point of fact, Lipton was never actually blackballed, his candidature being withdrawn before the election meeting in view of the anticipated opposition.

The subject was not, however, allowed to drop. Eighteen months later the *New York Herald* was remarking that Lipton's chances of election to the club were as remote as ever. "Should the King," it wrote, "exercising his royal prerogative, force the matter to an issue, many members of the squadron contemplate withdrawing and forming another organization. Already there is talk of building another clubhouse; but, in view of the deep-rooted opposition of such distinguished subjects, it is not likely the King will push matters further."

The committee's objection to Sir Thomas was probably due as much as anything to his inexperience as a yachtsman. In America, however, his humble origin was regarded as the sole cause of his non-election. His failure on those grounds added to his popularity. He was regarded as another victim of English snobbery.

By now he was an established feature of the New York scene. In a musical called *The Defender,* Henry Davenport impersonated him under the thin pseudonym of Sir Thomas Ceylon Teaton. And a third challenge was despatched in time for a series in 1903. "In thus desiring an opportunity of making a third attempt to obtain possession of the America's Cup," he wrote to the New York Yacht Club, "I hope I may not be deemed importunate or unduly covetous of the precious trophy so long and so securely held in trust by N.Y.Y.C."

This time he was opposed by a millionaire's syndicate—Cornelius Vanderbilt, William Rockefeller, Widener—for whom Herreshoff designed an extremely flat boat with a shallow body and a very deep keel, "a skimming dish" with well over 16,000 square feet of sail, over 2000 more than *Shamrock.* This time there was a special clause in the terms about not racing when the weather was rough, "If in the opinion of the regatta committee the weather shall at the time appointed for any race be or threaten to be of such character as not to afford a reasonable opportunity of fairly testing the speed of the two vessels . . . unless either contestant insists," a clause that was to cause trouble later.

His departure was attended by the usual fanfare, a dinner in his honour, a telegram from Windsor: "As you are just about to leave for America, let me wish you a prosperous journey and all possible good luck for the great race in August. Edward R.I." *Punch* carried a full-page cartoon by Raven Hill of Lipton dressed as a medieval Norwegian warrior riding the sea, with small vessels, bearing shamrock-inscribed sails, attached to his feet like snow boots. It bore the caption, "Last of the VI-KINGS and first of the TEA-kings."

Punch also ran for several weeks a feature called the "Bart's Progress," or "Lipton day by day," the quality of whose humour can be judged by such excerpts as: "July 2: Sir Thomas Lipton wins walking race from Wall Street to Washington. Dines and sleeps at the White House, which he paints red. July 4: A full day, Sir Thomas Lipton adjudicates as umpire in the walking race of waitresses in the American tea table company. In the afternoon he kicks off in a baseball match and in the evening saves a valuable life. July 19: Sir Thomas Lipton visits Poloniville, Pa., and is kissed at the station by 3000 ladies, each of whom remarks, 'This is a great day for Poloniville.' *Shamrock III* resumes a yellow tinge of green. July 20: Sir Thomas Lipton at Harvard. Is made honorary D.C.L. (Disappointed Cup Lifter). Returns thanks in an affecting speech and presents the students with a portrait of himself in Okomagarin."

On his arrival the familiar ballyhoo broke loose. Dorothy Dix, a young journalist who had yet to win her spurs, headlined him as a "three-volume romance bound in yachting flannels." She described the bedrooms on the *Erin* as "little dens all done up in dainty lace and silk like a beauty's boudoir." She catalogued the clocks, the bric-a-brac and statuary, the litter of ormolu and buhl, of brasses and bronzes, the royal blue Sèvres vases, the china cabinets; the water colours by the Chevalier de Martino and Parker Newton; the music room and the canaries, the harp that stood upon the hearthrug; the dining room that ran the whole length of the ship, its iris-blue lampshades, and the long luncheon tables on the starboard decks that could serve seventy at a time; the large gilt beds and wash-stands that could be converted into desks; the three thousand lamps by which not only the *Erin's* rails and masts and shroud but the whole water line could be lit at night.

In the same article she described his parties. On days when there was no racing he would invite his guests for tea, a meal that would be served at three. His teacups, with their saucers on top, were presented on a little tray with a slice of lemon, two lumps of sugar, and a minute milk pitcher shaped like a dragon's head. The tea would be made fresh for every cup. Hot crumpets and broiled birds would comprise the menu. Champagne would be served as well. Every guest would receive a present. At nine o'clock each night there would be a formal dinner.

Theodore Roosevelt was President that year and Lipton lunched at the White House in the state dining room, to sit on the President's right. William Fife, who designed *Shamrock III,* was on his left. Among the other guests were Senator Hanna, George W. Perkins, Andrew D. White, B. A. C. Smith, the vice-commodore of the New York Yacht Club, and General Corbin. The President promised to watch one of the races from the *Erin.*

The same day Lipton judged a beauty contest between the choruses of the Runaways and the Punch and Judy company. Miriam Falconer was the former's choice, Rose Earle the latter's; to each he sent a small gold shamrock but refused to discriminate between them. "Dear Ladies," he wrote, "When I agreed to act as judge I did not realize the difficulties of the position. Solomon himself might well hesitate at such a responsibility. It is impossible for me to arrive at a decision as to which is the more beautiful lady —the one is perfectly charming, while the other is delight-fully bewitching.

"I cannot refrain from congratulating both companies upon having among their number two such charming ladies."

His popularity was as great as ever. There was as much competition to be his host as to be his guest. For the naval review at Oyster Bay he was the guest of President Roosevelt on the *Mayflower*. The Lehigh Valley Railway ran a special excursion to Niagara. The smallest station was crowded with admirers; at every halt there was a female deputation bearing flowers. The publicity value of the races was as great as ever. At the same time the races were themselves a disappointment. *Reliance* not only won, but won very easily. *Shamrock III* did not make nearly so good a showing as her predecessors.

It was a big disappointment to Sir Thomas. "No one," he told the *New York Herald,* "has any idea of how I have worried and fretted over this race. No man was more confident of winning anything than I was when I came over. I don't believe in gambling, but I would have been willing to bet the *Erin* that I would win. It is the greatest disappointment of my life.

"What can I do? I have tried my best. I have spent months of sleepless nights worrying over the challenger. They tell me that I have a beautiful boat. I don't want a beautiful boat. What I want is a boat to lift the cup—a *Reliance*. Give me a homely boat, the homeliest boat that was ever designed, if she is like *Reliance*."

Disappointed though he was, his manner remained as

urbane as ever. When a woman sought to console him on his defeat with the suggestion that his opponents had put something special in the water to defeat him, his eyes twinkled and he replied with mock earnestness: "I knew it all the time, madam! What they put in the water was the cup's defender!"

The failure of *Shamrock III* was attended by no lessening of his personal popularity. Cartoons appeared in the press suggesting that he should be sent to Washington as Ambassador; American tourists announced that there were only two Londoners they really wanted to see, King Edward and Sir Thomas. On his departure he received the gift of a dinner service. *Town Topics,* which had never neglected a chance of making merry at the expense of what it called his *"opéra bouffe* style of cup racing," had written at the beginning of the series: "Since the days of the late-lamented Barnum no such past master in the art of humbugging the gullible public of all nations has risen and shone with such effulgent luminosity. He beats Barnum and goes him one better at least in one respect. The great showman, for the life of him, could not help chuckling and giving himself away whenever he successfully played the populace for suckers. Lipton, on the contrary, either candidly believes that he is a sportsman and philanthropist or is the finest actor that ever lived." But even *Town Topics* had to throw him a bouquet in the end.

"You may talk," it wrote, "about Lipton as you will; you may deride his penchant for bussing soubrettes square on their mouths—especially you of mature years who have outgrown such luxurious habits—but no matter what you may accuse our cup challenger of, you cannot say that he is anything but the most graceful loser we ever saw. He takes his defeat so pleasantly and gracefully that none can help applauding, and while congratulating him on his successful advertising, we can also compliment him on his manhood and his sportsmanship.

"There is nothing of the common scold about Sir Thomas. When you contrast his behaviour with that of Lord Dunraven, the dour, the sullen, and the sour, you are compelled to use generous adjectives and bless yourself that Dunraven is consigned to the limbo of dead dogs, while Lipton, of tea, jam, pork, and whiskey fame, is still with us and ready to challenge again when the fiat comes forth from the Regatta Committee that he has loved and lost once more.

"To lose his third attempt without one single growl at the men who sold him a gold brick in the shape of the third *Shamrock* shows a squareness of principle that endears him to all. I, THE HORSE-MARINE, offer him my most sincere and humble apologies for my flippant and envious talk about his girl conquests and take off my hat to him as a true sportsman."

This was good enough as a write-up, but at the same time it was not quite the kind of write-up that Lipton wanted. He might not, at this stage of his career, have been desperately anxious to "lift the mug." But he was anxious to make a good show. It was not necessary for him to win, but it was necessary for him nearly to win. A rout made him look ridiculous. And it was at this point that he recognised how considerable were the handicaps under which a challenger had to operate.

For the issue was no longer as simple as it had been in the days when the original deed of gift was made. That deed laid it down that the competing vessels, if of one mast, "shall be not less than 65 feet nor more than 90 feet on the load water line. If of more than one mast, they shall not be less than 80 feet nor more than 100 feet on the load water line. The challenging club shall give ten months' notice in writing . . . accompanying the ten months' challenge there must be sent the following dimensions of the challenging vessel, namely length on load water line, beam at load water line, and extreme beam and draught of water . . . vessels selected to compete must proceed under sail on their own bottoms to the part where the contest is to take place." It was further stipulated that the race should follow in the waters of the club defending the challenge.

The intentions of the original donor are very clear. The deed of gift was a challenge to a British yacht to do what the *America* had done, to cross the Atlantic and outsail her rivals in their own waters. Conditions had so changed, however, during fifty years that it had become increasingly difficult, had very nearly indeed become impossible, to build a yacht that was both strong enough to face the Atlantic and fast enough to sail in sheltered waters—particularly under a measurement rule that, by allowing great excess in the way of flat bodies and long ends, encouraged the sacrifice of everything for speed with an abnormal rig.

W. P. Stephens, one of the greatest yachting authorities of his day, whose daughter is now librarian of the New York Yacht Club, set out the position thus. There were three factors, he argued, which had a bearing upon speed: length, sail area, and displacement. But as only length of water line and sail area were taxed in the America's Cup races, designers could and did take the greatest liberties with the keel, cutting away the underbody and lengthening the water line so that there was produced a long flat body with a deep thin keel, practically amounting to a fin, carrying at its lower end a big chunk of ballast with long spars of steel to carry the tremendous sail area.

Models in the New York Yacht Club demonstrate how far less serviceable as vessels were the racing yachts of the period than the original *America*. They were too delicate for racing in rough weather, and their masts were always breaking. They were fast in smooth water but cockles in a sea. It was, Stephens argued, wholly opposed to the spirit of the original races for the challenger to be towed across the Atlantic, as *Shamrock II* had been; he was even more shocked when the rough-weather clause was introduced. "It was time," he contended, "to call a halt when 135-foot yachts could not go out in a breeze of over 12 knots' strength without danger of losing the entire rig overboard." The series, he maintained, was developing a freak type of yacht; a racing machine that was not really seaworthy and could only be used in the America's Cup races.

Many yachtsmen were in agreement with Stephens on that point, and after 1903 the New York Yacht Club took displacement into account, encouraging thereby a sharper, fuller-bodied keel.

In detail the problem is extremely technical, but the layman can resolve it into a straightforward issue. Under any conditions the advantages in favour of the New York Yacht Club were very great. The challenger had to race in strange waters; until a very short time before the race he did not know who the defender would be; while, owing to the ocean passage, the time which should be devoted to leisurely completion and trial races was lost on stripping

and refitting. The challenger could not, therefore, afford
to give away points in measurement rules that would affect
time allowances. For the issue was not simply one of seeing
whether one yacht was faster than another but of whether
one yacht was faster than the other in terms of the time
allowances that were conceded in relation to these measurements.

After the failure of *Shamrock III* Lipton realised that
the clauses of the deed of gift would have to be reinter-
preted in terms of modern conditions so that a vessel
strong enough to sail the Atlantic should have a fair
chance against a racing machine designed for sheltered
waters.

Ten years were to pass before Lipton and the New York
Yacht Club were to find themselves in agreement as to the
terms under which the next race was to be sailed. At no
point, however, were the discussions anything but amicable. Nor did this delay in any way lessen the frequency of
his visits to America. All the time, indeed, his links there
were becoming closer and more numerous. When the
Olympia, under Admiral Jewell, arrived in British waters,
he gave two hundred of the *Olympia's* crew a "typical
English lunch" at the Crystal Palace. When the *Olympia*
sailed, the crew presented him with a cup. Selling his
Chicago holdings to the Armours, he acquired with the
proceeds a large estate in Georgia that could supply his
English shops with fruit and vegetables. While the guest
in Boston of Mayor Fitzgerald, he was highly and approvingly publicised for refusing to attend the Boston Yacht
Club's dinner unless his host was invited too. His name was
linked with Jane, the daughter of Randal Morgan, vice-
president of the United Gas Improvement Company of

Philadelphia. In an article in the *Weekly Despatch* on his return he acclaimed American prosperity. "Americans don't bother to count their change," he said. When it was London's turn to welcome the Olympic Games, he entertained sixty-five American athletes on the *Erin*. "Boys, I want you to act as though you owned everything in sight." When the Harvard House at Stratford-on-Avon was bought by Mr. Edward Morris as a permanent American trust, Marie Corelli and R. C. Lehman were Lipton's co-trustees.

As far as England and America were concerned he was, so a reporter said, bilingual.

1897–1910—this was the high period, the peak in Lipton's life. He was forty-seven when it began; he was sixty when it closed. He ended it, as he began it, as a bachelor.

Inevitably, and particularly in America, this bachelordom of his was the subject of constant comment and conjecture; his name was linked first with one lady then another. There was a music-hall singer, Elfie Fay, then there was Alice Revell of Chicago, and after her Mrs. Edith Wyman Stuart, the widow of a Boston clubman, who acted as his hostess on the *Erin* in 1899. Once his engagement was rumoured to the daughter of Sir George Faudel Philipps. It was also rumoured that he had proposed to and been rejected by the daughter of John Fitzgerald. The actual facts of this proposal are a reasonable indication of the measure of truth that ordinarily lies behind such rumours. At a party in the Fitzgerald house, a group of friends were teasing Sir Thomas about his sloth in marrying. "Don't be so shy," they said; "who is going to be Lady Lipton?" He laughed and turned towards Miss Fitzgerald.

"Come along, Rose, stand up. We'd better let them into our secret." Miss Fitzgerald entered into the spirit of the charade. "Oh no, Sir Thomas, I couldn't marry anyone so fickle." That is the basis for the Fitzgerald rumour. There is no more solid basis of verifiable fact for any of the other rumours.

Once it was rumoured that he was married all the time. A more favourite story alleged that his heart had been broken as a boy. This story developed in time into a legend. Many years later Rose, one of the Dolly sisters, was to report his having said to her, "When the woman I loved ran off and married another man because he had more of the world's goods than I possessed, I came to the conclusion that matrimony was largely a matter of money." According to Rose's story, he had built and furnished a house for this fiancée. He told that particular story, however, to no one else, and reading it in its context, as part of a light-hearted interview, it is reasonable to assume that the confession was made banteringly by a man in his middle seventies to a young and attractive woman. All the same it cannot be denied that Lipton did not actually discourage the suggestion that he was the victim of a youthful disillusionment, and the publisher's blurb inside the American edition of his autobiography states: "Behind the bachelor love of ships and sea and the great store laid by jovial friendships all and sundry, one feels the sublimation of an early romance which left the good Sir Thomas rudderless."

Shortly after his death, moreover, endorsement of this legend came from an unexpected quarter.

During his lifetime Catherine McLeod Stewart, to whom reference has been made in an earlier chapter, had never spoken of her long-ago friendship with Sir Thomas. After his death, however, she mentioned to a friend that she had known him. The friend's son happened to be a journalist. A reporter called, and Mrs. Stewart, to her surprised embarrassment, found herself written up across the continent under such headlines as "Long-Lost Sweetheart of Sir Thomas Lipton's Youth Found at Last," "Why Lipton Remained a Bachelor." Eventually Sara Worthem Roberts was despatched to Duluth by *Good Housekeeping* for an interview, which appeared in the October issue of 1932. This interview provided the material for the earlier references.

Sara Roberts described in it how she found in the dining room of a clean, neat, modest little house far out from the centre of the town, high on a hill overlooking Lake Superior, a sweet-faced little gray-haired woman sitting at a table preparing a dish of dates. At first the lady was suspicious. She disliked publicity. In particular she resented the suggestion made in certain papers that she had jilted Lipton. She denied that they had ever been engaged. They had never been more than friends. In the end, however, she consented to be interviewed. One thing, however, she refused to tell. She would not say what Lipton had written on the back of the tintype he had given her. That was his secret and hers, and she had destroyed the tintype.

The *Good Housekeeping* interview was headed "Lipton's First Sweetheart," but in point of fact nothing is more unlikely than that Catherine was. She never claimed to be. Lipton was thirty-five when he met her, and an experience such as she described is not of the kind that "spoils a man for other women." The incident was caught upon at the time because it seemed to provide an explanation for the surprising fact that Lipton never married. But it is rather too obvious an explanation to be the true one.

There were in all probability a great many contributing factors. And in the first place we must remember that we know nothing about Lipton's early life except what he has chosen himself to tell us. He lived for the first thirty years of his life obscurely. There was no one in later years with whom he could discuss the personalities of his boyhood. He could discuss the picaresque details of his early struggles, but he could never be intimate. There could be no give and take about "his early days" conversation. By the time his new friends in "the great world" had become curious about him, the people who could have satisfied that curiosity were remote or dead. No one knew who they were.

Besides, unless a person is constantly appearing in the divorce courts, unless he is himself indiscreet or associates with people who are indiscreet, nothing much can be known about him. All we know about Robert Browning's private life is that he married Elizabeth Barrett. Yet before he met her he had written some of the greatest love poetry in the language, poetry that must have been inspired by personal and profound experience.

Let the reader consider his own position; suppose he were to become overnight the object of the pressman's curiosity. Suppose by meeting death in an act of gallantry he were to make the headlines; let him consider the number of his friends who could give a journalist those authentic facts without which no intimate biography would be complete. Would there be two, three, four? And would not those few, as often as not, be the very last whom it would occur to the reporters to consult?

Lipton was, besides, extremely reticent. In his autobiography he wrote, "To say that I dislike publicity would come rather badly from a man who has used publicity for his business affairs to an extent few merchants in the world have equalled! Yet the fact remains that so far as my own private life is concerned, I have never been anxious to write or speak about it." Any explanation of Lipton's bachelordom has to be based on guesswork. There are some things, however, that we know. We know, for instance, that mid-Victorian Glasgow was intensely Calvinistic in outlook and in conduct, that the Church was the social centre of each community, that Lipton was brought up by church-going parents, that he respected inordinately his parents' views, that in respect of those views he never smoked, drank, or played cards for money. Nor must it be forgotten that for the first forty years of his life he lived under his mother's roof.

It has also to be remembered that women in Lipton's youth were closely chaperoned; there were two separate classes of women, "the girls one's sister knew" and the other kind. In London, as Michael Sadleir has depicted in his two Victorian novels, *Fanny by Gaslight* and *Forlorn Sunset,* there was a wide and varied demi-monde, not without its glamour. But in Glasgow there was no such atmosphere, and even if there had been it is unlikely that Lipton, when he was living in his parents' house, would have tampered with it. He travelled frequently, and no doubt when he was abroad, in a foreign atmosphere, he was subject to the kind of transitory experience that has inspired so many locker-room stories about travelling salesmen. But it is reasonable to assume that such experiences were basically unimportant.

L

Only two things mattered to him during his early manhood, his mother and his work. It is exceptional for a healthy young man of twenty-five not to be in a continual state of emotional and physical turmoil and not to devote his time and dissipate his energies upon the pursuit and courtship of young women. But Lipton *was* exceptional. Only one man in many millions makes himself a millionaire before he is forty. Most millionaires take a short cut at some point of their career. Either they run an unjustifiable risk or they indulge in dishonest operations. Lipton did neither. He never gambled and he never cheated. He did not need to. He had that extra amount of time, that extra amount of energy. Or to put it another way, chastity may have been his short cut.

In an obituary article contributed to the staff magazine, H. A. Snelling, who was in later years Lipton's closest advisor and was eventually appointed as one of his trustees, wrote that his not having married threw his later life somewhat out of balance, adding that Lipton's comment that the only sweetheart he ever had was his mother shows the biggest mistake he made in his life; and there is little doubt that his mother's influence arrested his emotional development. While his mother lived there was no room in the life of such a busy man for another woman, and immediately after his mother's death he worked harder than he ever had before to counteract his loneliness. By the time, however, that he had come to convert his business into a limited company, his mother had been dead ten years. He was healthy, buoyant, rich, and youthful. He was full of a zest for living. It is certainly surprising that he did not marry during the first ten years of the century. One would have expected that a man of such limitless ambition should have wanted to perpetuate his name and title.

As to why he did not we have to rely on guesswork once again. But we have to note that many of the factors which may have earlier prevented his falling seriously in love with the kind of woman that he would want to marry were still operative. He was no less busy, though now he was as busy playing as ten years earlier he had been busy working. He had no more spare time now than then. In America as in London his diary was black with entries. A new, all-absorbing passion—yachting—had come into his life, filling, partially, at any rate, his mother's place.

He had been, moreover, on his own for thirty years. He had developed his own tastes and habits; he may well have wondered how any woman who was not a mouse—and he cannot have wanted that—could fit into the framework of his routine. He must have known that part of his strength was the absence of encumbrances. And he had now the divided allegiance that complicates the lives of all those Britons who find themselves as much at home in America as their own country; who on the whole are happier, feel more themselves in America than in England; who would give a great deal to have been born Americans, yet whose roots go too deeply into their native life for them not to appreciate the impossibility of their becoming citizens; who also recognize in what large part the strength of their position in America depends on their being Britons, in having the status there of guesthood.

Such Britons, and Lipton pre-eminently was one, realise the inevitable divergences of taste between the Briton and the American. A large part of their time in England they are explaining the American point of view to the English; while in America they have to justify their countrymen. They know how hard it is for British and Americans ever really to like each other, except as individuals. They recognise how difficult it would be for an American woman to fit into the English scene as the wife of an Englishman; they also know how difficult the English wife of an Englishman would find it to adapt herself to an expatriate life. It is hard to believe that these influences were not, subconsciously at least, at work in Lipton, just as it is hard to believe that he did not fall in love at some time or another with an American.

Every suggestion that one makes in this connection must obviously be based on guesswork. Lipton's was an uncomplicated nature. "A very simple man, the most simple man that I have ever met," was Lord Inverforth's estimate of him. He was not a man who brooded. There are certain men who are born bachelors, who when they marry fail to adapt themselves to the discipline of marriage, and it may well be that that sense of timing, that subconscious sense of self-direction which led Lipton so infallibly from one success to the next, that interior need to develop a career rather than a personal existence always at the last moment stayed him.

He was to say in his last years that he regretted two things only—that he had not married and that he had not lifted the cup. But even when he said it he must have recognised that the odds were always heavily against his victory in the races, that in order for him to have won, luck would have had to be more on his side than any man has the right to ask it to be. He may at the same time have recognised that the betting against a man of his position and temperament's finding a wife who would be an asset and not a liability was as great as it was against his "lifting of the mug." His life would probably have been happier had he never returned to Scotland in 1870; but once started on a career in Britain, once dedicated to that career, it may well have been not only inevitable but better that he should have led the life he did.

Certainly in the days when he might well have been expected to be looking for a wife, he never indicated that he had any matrimonial intentions. He once said, "If I had been a Mormon I should have been married many times by now." Once he said, "If I lift the cup I suppose I should take back an American lady to help me look after it." But that was all he said. There is no indication of any kind that there was ever anyone in his life whom he really wished to marry. It may be, of course, that his life was involved with someone whom it was not possible for him to marry, that he was the victim of an "impossible situation." It may have been. It may well have been. But even so, he was a man who was always busy. It is quite possible that he never had the time to fall whole-heartedly in love.

§ 13

His peak years were 1897–1910. No one could have savoured them more fully. And in this, too, the time factor was on his side. This great period ended before he had grown weary of it.

In the late spring of 1910 a bronchial attack that the King had developed while on a holiday in Biarritz became unexpectedly serious. On his return to London, when he went round to Mrs. Keppel's house for a game of cards, though he tried to pretend that there was nothing wrong with him, his attempt to smoke a cigar brought on such an attack of coughing that she had to beg him to go home. It was the last time he left his house. Though he refused to stay in bed even on the last morning of his life and insisted on seeing Sir Ernest Cassel, the strain on his heart was now apparent.

By lunch time the news was out. One of his horses, Witch of the Air, was to run that afternoon at Kempton, and his trainer rang through to ask if she should be scratched. The King shook his head. The news of his horse's victory was almost the last thing he was conscious of. Later that evening the Queen sent for Mrs. Keppel and led her by the hand to the King's bedside. That gesture, that queenly, that gracious gesture, was an appropriate curtain to a way of living that was to exist no longer in the world, when King Edward, later that night, subsided into the coma that preceded death.

It is easy and it is tempting to map out the destiny of nations by the deaths of kings and by the dates of battles, and it would be very easy to argue that a new epoch began with the accession of George V. Nineteen-ten is a big date in English history. It marks the end of the power of the House of Lords. The Lords had challenged the Commons and been defeated, and the way lay open for the elected representatives of the people to legislate as they thought fit for their own interests. The English version of "the dictatorship of the proletariat" had begun.

It was merely chance, however, that this should have happened in the first year of King George's reign. The logic of history had been moving inexorably through the centuries to a certain point. The death of a king was incidental. The constitutional crisis would have come at precisely the same time, in the same manner, if Edward VII had lived ten years longer.

In the same way it is easy now to see the first four years of George V's reign as the start of a pre-war period, to mark by the death of Edward, who had such a gift for amity, the end of a period of appeasement. But in point of fact the German war machine had been set in motion many years before. The death of the Kaiser might have postponed the war, but nothing else could have. The stream of events that was leading to 1914 was also leading to the breakdown of hereditary rule in Europe, both of thrones and families. Historically the death of Edward VII is a convenient landmark, but nothing more.

For certain individuals, however, it was to mark the finish of an epoch. It did for Lipton. English society has always been divided into two classes, the King's set and the heir apparent's set. There may not be opposition between the sets, but there are different standards. There have always been two sides to the English temperament, the Cavalier and Roundhead, the side that has stood for convention and protocol and the side that has stood for dash and colour. King Edward VII had stood at the apex of a set that loved display, gaiety, and, in a sense, frivolity. The Prince of Wales, the future George V, had stood at the apex of a set that placed more store upon the domestic virtues. Both father and son saw kinghood in terms of duties and responsibilities. But they had different conceptions of what "duty" meant.

Shortly after the death of Edward VII the following paragraph appeared in a journal called *Week End*: "There was a strong current of commercialism in his late Majesty's choice of companions. It is true that many men of light and learning were honoured with the acquaintance of King Edward, but his closest friends, his 'cronies,' were chiefly drawn from commerce and finance. The Rothschilds, Sir Ernest Cassel, Sir Everard Hambro, the Sassoons, Sir Thomas Lipton are all men great in ability and worthy of a king's friendship, yet strongly though they appealed to the late King, it is hardly likely that they will occupy the same position with his son."

Not only did a new reign introduce new standards; it brought a new generation into power. Lipton was now a man of sixty. To Edward VII, who was close on seventy, Lipton had seemed young. To George V, in his middle forties, Lipton, in spite of his health and vigour, was a man on the brink of being old. The court became the centre both of a different and a younger group.

To an Englishman those four years, 1910–14, maybe because of their short-lived tenure, seem in retrospect a period of striking vitality and promise. There was a Liberal government in Westminster: Lloyd George and Winston Churchill, Lord Haldane and Sir Edward Grey, Morley and John Burns. Asquith was Prime Minister, with 27 Bedford Square not only a diplomatic but a cultural centre. The social limelight fell on such women as Lady Diana Manners (now Lady Diana Cooper).

There was the Poetry Bookshop and the Georgian poets—
Rupert Brooke, Flecker, Lascelles Abercrombie, de la
Mare; there were the new novelists, Compton Mackenzie,
Gilbert Cannan, E. M. Forster, Hugh Walpole, D. H.
Lawrence. Youth was in the saddle, and Lipton was no
longer young. He had had his twelve years with the spot-
light on him. Now the wheel had turned.

To what extent he was conscious of that change it is
hard to tell. But there were signs in him now and then of
a growing irritability, as though he realised that he was on
the brink of being a back number. In business he had
always been quick-tempered, resenting opposition, want-
ing everything done in his own way, firing at a moment's
notice the employee who did not give satisfaction. Something of this irritation appeared now in his general manner. He suspected criticism, and perhaps there was criticism. A slightly uncharitable reference to him in the
Bystander may, for instance, be taken as symptomatic. The
heading, "Personalities Who Must Be Kept in the Public
Eye," appeared under a photograph of Lord Dewar and
himself. The caption read: "They are both obviously embarrassed by the photographer. Query, how did he get on
the yacht?"

His interests had been moving more and more towards
America during the last few years, and he showed himself
now and again antagonistic towards certain aspects of
English policy. He was impatient, for example, with
Whitehall's attitude over the Panama·Canal. "England,"
he said, "is trying to drive the best bargain she can; some
of her public men are indulging in jingoism. America
owns the canal and has the right to benefit over that ownership." He was angry when England decided not to be

represented at the Panama Exposition in San Francisco in 1915. When he was asked to contribute to Oliver Bainbridge's book, *Lesson of the Anglo-American Peace Centenary,* he retorted that it would be better if we talked less and did more to show our friendship with the United States, adding that "friction between countries was always due to some trifling misunderstanding."

He indulged in several comparisons between English and American prosperity. There was nothing new in this. As far back as 1903 he had been arguing that too much of England's prosperity depended on the loans she made other countries, that her imports were dangerously in excess over her exports. But those previous comments had been made in a different tone. He was fractious now.

In many ways he was as jovial as ever. When he was checked by a police officer for speeding, he said: "You have your duty to do; I have always found you to be correct, boys. I am sorry," and accepted cheerfully his ten pound fine.

In many ways his old life seemed to be continuing unchanged. He was yachting with no less enthusiasm.

A few years earlier, in 1907, with the New York Yacht Club still continuing to decline his challenge, or rather with his failing to agree on the conditions under which the New York Yacht Club would accept a challenge, he decided to build a yacht in the 23-metre class and race her in home waters. He christened her *Shamrock*. "Just *Shamrock*," he insisted. "I'm keeping number IV for Sandy Hook."

She was designed by William Fife. He appointed Captain Sycamore as the skipper. Expense was not considered. The forecastle, the messroom, and the captain's berth were in African mahogany. Honduras mahogany was used in the main living rooms. The passages were of Australian oak. The sideboard and the locker were silver-mounted. There were tapestry panellings in the saloon, rose carpets and green embroidered tapestry in the staterooms.

It is customary to think of Lipton's yachting in terms of failure because he never carried off the mug, but his successes in Europe were considerable. The display of his trophies in the Glasgow Art Museum testifies that he was one of the most successful yachtsmen of his day.

Yachting critics, when they wrote their surveys of his first year's racing in home waters—the most brilliant, they all agreed, since the days of the *Britannia*—jokingly remarked that 1908 had suffered from Shamrockitis. Against three main rivals, Miles Kennedy's *White Heather*, Sir James Pender's *Brynhild*, and R. W. Young's *Nyna*, unquestionably it was *Shamrock's* year. She won her very first race, the Thames Yacht Club's, from Southend to Harwich; she won the King's Cup at Gravesend. In thirty-five races she won thirty-one flags, twenty of them first prizes. It was from this point, indeed, that Lipton's real love of yachting as distinct from his attempts upon the mug may be said to have started. Whereas before he had been a visitor, a spectator at the regattas, now he was a part of the parade. He was no longer the host of the *Erin;* he was a participant, a competitor. Yachting was a part of his life now in a way that it had never been before.

In 1910, when there were few social festivities owing to King Edward's death, he again asserted his superiority, winning eighteen first prizes against *White Heather's* nine. In 1912 the Kaiserlich Yacht Club celebrated its twenty-fifth anniversary. As a host the Kaiser proved less offensive than he had as a guest at Cowes. The regatta passed off harmoniously for everyone. *Shamrock* won six cups.

Yes, on the surface everything was going well. His visits to America became more frequent, also his winters in Ceylon. One Christmas there he entertained the White Sox and the Giants. His friendship with Dewar was growing firmer. The one was called "Whiskey Tom," the other "Tea Tom." At the Alhambra, Robert Hale was impersonating him in the revue, *Keep Smiling*, while across the Atlantic, Chauncey Olcott had the following hit number:

> Come over, come over, come on over here
> It's a wonderful place, it's a wonderful place;
> Sir Thomas Lipton from over the sea
> Is making a fortune in cocoa and tea;
> At the Waldorf you'll meet all the swagger set bunch
> And a dollar will buy you a lovely milk punch;
> I have heard that for ten you can buy a light lunch,
> It's a wonderful, wonderful place.

In December 1912 he was in New Orleans, telling American girls that they were the best dressed in the world and that they should not seek titles abroad since American husbands were the best. A week later he was in Boston, buying the biggest doll for Gaby Deslys. He was planning for the *Erin* to be the first yacht through the canal. Then he was in California with Mack Sennett and actually acting in a film there. On his return to London he remarked that he had left behind him in America his best friends in the world. At the Hippodrome he was being caricatured in *Hullo Ragtime!* In March 1913 he sent a thousand dollars to the destitute of the Dayton disaster. He attended the memorial service for J. Pierpont Morgan at Westminster Abbey and was photographed next to Mrs. Asquith. At Cowes the Duke and Duchess of Santonia were his guests on board the *Erin*.

And now at last, a final gift of providence, his discussions with the New York Yacht Club reached a head. He was weary of having his challenges refused. He wanted to race again. His attitude became "Gentlemen, I challenge you. You choose the weapons." He waived his previous claim to challenge with a 75-foot and offered to meet them with a 90-foot boat. His gesture was a clever move. Public opinion in America had become critical of the yacht club's attitude. There was even talk of some other club arranging a match to meet a Lipton challenge. The completeness of Lipton's acceptance put the yacht club at a disadvantage. To the general surprise the committee accepted what previously it had refused, a 75-foot boat under the universal rule. The challenge was accepted in May 1913 for a race to be held in September 1914.

It was the kind of challenge he wanted. The old essential problem of any challenge remained: the Atlantic had to be crossed. *Shamrock IV* had to be entirely dismantled, the hull specially strengthened, and a new ketch rig fitted for a passage which might easily pull such a boat out of shape. On arrival in the States the boat had to be retrimmed, rigged, and generally adjusted. She had to meet the American boat untrimmed, unbalanced, and untried. Moreover, Nicholson would be building for the first time under a rule with which American yachts had several years' experience and, as *Land and Water* said: "To sail a boat that must be seaworthy across the Atlantic and compete in the light fleecy airs off Sandy Hook against a volatile cockleshell kind of racing machine built with all the foreknowledge of a rival's plans and lines of construction must obviously be a stupendous obstacle to a challenger's success." At the same time he had got the kind of challenge he had been seeking for ten years, a 75-foot boat under the universal rules, with measurements that would take displacement into account.

On the surface everything seemed to be going well with him. To the public it must have seemed to be. He was looking a little older, but the yachting cap still sat jauntily upon his curls. In a sense everything looked the way it was, but beneath the surface there was a suggestion of impatience, a suspicion that everyone was not quite on his side in the way they had been. And it was just at this of all moments that the first, the only real scandal of his life should have had the ill luck to break; a scandal that in point of fact reflected no discredit on Sir Thomas but caused him, nevertheless, a great deal of pain.

As such it must be recorded here in detail. And indeed it has its own interest and value as a picture of the times. It is a story whose genesis went back quite a way.[5]

In 1903 the Hon. Cecil Twistleton-Wykeham-Fiennes,[6] heir of the seventeenth Baron Saye and Sele, a colonel of militia and a retired Regular Army officer who had served with distinction in the Zulu War, figured on the pay roll of Messrs. Style and Winch, a firm of brewers. His activities were mainly of a liaison nature, and it was in this capacity

---

[5] I have changed the names of those defendants in the case whose descendants might be embarrassed by the recalling of it.

[6] Fiennes is pronounced "Fines," and it has been claimed that the Banbury Cross rhyme is a tribute to the family and that the original poem ran:

> Ride a cock horse to Banbury Cross
> And see a Fiennes lady upon a white horse.

that he wrote the following letter to the commanding officer of the 2nd Loamshire Regiment, a unit which was then recuperating in Malta after an exacting period of service in the South African war.

"Dear Savage, I know you are of an enterprising nature. I wonder whether you would care for a free trip to Cyprus and Crete; our agent there is in a very great state of mind about the Dublin Fusiliers. He appears to have got into trouble with Col. Marsh. He is wondering whether you would feel inclined to take 10 days leave and do Crete and Cyprus. You could play globe-trotter and at the same time give Marsh a pat on the back and put him right with us."

Colonel Savage availed himself of Colonel Fiennes's offer and transacted his commission satisfactorily. In the course of these transactions he met Messrs. Style and Winch's Malta agent, a Mr. Morris. This Mr. Morris was also the Malta agent for Lipton, Ltd. His duties in this latter capacity were concerned with the supply through army canteens of a number of articles that were not issued to the men with rations. By what was then known as the Tenants' System, each unit had its own canteen, and the colonel of the regiment decided which out of a number of competing firms should supply his men.

The commanding officer gave the order. But the order was given or withheld on the strength of the reports received from the men's representatives, from the quartermaster, the colour sergeant, and the cooks. It was important from the caterer's point of view that such persons should be kept content, and it was one of the chief duties of a man like Morris to see that they were satisfied with the Lipton service. An annual Christmas present was a useful way of securing and maintaining that satisfaction.

It was "the custom of the trade" but was at the same time against "the law of the land."

At about the same time that Colonel Savage was executing his commission on behalf of Messrs. Style and Winch, a Mr. Evans joined Lipton's staff in London, where the same Tenants' System operated, and one of his duties was the disbursement to his inspectors of the various sums that had to be handed over to the respective quartermasters. Evans had to make these payments out of his expense account. It was a system that made the exact fixing of a salary for Evans extremely difficult. His relations with Lipton's were never cordial, and finally in 1911 he resigned to enter the employment of the Canteen Mess Society, a rival organisation which supplied army units on a co-operative basis. At that point the trouble started. For when Evans joined Lipton's he had signed an agreement not to work for any firm engaged in competitive activities for a year after leaving their employ. By registering with the Canteen Mess Society he broke this agreement, and Lipton's brought an action for breach of contract.

Litigation is usually a mistake, and more short-sighted proceedings than these can rarely have been undertaken. Any discussion of Evans's position was bound to raise the issue of his salary, and any discussion of his salary was bound to raise the question of "expenses."

By settling the case out of court and issuing a public announcement that any payment by their inspectors to army personnel had been made without their knowledge, Lipton's no doubt believed that they had escaped the consequences of these hastily instituted proceedings. And ninety-nine times in a hundred they would have done.

This was, however, the hundredth time, for the firm now employing Evans, the Canteen Mess Society, worked as a co-operative and did not follow the general practice of giving Christmas presents to cooks and colour sergeants; they were well aware that by not doing so they lost a good deal of business, and they were naturally not sorry to have an example they could exploit. The directorate informed Evans that he had to clear himself or be dismissed. Unfortunately for Lipton's, Evans had kept not only all the correspondence he had received but copies of all the letters he had written. The evidence he gave to the Bribery Prevention League was handed to the Public Prosecutor, and on Saturday, January 17, 1914, the case was opened at Bow Street before the chief metropolitan magistrate. Eight of the sixteen defendants were army officers, the other eight were on Lipton's staff. For the next four and a half months the case was to provide the firm of Lipton's with more publicity than was attending the birth of *Shamrock IV*. Evans was in the witness box for nearly fifty hours, and his evidence left no doubt whatever that the tenant canteen system was built on a system of competing bribery.

On the first day of the trial the eight military defendants, though officers, were men who had been promoted from the ranks. On the second day, however, the public was astonished by the appearance in the list of a Colonel Savage who, while he had been stationed in Malta in charge of the 2nd Loamshires, had been in receipt of a yearly allowance from Lipton's of three hundred pounds, a sum that had been paid to him by Lipton's Malta agent, the same Mr. Morris who handled Messrs. Style and Winch's beers.

M

This yearly allowance came clearly in quite a different category from the Christmas presents that had been paid to quartermasters and colour sergeants, both in size and in the nature of the service that it rewarded. In every army in the world the quartermaster's stores is the centre of a certain amount of "wangling," and it is doubtful if any commanding officer, whatever he might have said in public, would in private have been surprised to learn that his quartermaster had been receiving Christmas presents, provided the men were satisfied with their canteen and the goods on sale there compared favourably with the current prices in civilian shops. But it is quite another matter for a commanding officer of a regiment to receive money from a commercial firm in return for concessions affecting the welfare of his men.

The colonel's appearance in the case heightened the whole level of what the prosecution described as "the conspiracy." It also raised the dramatic content of the trial. Colonel Savage had retired from the service in 1906. He had received not only the Victorian Order from Edward VII but a medal from the Royal Humane Society for saving life. For eight years, after thirty-eight years of service, he had enjoyed an honourable retirement. He had three sons, two of whom were gentlemen cadets at the Royal Military College, Sandhurst. Now he was suddenly called to the dock to answer charges for an offence committed eleven years before. It was not surprising that public interest in the case ran high. From the middle of January to the beginning of April the hearing of the evidence continued. Then the defendants were committed for trial at the Old Bailey.

The case was heard five weeks later in the Central Criminal Court before Mr. Justice Darling. Lord Darling was one of the greatest English judges; he was also one of the wittiest. A caricature by Max Beerbohm shows him handing to his marshal the black cap which a judge wears when sentencing a prisoner to death, with the remark, "Please have some bells sewn on." The cartoon was reported to have annoyed Lord Darling. He never jested, he said, in a murder trial. It was the only kind of trial in which he refrained, and this case clearly was one that provided him with ample scope. From the point of view of adverse publicity, Lipton could not have been unluckier in the court where the case was tried.

Nor could Lipton have been unluckier in the line of defence adopted by Colonel Savage. Represented by Mr. Tim Healy, an Irishman as well known in politics as at the Bar, Savage denied that he had received this yearly salary in return for his concessions in regard to the canteen of the 2nd Loamshires, but as a commission for the good services that he had done in Crete and Cyprus on behalf of Style and Winch's beers; and he entered as his defence the letter written to him eleven years earlier by Colonel Fiennes. As the prosecution had not been able to locate Morris, there was no one in the witness box to deny this story. Savage argued that he had earned this commission while he was on leave, which he was entitled to do. He insisted that he had only been brought into touch with Morris through Colonel Fiennes.

Against this defence Sir John Simon, as Attorney General, had an easy task. The judge could not believe, he said, that the commission on an order of beer would amount to three hundred pounds for three years. He

called it "a trifling service." Moreover, the money had
been paid through Lipton's, a fact Colonel Savage tried
to explain away by alleging that Morris was a muddle-
headed fellow who confused his accounts. The story cut no
ice in court, but a good deal of dirt got thrown by Mr.
Healy. Colonel Fiennes had now become the eighteenth
Baron Saye and Sele. He was controller of the King's
household. Mr. Healy made play in plenty of the fact that
Lord Saye and Sele, as a peer, could not be tried in the
Central Criminal Court but only in the House of Lords.
"Colonel Savage is in the dock," he said. "Lord Saye and
Sele is in the Palace."

Mr. Healy could, of course, have called Lord Saye and
Sele as a witness, but that in the circumstances would not
have helped his client. His line of defence made the headlines none the less. It also gave Lord Darling an excellent
opportunity for pungent comments. His Honour deplored
that a nobleman whose ancestor had set his hand to
Magna Charta should have set his hand to this letter and
should have induced the colonel of a regiment to act as a
sort of envoy on behalf of a brewery firm, to smooth down
an angry colonel and get him to think better of a certain
beer. It showed, he said, a sad decadence from the tradition of a great family. It was better for such a man as
Lord Saye and Sele to starve than get his living by cadging
orders for beer: a comment that throws a curious light
on what was and what was not considered fitting conduct
for an English nobleman in 1914—a comment which also
in part explains why Lipton found obstacles to his election
to the Royal Yacht Club.

Lord Darling's strictures on Lord Saye and Sele were
of course incidental and irrelevant to the real issue, which,

as he proceeded to point out, was that a colonel had con-
spired with a tradesman that money should be given him
as an inducement to show favour and abstain from showing disfavour to a commercial firm in relation to catering
contracts with his regiment.

In giving judgment Lord Darling went on to say that
the evidence before the court satisfied him that those defendants employed by Lipton's, in so far as they made payments for the profits of persons who were capable of in-
fluencing contracts in favour of Lipton's, were acting upon
a system which was known to the directorate, encouraged
by the directorate, and persisted in by the directorate. . . .
As to the amount of responsibility of any particular director, he knew nothing except as to those whose names had
been mentioned here. Colonel Savage was given six
months' imprisonment.

Next day, forty-eight hours after *Shamrock IV* had
been launched by Lady Shaftesbury, every paper in the
country headlined an article on the canteen scandal. *The
Times* leader set the general note: "The time has come
when the whole of the present canteen system should become the subject of searching investigation on behalf of
the government."

Nor did the case end there. The particular line of defence taken by Mr. Healy had assured that. Three days
later the following letter from Lord Saye and Sele was
prominently displayed on the leader page of *The Times:*

In view of the attack that was made on my personal honour in
the Central Criminal Court on Wednesday of last week, I have
cancelled all public engagements pending the opportunity at an
early date of vindicating my character in the only place open
to me.

That place was the House of Lords. A month later, when Parliament re-opened, he rose to "repudiate the mischievous and dangerous idea that the possession of an illustrious ancestry debars a man from earning an honest living." His letter to Colonel Savage was, he argued, "nothing more than a request to a satisfied customer to speak to one who had once been a satisfied customer." He emphatically denied that he had started the unfortunate colonel on the career that had brought him to his present fate.

At that point Lord Newton rose. Lord Newton was at that time a man of fifty-seven, of prominence and responsibility, a diplomat and a soldier who had represented a constituency for thirteen years in the Conservative interest before inheriting his title, and who later, during the war, was to hold important appointments, as Paymaster General, as Assistant Under-Secretary of State for Foreign Affairs, and Controller of the Prisoners of War Department. He was a man whose word carried weight.

Why, he asked, did not Lord Saye and Sele give evidence in court? And when Lord Saye and Sele replied that he had been awaiting anxiously to be called, remarked caustically, "You have a will of your own, haven't you?" Lord Newton then proceeded to attack Lipton's in general and Lipton in particular. It had now, he contended, been shown to the world that it was the deliberate practice of Lipton's firm to engage in a campaign for the purpose of debauching a certain class of officers in the Army. It was the deliberate policy of the board. Sir Thomas Lipton was chairman of the board and yet not one word of condemnation had fallen from this man who was really responsible. If he were chairman of a company which had been engaged for many years in practices of this kind he should be more inclined to seek temporary seclusion than to advertise himself in every conceivable way. He wanted to know whether Lipton's was still on the list of contractors to the War Office or had it been removed.

Lord Crewe at this point interposed. He did not think it desirable or that the House should wish this discussion to be prolonged. He accepted Lord Saye and Sele's statement and made the comment that the defence had not been sufficiently careful to avoid casting blame upon persons such as his noble friend who were not directly concerned with the case.

Even there the matter did not end. On the next day it was announced in *The Times* that Lord Newton proposed to ask in the House of Lords whether Lipton's was still on the War Office list of contractors. The speech in which he asked this question is the biggest personal attack that was ever made on Lipton.

It must be perfectly plain to everybody, he said, that the employees of Lipton, Ltd. were associated in a flagrant conspiracy with government functionaries and that large sums of money were actually expended in bribing those officials—money which presumably came out of the pockets of the shareholders. The head of this engaging enterprise—not the ornamental head but the chairman and managing director—was Sir Thomas Lipton, and in view of the well-established facts, it might have been reasonably expected that some adverse comment on their proceedings would have appeared in the press and that there would have been some condemnation expressed. On the contrary, they were invited daily, he might almost say hourly, to admire this gentleman as a sort of national hero, a magnificent sportsman of the true British type, a com-

pendium of all the British and all the other Christian
virtues, and he frequently saw it suggested that his transcendent merits could only be recognised by making him
a member of that House. He went on to sympathise with
the victims. He criticised the system. Lipton's might say
that they had been unfortunate in having been found out
and that it was the practice of other firms as well as their
own. That might be the case, but it seemed to him that an
example should be made. If it was announced that in future the War Office and other bodies concerned would
have nothing more to do with Lipton, Ltd., he felt convinced that that decision would meet with greater approval from the public generally than many actions with
which the government had been recently associated.

Lord Lucas replied that Lipton's had not held any War
Office contract since 1912. Their name had been removed
from the lists of firms eligible to hold War Office contracts,
and instruction had been issued that no new contracts
were under any circumstances to be entered into with Lipton, Ltd., and that steps should be taken that all contracts
with canteens now held by that firm be terminated as soon
as possible.

A week later the annual general shareholders' meeting
of Lipton, Ltd. took place at Winchester House, Old Broad
Street. *The Times* described it as an "animated meeting."
The year's trading showed a profit of nearly two hundred
thousand pounds and a half yearly dividend of 6 per cent was
declared, but the shareholders who attend annual general
meetings are a contentious race, and Lipton was not good
at handling adversaries. He could not be bothered to pla-
cate them. His speech referred to the canteen scandal in

an offhand manner. It was unfortunate, he said, that an old story had been brought up, but the practice had been abandoned many years before the case was brought. It was a pity that they had lost their canteen contract, but it was a very small and unimportant branch of their activities. The yearly profit on the whole business was a bare four thousand pounds. The thing was a pity, but there it was. And he passed on airily to the next point.

The shareholders, however, were greedy for their pound of flesh. There were protests and interruptions. When Lipton spoke about reorganisation and the appointment of new directors, there were shouts of "We want them." As he sat down half a dozen shareholders were on their feet. Questions were asked about the cost of the defence. Why should the shareholders pay twenty thousand dollars for the defence of a man who had been fined as a criminal at the Old Bailey? Someone else shouted, "Attend to your business and leave yachting alone." Someone else shouted, "Never mind about dividends, bring back the cup!"

Sir Thomas listened for a little, then rose to move the adoption of the report. A number of people were still on their feet, shouting and being shouted down, but he announced blandly that the resolution had been passed unanimously, although, as *The Times* said, very few of the shareholders had voted.

It was a bad day for the owner of the *Shamrock,* but he had good friends among the press, and the meeting received less publicity than might have been expected, the *Daily Mail* giving a column to Lipton's speech and, without mention of the protests and interruptions, reporting that the meeting terminated with a unanimous acceptance of the report and cheers for Sir Thomas and the *Shamrock*.

Even so, it was a bad time for Lipton. And all this happened, it must be recalled, during what should have been one of his proudest periods. At last, after eleven years, another *Shamrock* was in quest of "the old mug." Every week some section of the London and provincial press was covering the story. Keen curiosity had been aroused. So that America should have no inkling as to the kind of yacht that was being sent against her, the strictest secrecy had been maintained, and the publicity value of this secrecy was being exploited to the full. No married man was allowed to work on the construction. Married men, Lipton insisted, would gossip to their wives. The correspondence columns of half the papers in the country debated the wisdom of this embargo. It made a capital "silly season" controversy, "were married men indiscreet?"

As might be expected, the launching of *Shamrock IV* by Lady Shaftesbury was admirably stage-managed. A hundred pressmen travelled down in a specially decorated shamrock train. A party of five hundred lunched in the shed; telegrams of well-wishing arrived from the five continents and the seven seas. Lord Dewar presented a monkey as a mascot. It was the Queen's birthday, and the warships were dressed in Portsmouth Harbour, the old *Victory* firing a royal salute only a few minutes before *Shamrock* struck the water. It should have been one of the big days of Lipton's life. In a way it was. But what peace of mind was there for him at the very hour when Mr. Justice Darling was summing up at the Old Bailey?

The law-court proceedings poisoned the whole year for him. Up to now both his private and his public life had been clear of scandal. He had been brought up in a rigid Calvinistic atmosphere. He neither drank nor smoked. He had promised his mother not to gamble and he had never bet on cards or horses. Though he had moved in what was then accounted a fast set, he had never been associated with fast living. He had retained the rectitude of his upbringing. He was not one of those business men who, keeping on the windy side of the law, expect to find themselves every so often on the verge of trouble. The whole case was a torture to him. His acute sense of publicity magnified its importance. He fancied himself disgraced. In forty-five years of business not one word of criticism had been made against him. Now the beloved business, built up on his mother's pattern from that single shop in Crown Street, was exposed to contumely. His name had been struck off the list of War Office contractors. He was being criticised in court, vilified in the House of Lords.

He saw the whole issue out of focus. He did not realise that no one seriously considered that he was himself to blame. He did not recognise that Lord Newton, in his capacity as a Tory politician, welcomed in the canteen case an opportunity to attack the Liberals, Lord Saye and Sele's position in the royal household providing him with a wide-stretched target. Lipton did not realise that. He saw himself dishonoured and disgraced. Stories of his distress ran round the clubs. "There's old Tommy Lipton," they said, "with the *Erin's* steam up, wondering whether to make a bolt for it." Such stories were an exaggeration. But they had a basis of truth in them. He was upset and worried, and because he knew himself to be completely innocent, his distress was converted into a resentment against the world in which such a thing was possible. This could not have happened in King Edward's day.

He was angry and resentful, in a mood to do something

rash, something foolhardy. He had reached the grand climacteric. It may be that he went very near to danger then. How near we shall never know. His guardian angel, that sense of timing which always made things happen at the right time for him, intervened. When the *Erin* sailed from Portsmouth in July, the Grand Fleet was already assembling at Spithead. Before she was halfway across the Atlantic she had intercepted a message from a German cruiser announcing that war had broken out.

For many Englishmen in August 1914, as in September 1939, the declaration of war came as a relief, as a simplification and a cancelling out of personal problems. For Lipton very certainly it did. It may have postponed his challenge for the cup, it may have prevented his racing in San Francisco during the 1915 exposition, but at the same time it stifled completely and forever the canteen-scandal gossip. No one had time to bother about that now. There were other things more important. And Lipton was one of the first to be among them.

By mid-October the *Erin,* having taken *Shamrock* into sanctuary first in Bermuda and then into wartime hibernation at a pier in Brooklyn, was safely anchored in home waters. The Duchess of Westminster, who had been one of Lipton's prospective guests at Sandy Hook, had an alternative scheme ready. Why should she not have her trip in the *Erin* after all? Why not equip a hospital and take it across the Channel? Within a month the *Erin* was loaded with ten doctors, twenty nursing sisters, sixty-two orderlies, and much medical equipment. When they were held up in Southampton by submarines in the Channel, Lipton chuckled. "I suppose the Kaiser wants back the cups he presented to the *Shamrock.*"

While the *Erin* was waiting, a cable had arrived from the *Chicago Examiner* suggesting that Lipton and Hiram Maxim form a committee to decide how the war could be brought to the speediest conclusion. Lipton found a tactful answer. Soon, he hoped, the United States would be presiding, in terms of its neutrality and history, over a peace conference. He knew how to say "No" without offending.

On the whole, the *Erin's* first piece of war work was not too successful. Kitchener disliked amateurs and he gave no encouragement to private hospitals. Nor did the Duchess have the press, certainly not the American press, on her side; several malicious comments were made about the favourite wolfhound and the volume of Longfellow's poetry with which she was inevitably photographed, and the story was somewhat uncharitably if appositely revived of how the Duke, in the Boer War, had fallen in love with a mature but entrancing nurse from whose charms he had been detached, unwillingly and under royal orders, to the fiancée who was awaiting him in England. *Erin's* second experiment fared much better. It was indeed an altogether more serious business, the transportation to Serbia and Montenegro of a hospital unit consisting of seven surgeons, seven nurses, and three orderlies under the joint auspices of the Order of St. John of Jerusalem and the British Red Cross.

There was considerable competition to join the unit, and among the letters which Lipton received was one bearing a Glasgow postmark. It also bore a familiar letter heading. It was from the chairman of a company, requesting that Lipton show special consideration to a female mem-

ber of his staff. It was almost fifty years since Lipton had
seen that letter heading. He had seen it last at the head of
a pencilled note on which a cashier had told him that he
was getting as much as he was worth and that he was "in
a devil of a hurry asking for a rise." The initials on that
note had been D. A. S., and the signature on this letter was
D. A. Sinclair. He smiled as he put through his call to
Glasgow. "I'll keep an eye on the young girl," he said,
"and I'm glad to see we've both come up in the world since
the cashier told the office boy that four shillings a week
was all that he was worth!" The chairman would no doubt
have been embarrassed had he not heard the chuckle in
Lipton's voice.

The mission started at the turn of the year, with the
Erin repainted white and with a broad red line above the
water and a red cross upon her bows.

To the infantrymen up to their knees in the flooded
ditches of northern France, the account of the expedition
in its early stages must have read like a pre-war pleasure
cruise. The first stop was Monte Carlo, and in spite of
the uniforms that thronged the Casino Gardens the war
seemed so remote that the Red Cross personnel were
highly indignant at not being allowed into the Casino.
Nevertheless, they enjoyed the palm trees and the sun.
Then they moved on to the Piraeus, to be welcomed in a
mood of carnival; the Athenians in masks and *travesti*
scattering confetti, the guns roaring a salute with the ships
"dressed rainbow," and the King and Queen of the Hellenes lunching on board the *Erin*.

A photograph was taken on her sun deck that looks in
retrospect like the final glimpse of a dissolving world—the

Greek King and Queen are there, the Grand Duchess George of Russia, Prince George and Prince Alexander of Greece, Princess Henry of Battenberg. The photograph with the King of the Hellenes on the deck, seated in Arab fashion with his knees tucked up, was to be reproduced in a hundred papers. There had been so many photographs of that kind taken on the *Erin*. There was never to be another.

They sailed on through the Corinth Canal to what is now Jugoslavia, and there the pleasure-cruise side of the expedition began to end. Standing beside Prince Paul on the balcony of the Royal Palace, its organiser watched the shelling of Belgrade. Next day the English and American press was headlining "Lipton under Fire." The nearest shell dropped within a hundred and fifty yards of him, which seems a comparatively wide berth today, when so many civilians have seen the house across the road collapse in rubble. All the same he was within range of war.

His next stage was nearer still—Nish, a miry semi-oriental town, sweltering at the mountain's base, that had suddenly become the centre of big events, its population of 25,000, quadrupled overnight by a spate of refugees and ministries, with every house requisitioned and every café converted into an *hôtel de premier ordre*. Chaos was in charge. Ragged soldiers from the line, bootless, with a rifle over one arm and a loaf of bread under the other, limped towards back areas. The few Austrian prisoners who could walk were allowed full liberty of residence and movement, provided they assisted in the hospitals. Typhus was raging, and no one effective was there to cope with it apart from a British unit under Lady Muriel Paget, an American Red Cross unit under Dr. Ryan, and James Donnelly, that very gallant doctor, who a few months later was to fall a victim to the very disease he was fighting. All day long the streets were filled with oxen-drawn plague carts. The cemeteries were full.

In the fight against typhus Lipton played an important part. It was not only that the *Erin* conveyed a Red Cross unit and large quantities of medical equipment, but that his presence publicised Serbia's problems in England and America in a way that no ministerial oratory could have done. During the three weeks he was based in Nish he travelled extensively through the interior. These travels were, of course, attended with all the limelight, if not the comfort, to which he was accustomed. The familiar figure with the yaching cap and polka-dot blue tie was presented against a background of hospitals, derelict railway stations, fortifications, artillery emplacements. He was photographed on horse and on foot and in army transport, in the company of princes, generals, prisoners, and wounded.

Before the close of World War I, front-line soldiers were to become somewhat cynical about such "Cook's Tours." In World War I an officer at divisional headquarters was accounted to have "a cushy job." The civilian was immune. No doubt the gunners beside whom Lipton had been photographed thought as his pony trotted away towards the base, "Well, he picked a nice day for it," reflecting that in ten days' time Lipton would be aboard the *Erin,* while they would be in this same emplacement being shelled.

It is idle to pretend that Lipton's mission was an affair of danger. It was, however, a considerable undertaking for a man of sixty-four, and it did serve a useful purpose. On his return to England he addressed a letter to the press calling the public's attention to Serbia's plight, which was printed in practically every newspaper; he then organised a relief fund and with its proceeds took the *Erin* out for a second journey. By now he was as prominent a personality in Serbia as in London. He was known throughout the country as Tchika (Uncle) Tom: he was made a Grand Commander of the Order of St. Sava. By midsummer the typhus epidemic had been checked, in large part owing to his efforts.

It was an enterprising and successful piece of war work, of a kind, too, in keeping with his technique. Here, as at all other points of his career, his unfailing sense of gesture counselled him as to which course would most effectively combine the useful and spectacular. He was doing what no one else was. Quite a number of notables were in France. Only under exceptional conditions was an individual "news" there. But the photographs of Lipton's Serbian campaign filled five pages of the *New York Times* roto-gravure. The sixth page, ironically enough—America was a neutral then—was filled with studio portraits of six titled Hungarian ladies resident in America who had sold their jewels for the benefit of the other side.

By the autumn he was back in England, with the *Erin* handed over to the Admiralty for patrol work under her original name *Argusa*. He was never to sail in her again. In June of the following year she was sunk in the Mediterranean as she hurried to the assistance of a torpedoed cruiser.

For the next three years and a half Lipton remained in England. From time to time he made half promises to cross the Atlantic, and Big Bill Thompson of Chicago promised to turn out the town for him. But his intuition warned him that all social activities in wartime, even in a neutral country, had a subfusc quality. He had to be in the limelight or in the dark. He had use only for superlatives and extremes. Moreover, his business needed him.

A great many of his junior managers were on active service. Warned by the canteen scandal, he had taken stock, and taken it so thoroughly that out of his own pocket he had paid a million dollars which the incapacity and dishonesty of certain employees had lost the company. With no yachting to distract him, with *Shamrock IV*, after a few weeks' sheltering in Bermuda, safely anchored against a pier in Brooklyn, he resumed the rigorous routine of the period after his mother's death when he had worked eighteen hours a day, using work not as a hobby but as an anodyne. Such public activities as he found time for were a kind of war work: entertaining nurses, presenting trophies to cadet battalions, kicking off at a charity football match. In 1917 the London *Mail* was enquiring under the column "Things We Want to Know" if Lipton's increased weight was due to his lately renewed devotion to business, and in 1918 Lipton's was once again paying a dividend of 12 per cent.

In a way it was an impersonal period for him. He was alone in the world, without a single relative. No one close to him was in the Forces. He could study the casualty lists with a steady pulse. His heart never beat quicker at the sight of a telegraph boy's bicycle on the hill. He never had to ask himself, "Is that a War Office telegram for me?" He was spared anxiety and sorrow. It was only vicariously that he experienced them through others, particularly through Harry Lauder, whose son John was killed in action at the end of 1917. As soon as Lipton heard he called up Lauder. But from the sound of his friend's voice he knew at once that the father had not yet been told. Lipton had not the heart to tell him; he could not rob his old friend of those few extra hours in which he could build dreams and hope. He turned his telephone call into a New Year's greeting and rang off.

It was only on such occasions that the tragedy of war drew close to him. In the main he was apart from it, cut off by his age and by his lack of relatives from a whole cycle of experience. He was spared its tragedy and he missed its glamour, never knowing the excitement of unexpected leaves, the sense of heightened living in the moment. He went into hibernation. For the first time in his life he lived in the past more than in the present.

Often late at night when the last conference was ended he would bring out his press-cutting albums—there were more than fifty now—picturing as he turned the pages Sandy Hook during those first races in '99; picturing Cowes on the week of his first triumphs there, Cowes in 1908, with its elms and oaks and meadows, like an immense garden stretched along a lake, with the sun shining on its hotels and villas and the turrets of the squadron's castle; remembering as he read, the whole routine of it, the leisurely mornings with the shopping in the narrow street; the women, nearly all of them in white, linen, or piqué, with their long leg-of-mutton sleeves and high stock collars, their straw hats and voile scarves and white buckskin shoes. He remembered the acrobats and minstrels on the esplanade, the patient little crowd at the squadron landing stage, and the evenings when the roadstead was a mass of lights, as though Venice were in the Solent.

Night after night he would sit there brooding over his albums, picturing as he turned the pages the summer-long succession of regattas. Torbay, Weymouth, the Clyde fortnight, the crowded sea front at Hunter's Bay, the programme sellers and the carriage touts and the dinghies at the jetty; and after dinner the strolling in evening dress along the Shore Road out to Lazareth Point, with the fleet's riding lights bobbing against the background of Finnackmore. One day it would all come back, he told himself.

A kind of hibernation; that was what the war was for Lipton. Yet all the time the Lipton story was developing. The world was changing fast, and Lipton was the expression of his day. The purpose, the significance, of the Lipton story is the reflection it gives of his day, the light it throws upon his day. Because of him we see that day more clearly.

Though Lipton spent those three years from the autumn of 1915 to the eleventh of November 1918 unspectacularly and undramatically, driving down each morning to City Road, lunching in his office, sitting late over reports and files, taking back with him to Osidge two or three of his colleagues for the dinner that would become a conference, with the only variation to this routine the frequent trips into the provinces, the unheralded visit on this and the other manager, the constant checking upon his markets; although on the surface nothing seemed to have been happening to him, below the surface the entire fabric of his world was changing.

In England in the spring of 1916 the first Conscription Act was passed, and from that point not only the whole basis of the war but the whole basis of government in relation to the individual was changed. From that point on what has since been called "the common man" had a new stake in his country's welfare. In feudal days the country was the throne; the French kings talked of "their brother England"; the King was defended by his barons, each baron the general of a private army, the men of his estates. Later, when the estates dissolved, with the nation's wealth derived in the main from cities, the country was defended by mercenary armies and by volunteers. But the principle was constant. In August 1914 the recruiting posters placarded their appeal: "Your King and Country Need You." The Battle of Loos was fought in the same mood as Agincourt, by freeborn men identifying their fortunes with their country's. "Who stands if freedom fall?" It was not in that same spirit that the Somme and Passchendaele were fought. After Loos, Government had assumed the right to demand of the King's subjects military service; it assumed the right to break up homes, to interrupt careers, to inflict loss of life and health. It was a right that no English King, not even Charles I, had dared to arrogate, and the government that assumed that right assumed at the same time responsibilities that have not yet been reckoned towards those of whom this service was demanded.

You can say to a volunteer when a war is over, "Thank you for helping me. Good luck, and if you ever find yourself in trouble I'll try to do you a good turn." You can say that to a volunteer, to the man who has come to you of his own free will, but you cannot say it to the man you have coerced. At least you cannot say it with impunity. The man who is coerced will revolt if he is not satisfied. And the man who has been conscripted for the forces demands to know what he has been fighting for. Has he been only defending other people's property, other people's lives? Before the conscript can feel satisfied he has to be convinced that he has been fighting in self-defence, that he has been defending what is his own. His country has ceased to be the throne, has ceased to be one man—though the throne can remain or become, as it has in England, the symbol of the country. A country is now the various small stakes held in it by those who have defended it.

In England after 1916 the relationship of Government and governed was completely altered. By assuming a right over the life and livelihood of the individual in time of war, Government became responsible for the maintenance of the individual in time of peace. If you are going to demand that a man risk his life for you, you are responsible for his welfare not only after you have exercised that right but before you have. This is a self-evident fact that does not need arguing.

As far as it affected Lipton, the Conscription Act was the curtain drop upon a way of living based on the survival of the fittest; the principle on which Lipton's own career was based. When he was a boy the weak went to the wall. That was the law of nature. In the failure of the weak was implied no criticism of the social sytem. The social system was only criticised when, as in the case of Russia, red-tapism, backwardness, and inefficiency made it difficult for the strong to operate effectively. That was the world into which Lipton had been born. The social system of his youth was justified to contemporary opinion by its provision of opportunity to men such as himself. But in the post-war world, as a corollary to this changed relationship between the governing and the governed, the social system was appraised not by the opportunities it offered to men like himself, but by the number of the unemployed. The weak set the standard, not the strong. It had become the duty of the state to provide employment for its citizens.

It was a change of attitude that was to affect profoundly the status of a man like Lipton. Though nothing seemed to be happening to him during those three slow-passing years, the Lipton story was galloping towards its climax.

§ 14

O NE DAY it would all come back. That was what he had told himself as he had turned over his press cuttings during those long wartime evenings; one day *Shamrock IV* would be taken out of her shrouds in Brooklyn; one day he would fly his personal flag again, the field of gold with the green shamrock worked on it. One day it would all come back.

When it did, in July 1920, to many millions on both sides of the Atlantic it seemed as though the clock had been put right back to pre-war summers. Empires had been overthrown and crowned heads exiled; casualty lists had darkened every home; revolution had ceased to be a topic for academic argument and become an actual menace. In speech after speech, sermon after sermon, article after article, an exhausted world had been assured that the old ways had gone forever, but here at Sandy Hook, as a reassurance of continuity, was old Tommy Lipton with his goatee, his polka-dot blue tie, his jauntily tilted yachting cap, looking not one half-hour older, challenging again with another *Shamrock*. The *Erin* might have been sunk, but here was the *Victoria* to take her place.

On the surface it was all just as it had been, and the papers were once again crowded with descriptions of the challenger.

Shamrock was, Lipton had said in 1914, "a hit-or-miss" proposition. She was a big boat that would have to carry an enormous sail. With her snublike nose, her bowsprit of a few feet length, her straight stem, with the body squeezed in at the bulwarks, rounding outwards to the waistline, going in almost flat, then tapering towards the keel and expanding outwards at the foot, she looked in silhouette more like a giant's wineglass than a yacht. Francis B. Cooke did not hesitate to describe her as a freak. But though she was unusual, she was tough. She would, however, have to face a time allowance of six and a half minutes.

In view of this time allowance, America's hope was for a moderate breeze. Designed by Herreshoff, who had died during the war, the defender, *Resolute,* was Boston-owned and Boston-manned. Chris Christensen, who had been mate with Charlie Barr, was the actual skipper. But Charles Francis Adams was at the wheel. Robert W. Emmons was the manager, with George Nichols, a son-in-law of J. P. Morgan, as the navigator, and John Parkinson, the famous Harvard centre, as the strong man of the afterdeck crew to relieve Charles Adams when the sloop ran down-wind. *Resolute's* crew was mainly Scandinavian by birth. *Shamrock's* was composed of Essex fishermen, with William P. Burton at the helm and his wife a member of the crew.

Critics of the races over a span of years have generally conceded that *Shamrock II* was the best of Lipton's challengers, but *Shamrock IV* came nearest to victory. With the least extra luck she would have won. At one point she was two up. At the same time she scarcely deserved to be. She won the first race luckily, after making a bad start and being well behind in a drifting match, only because *Resolute's* throat halyards parted. It was a victory that gave Lipton little pleasure. He did not want to win by a fluke and offered to call off the race. It might be the way of winning according to the rules, but "It wasn't Tom Lipton's way," he said. And though his friends overruled him, he felt no confidence for the future contests from the way in which *Shamrock* had been handled.

He felt even less confident after the second race, when *Resolute,* in a light breeze, completely outsailed *Shamrock* but was unable to finish the course in time. That evening the odds against *Shamrock* lengthened. And it was widely announced that Lipton was proposing to change his skipper. It was also rumoured that *Shamrock's* crew resented having Burton's wife aboard. A woman, they said, put a hoodoo on them. Eventually Lipton decided to persevere with Burton. But the atmosphere cannot have been anything but tricky.

Twenty-four hours later, however, Lipton was congratulating himself on his decision. For the first time in a real race he had seen his green cutter pass the finishing line first. "I'm the happiest man in the world," he said.

It could not have been a more popular win. As *Shamrock* went past the line not a whistle saved its steam. They all let loose on her. At the same time it was not a convincing win. In another drifting match, and on a day of fitful breezes, *Resolute* had the bad luck to become becalmed. *Shamrock* only just got home within the time.

Ring Lardner wrote, "You can get up to Yonkers and back on the subway in one eighth of the time it takes to sail the distance in one of these yachts. And it don't make no difference if the wind is blowing or not."

Shamrock was two up, and Lipton was ordering a special case to take the cup back to England in, but the experts were by no means confident that the cup was lost. There had not in their opinion been a real race yet. Still, "two up" was a big margin to pull back, and there was a general belief that if the green yacht caught the defender on a broad reach in a strong breeze there would be only one boat in it. *Shamrock's* supporters were praying for a fifteen- to twenty-five-knot breeze.

The next race was not to produce those conditions. From the defender's point of view, from the point of view indeed of everyone but Lipton, conditions were ideal; a steady but not a violent breeze was blowing. It was the first real racing day. It was not, however, the kind of day on which *Shamrock* could afford to give away six and a half minutes' time allowance. She put up a good performance and actually crossed the line ahead of *Resolute,* but against that handicap she never looked like winning.

All the same there was no lack of confidence that night on the *Victoria*. If only the wind would blow. In all these dozen races it had not blown a single time in the way that would suit a boat tough enough to have crossed the ocean.

A fifteen- to twenty-five-knot breeze. That was what Lipton hoped for at the end of the third race. That was what he was hoping a little later when the score stood even, with *Resolute* on the triangular course in a five-knot breeze, having beaten him by more than three minutes without reckoning the time allowance. That was what he was praying for on the eve of the fifth race. And that was what he woke to on the following morning, a grey sky and a twenty- to twenty-five-knot wind. His heart bounded at the news. At last, after all these years!

As the *Victoria* came up from Brooklyn towards Sandy Hook the wind began to blow more strongly. Several of his party went below. It was almost rough. But Lipton could have wished it rougher. It was *Shamrock* weather. It was his chance, his greatest chance. At last the luck had turned. He couldn't—how could he?—lose on a day like this. His heart was jubilant. And then suddenly, to his astonishment, he saw the "No Race" signal going up.

Lipton was not the man to show undue patience when he was thwarted. In a fury of red rage he hurried over to *Shamrock;* he hardly waited to hear the explanation, that the judges, feeling that the weather was too rough, that sailing would be dangerous, had asked the boats whether they would agree to a cancelling of the races, and that both *Resolute* and *Shamrock* had agreed.

No one knows what exactly transpired in the interviews that followed. Bitter words must have been exchanged. The race had been called off without Lipton's having been consulted. His habitual smile had gone when he rejoined the *Victoria*. His comment was significant: "*Shamrock* had much worse weather than this coming over. She had her ocean rig and not her racing rig. But there was no more protection for the crew then than now." There was no doubt at all of what he thought. Later he was to retract that initial comment. He was to agree with the judges and the crews that it would have been dangerous to race. But no one believed that that retraction was occasioned by anything but the wish to avoid unpleasantness.

The press comments on both sides of the Atlantic were extremely caustic. An American critic, John C. Spears, talked of these "paper-napkin sailboats" and wrote in describing the next day's racing: "The wind-shy regatta committee and the skippers of the blown-glass *Resolute* and *Shamrock* were rewarded yesterday by weather exactly suited to their capacities. There was absolutely no danger at any time of losing top-hamper or of throwing spray over the well-polished shoes of the racing crews." While another American critic said: "To keep the races from degenerating into a joke it is necessary to change the rules of construction so as to insure that the boats will be able to stand at least a twenty-five-mile wind with racing rig." On the English side a typical comment was: "Sandy Hook is sheltered on three sides by the land, and the Yankees have the frankness to ask the sporting world to be fooled by the calling off of the race because their cockleshell was unable to stand up against a summer squall in a sheltered bay, while the sturdy British challenger that had stoutly weathered Atlantic storms was not allowed to sail the course."

That was, of course, an unfair comment, the kind of unfair accusation that is made so frequently in international sport. *Shamrock* could have sailed the course if she had wanted. A race can be called off only when both sides are in agreement. That was why Lipton was indignant; that also was why Lipton was in a spot. He would have had to order his men to do something that he was not able to do himself; to undergo dangers that he could not share. It was a responsibility he could not take. He had to accept his captain's decision, particularly in view of their previous disagreement. But he had good cause to be indignant.

Any sport that is worth anything is dangerous, and yachting is more dangerous than most. Fatal accidents are not uncommon, and it is indeed possible that the risk of taking out *Resolute* on such a day would have been considerable. At the same time it is hard to believe that a boat that had sailed right across the Atlantic could not manage a twenty-four-knot wind. It would not have been a pleasant day for racing, and *Shamrock's* crew were not on harmonious terms with one another; there was no true team spirit. But it is impossible to doubt that if Harold Vanderbilt had been on such a day at the helm of a challenger that had sailed across three thousand miles of open ocean he would have done anything but put his hands upon the wheel and shout out to his crew, "Come along, boys, we'll show them we can sail the course. They can follow or not, just as they feel inclined." Lipton was in no position to do that. He was seventy years old and he was not a yachtsman. He did the only thing he could do—but which a great many others would not have done—he accepted the inevitable like a sportsman.

Within a few hours the wind had blown itself out and *Resolute* won a final drifting match. *Shamrock IV* would have been very lucky if she had regained the mug, but at the same time she very nearly did.

§ 15

NOT EVEN in 1899 had Lipton's personal prestige stood higher than it did that autumn on his return to England. He was now a man of seventy; during not one week of those seventy years had he spared himself an hour either in work or play. But though he had lived hard, he had lived frugally. He was strong and healthy and erect. He did not look an old man; he did not feel an old man. He lived in the present and the future. There was no reason why they should not match the past. He had every reason for believing that years as good as he had known still lay ahead.

He was returning, it is true, to a world very different from that which he had known in boyhood and from that which he had known in London in the Edwardian day. Different ideas were in the air. The war had telescoped events. Changes that would have taken place slowly over fifty years had been compressed into five. Women had the vote. There had been revolutions in Russia, in Turkey, in Germany, in Austria. English life and business were being paralysed every few months by strikes. Manual labour had learned its power, or was learning it; was conscious of it but was afraid to use it. The old world of privilege and property was threatened. The world no longer felt about capital as it had forty years earlier when Lipton had gone to America for his first deal in pork. Basic income tax stood then at 3 per cent; now it stood at 33, with a mounting scale of supertax carrying it into the eighties. But that was not the only difference. In the 1870s and 1880s, when rapid fortunes were being made on both sides of the Atlantic, the doctrines of Samuel Smiles had been held in reverence. The man who made a fortune, provided he did not do it by swindling his fellows, was held to be conferring a benefit upon the human race; it was believed that wealth created wealth, employment, a raising of the general standard. "America's business is business. What is good for business is good for America." That was the transatlantic attitude, while the fact of earning money, of owning property, was regarded as a proof of merit. No justification was more eloquent than a large bank balance. In 1904 Lipton had been loudly applauded when he had said at a public dinner, "A man may have many friends, but he will find none so steadfast, so constant, so ready to respond to his wants, so capable of pushing him ahead, as a little leather-covered book with the name of a bank on its cover." That was not considered a cynical remark in 1904: on the contrary, it was felt that he was offering a worthy goal of ambition to the young.

But in 1920 that remark could only have been made with a raised eyebrow. Too many fortunes had been made in the war at the expense of others. Where *Punch* in the 1860s had mocked the vulgarian Sir Gorgius Midas with his rows of footmen and his diamond shirt studs, now it made fun of the city director standing on the lawns of the ducal estate that he had snapped up at a bargain price owing to the demands of death duties. Money was no longer a test of merit. For four and a half years the best of the young men had taken soldier's pay; many of them were now dead and many more disabled, while the men of fifty, sitting at their city desks, had sold them greatcoats and rifles and canned groceries at a mounting profit. Large fortunes were suspect in the 1920s. The millionaire was no longer necessarily a hero.

Was Lipton aware of this when he returned to London in the autumn of 1920? He may have been. Probably he was, though he was not by any means politically minded. In the memorial postscript to his autobiography William Blackwood wrote, "Science, politics, the arts interested him not at all. I never heard him discuss the daily events of the hemispheres as they were reported in the newspapers." But though he was uninterested in the ideas that were in the air, his unfailing, unfaltering sense of the slogan, of the right thing to say at the right moment, must have briefed him to the changes that had taken place.

Those changes were not, to begin with, of a kind that threatened his enjoyment of the next decade. The world had changed since the summer of 1914, when Lord Newton was attacking him in the House of Lords, but his own position had changed with it, and to his advantage. Ten years ago, when George V had come to the throne and a new court set had come into power, Lipton was in the unenviable position of the displaced favourite. He was no longer the New Thing. But now, though it was only ten years later, so much had happened in the past decade that the Edwardian Era already had an air of distance; those who had been a part of it possessed the attraction of a period piece. Lipton particularly. He had been there as long as anyone remembered—first with his shops and groceries, then with his tea, later with his *Shamrocks*. He had been there so long that he seemed to have been there forever. The war had come and gone, spoiling, shattering. It was reassuring now when the smoke had cleared to find old Sir Thomas as alert as ever with his rattle of anecdotes about the Kaiser and the Czar. England in that late autumn took Lipton to its heart in a way that she never had quite before. He was an institution now, and the English are very devoted to their institutions.

The new court set of 1910 might have been hostile to the cronies of the old regime, but the "Bright Young People" of the twenties, the English Scott Fitzgeralds who read *The Green Hat* and *Antic Hay;* the young men who wore Oxford trousers and high-necked jumpers; the girls who crooned "Limehouse Blues" and shook their short skirts about their knees to the syncopation of "Dance Little Lady," who wept shallow tears over the sorrows of "poor little rich girls," who wore Russian boots, carried short stumpy umbrellas, and pulled hats like inverted pudding bowls low over their eyes, whose most serious problem was summed up in the song "Shall I Have It Bobbed or Shingled?"—the wild, irresponsible young people of the early twenties were ready to respect and love the man of the people who had entertained crowned heads. For royalty, too, had acquired the fascination of a period piece now that the Almanach de Gotha was becoming increasingly a social register of displaced persons.

In the early twenties Beverley Nichols, who was then working in London for the *Weekly Despatch,* obtained an interview with Lipton. This interview, which was published later in his book *Twenty-Five,* though only four pages long, is the most vivid pen portrait we have of him. It is also one of the few interviews in the book that is entirely respectful. Nichols heads the chapter in which the interview is printed, "Two Big Men and One Medium." The other big man was Kipling.

The interview followed the familiar course. Lipton had never anything new to tell his interviewers. He recounted the old anecdotes: the "orphans," the bank note, the cheeses; he gossiped about royalty; he concluded as always by talking of his mother. "You stick to your mother, laddie, as you would stick to life. As long as you do that, you won't go far wrong."

Beverley Nichols could not help being startled at Lip-

o

ton's decorative scheme. "As soon as one entered the hall," he wrote, "the fun began. There were black china negresses, 'nice bright' wallpapers, heads of healthy animals and at every turn photographs of some royalty in a large silver frame. One object in the billiard room I particularly admired. This was a sofa covered with cushions of really inspiring colours. One cushion which was placed between a blue and orange stripe and a white and black check had for its main design the star-spangled banner worked in blue and crimson wools." He could not help smiling a little at all the silver-framed photographs with "the signatures written in that curious scrawl which denotes either a royal origin, success behind the footlights or delirium tremens." Yet all the same he was impressed by Lipton. "He was simple and charming. His pride was so naïve one could not possibly object to it. 'The Kaiser said to me . . . Her Majesty remarked . . . The Prince of Wales . . .' They were all only little pats on the back of the ex-factory boy." *

Lipton was more in tune with the 1920s than with the 1910s. He was more at home in England than he had been for a dozen years. He had recovered all the ground that he had lost in 1914. The canteen scandal was forgotten. During the war his firm had been replaced on the list of army contractors. In 1920 there was a new issue of shares, and though at the shareholders' meeting in 1921 he had to report a drop in profit owing to an increase in wages of a hundred thousand pounds and an increase in carriage rate of nearly the same amount, he still paid a dividend of 12½ per cent. His credit stood as high as his prestige.

* *Twenty-Five* by Beverley Nichols. Jonathan Cape, 1925

It was standing high, too, in America, particularly in New York. In August 1919 he opened his new offices. Until then his business had occupied small and obscure premises in Franklin Street. The turnover, though satisfactory, was by no means large, and his New York staff were astonished when he cabled them to take over a large twelve-story building in Hoboken. The staff to-day realise his far-sightedness. Every cubic foot of that building serves a purpose, and the large sign, "Lipton's Tea," is seen by every boat that steams up the Hudson. Lipton had recognised the publicity value of that sign and site. With the movement into these new premises, his turnover began to increase rapidly, and there is little doubt that prohibition assisted the sale of tea.

He had entered, it seemed, upon a happy and a tranquil autumn. His life's work lay behind him. His achievements lay before his eyes: the tea gardens in Ceylon, the six hundred markets, the steadily maintained dividends, the rising profits in America, and always there was the hope that one day he would see a *Shamrock* coming home first at Sandy Hook. That last decade should have been, if not the most exciting or the most dramatic, at least the most satisfying of his life.

And certainly the first five years were all that he could have asked of them. He was living more quietly now, as befitted a man of over seventy. But he was still a socialite. Until the age of fifty he had barely been inside a theatre, but now he was a regular first-nighter. He frequented rather different company. He was no longer moving in court circles. He was on friendly terms with royalty. He regularly attended the garden party. He was photographed

talking to the King at the Richmond Horse Show. When
the Duke of York visited Cathcart he lunched with him.
But he no longer appeared in the Court Circular as having
been "honoured with an attendance on the King"; he was
not one of the guests at Princess Mary's wedding.

His cronies now were big business men like Dewar, Lord
Inverforth, and Gordon Selfridge. Possibly it was a more
congenial set. For the first time in his life in England he
was mixing with his opposite numbers. In his boyhood and
his youth he was in the company of boys whom he would
—he must have known it—be very soon passing in the
race. Later, in the company of aristocrats and persons of
royal birth, it can hardly have been possible for him to
relax completely. Even with Edward he must have been
a little on his guard. With Dewar it was different; though
Dewar had been born, as the son of a distiller, to a more
prosperous environment than Lipton had, he, too, was a
self-made man. They could talk, he and Lipton, in short-
hand with one another. Each knew what the other was
about. They understood each other's problems, understood
them so well that there was no need ever to refer to them.
Everyone who ever saw them together spoke of their happiness in each other's company. They were always laughing, always playing practical jokes on one another. They
had been close friends for fifteen years. They were insep-
arable during the post-war period.

The autumn of 1923 saw Lipton once again at Glasgow, to have the freedom of the city conferred on him. It
was one of the great days of his life. The ceremony took
place in St. Andrew's Hall with Sir James Bell, a prominent civic administrator, at his side. "Oor ain Folk" was,

according to the *Glasgow Herald,* "the dominant note of
the ceremony.""There was," the report went on, "an atmosphere of homeliness. In the hall were representatives
to the general life of the community—staid business men
and their womenfolk, sober and sedate in dress and
demeanour, not readily moved to demonstration but
suggestive of that sound commercial element upon which
the prosperity of the city has been built and which was so
well typified by the chief figures in the ceremony." They
were both called by the Lord Provost "worthy citizens of
Glasgow."

On Lipton's behalf the sederunt stated that the honour
was given "in acknowledgment of the exemplary and patri-
otic services which he had rendered to the country, particularly during the Great War, and to the corporation
and the community by his repeated and generous gifts for
the benefit of his poorer fellow citizens in time of hardship
during unemployment and in recognition of the credit and
renown which from far and near he had brought to his
native city by his devotion to and success in trade and
commerce to the great advantage of the people and to
the promotion of British-American friendship and his de-
termination as a sportsman to regain for this country the
America's Cup and also as an expression of the respect
and admiration in which he was universally held."

In his speech the Lord Provost spoke of Lipton as one
who had never been ashamed of his background, who had
never ceased to declare that he owed all he was or had
been to his early training in Glasgow. In his reply Lipton
spoke of his early days. He told of how as an office boy
earning half-a-crown a day he had promised his mother
that one day she should have a carriage of her own. He

told that story, he said, because he wanted every ambitious lad of Glasgow to feel that the way was open for him to succeed in life if only he would take his mother for "his guiding star."

In many ways that day was the proudest in his life. Far though he might have wandered, his loyalty to Glasgow had never lessened. "I am prouder of this," he told an interviewer, "than I would be of a peerage, and indeed I have refused a peerage." Many times he must have looked back to that day in the years to come, wishing perhaps that the curtain could have descended then. Most people live too long; most people outlive their reputation. Most people look back to a certain day, a certain moment that acquires in retrospect a significance that at the time it had not possessed; a moment to which they look back, thinking, "If only it could have ended then."

At the moment nothing seemed less likely than that Lipton should experience such a mood and moment. The years were passing pleasantly. His name was still constantly appearing in the papers. Every summer there was Solly Joel's vast five-hundred-guest luncheon party at Maiden Erleigh. Colonel and Mrs. Knowles Stansfield were giving a luncheon party in their Wimbledon house with its amusing Japanese garden for the ex-King and Queen of Greece, with Lady Oxford, Lady Mond, and Lord Winchester among the guests. Will Rogers was making his London debut in Cochran's revue at the Pavilion and getting a slightly mixed reception owing to his trick of wisecracking at members of the audience. His spotlight often fell on Lipton. There was a party for Will Rogers in the Pinafore Room at the Savoy, for which Michael Arlen specially hurried back from Paris. In '24 a town in Canada was named after him. Next year he celebrated his seventy-fifth birthday. In its honour he handed over Johnstone Villa as a Lipton memorial nursing home. He planned to take advantage of prohibition with a big tea-drinking campaign in the U.S.A. He acquired a second *Erin*. He brought back from America his 23-metre *Shamrock* that he had taken over there four years earlier to race against *Shamrock IV;* he resumed the pleasant routine of Cowes, the Clyde fortnight, and all the other regattas round the coast. The big-class races might not be quite the same thing now, with no German challengers, with the lists of royalty diminished. But then nothing anywhere was quite the same thing.

There were new things, and agreeable things.

We have several contemporary accounts besides Beverley Nichols's of his life at Osidge. Elizabeth Craig wrote one in '26. She wrote of the dining room, with the set of dessert silver presented "by the people of U.S.," of the statuary in bronze and marble, the gold brocaded curtains, the red damask wallpaper, the oak chair padded in red morocco so that the room, "seen through half-shut eyes, presented a mellow picture of black and brown, relieved by gold and red." She wrote of the billiard room with its white marble bust of Edward VII, of the snake poised on top of the piano as if ready to strike. The cushions that had so struck Beverley Nichols had been worked, she tells us, by the sisters of the St. Bridget convent in Ceylon.

By now Osidge was clearly overcrowded with furniture and trophies. Lipton acquired fresh souvenirs on every trip. He was the constant recipient of presents. A friend who was there once for his birthday has described him as no more than opening, glancing at, then closing down the boxes. His secretary, John Westwood, would go through them afterwards to organise the letters of acknowledgment and thanks, but the safe was always stacked high with partially unpacked parcels. Only a small portion of the presents took their place upon the mantelpieces, cabinets, and occasional tables. But each birthday added to the accumulation of bric-a-brac. Moreover, Osidge was now housing many of the objects that had previously been in the original *Erin,* such as the gold loving cup of 1899 and the Nelson relics. The collection of photographs increased with every Christmas. By one in particular Elizabeth Craig was struck. "Imagine," she wrote, "four silver hearts so grouped that the points met inwards, frame a photograph in each heart, and then read the inscription above and the autographs. 'The Order of the Four Hearts.' The order carries the signatures H.R.H. Duchess of Hess, H.R.H. Princess Hohenlohe Langenburg, H.R.H. Princess Beatrice of Saxe-Coburg, H.H. Princess Ena of Battenberg, who after a week's yachting hung it round his neck." .

Elizabeth Craig, very appropriately in view of her culinary skill, is the only one of Lipton's interviewers to provide us with his favourite recipe for rice. "Three tablespoonfuls in cold water, boil till tender, drain off water, place in a buttered pie dish, mix a tablespoon of sugar and a tablespoon of butter, a pint of milk, a little vanilla, then bake slowly for two hours. Add very thick cream."

Rice appeared in some form at every meal. And it was extremely difficult for his guests to avoid their share of it

There was indeed no surer way of pleasing him than by asking for a second helping. He would immediately deliver a homily on the excellencies of rice and of what it had done for him. He was, as is inevitable for an aging bachelor, faddy and autocratic. The house was run on his own lines, to please himself. The temperature was maintained at a level which his Scots friends who had not learned the transatlantic habit of wearing light clothes and underclothes found overpowering: a temperature that was rendered even more testing for Caledonian tastes by the strict instructions that no curtain or window was to be tampered with, since every door and window was connected with the burglar alarm and the slightest lowering of the sash would set bells ringing throughout the entire house. Lipton was nervous about thieves, and the sleepless guest would listen to the crunch of the night watchman's footsteps on the gravel.

The house ran smoothly. He had three Sinhalese servants who moved on silent feet in long white skirts, with long black hair held in place by combs. There was John, the chief butler, also a Sinhalese, and Louis, his English valet. Louis ran the house. Guests who wished to go in to London for the evening were always provided with a car. No matter how late you returned, Louis would appear upon the landing with a little book and a questionnaire: When did you wish to be called? When would you like your bath? Would you prefer to be shaved or to shave yourself? Where and when would you like your breakfast, upstairs or downstairs? Which papers would you like? What kind of fruit? The fruit was a specialty of Osidge. Even in winter there would be pears and strawberries, grapes and cantaloupes. Then would come Louis's final warning. Don't touch the window.

Next morning you would not see your host. He breakfasted in his room. He was also medically examined daily. Though his health was good, he maintained that the body was a piece of mechanism that required as much care as an automobile. His doctor should give him a going over in the same way that the chauffeur went over the car. He wanted to be sure that nothing would go wrong during the day.

He left for his office soon after nine o'clock. He would not be back till late in the afternoon. When he did, it would be to retire at once into his study. He had, in addition to Westwood, two business secretaries. He had a tape machine at home and he would work for a couple of hours or so, watching the New York market. He did not invariably change for dinner. Though he usually had guests, he did not entertain formally. There was no "even numbers"; there was no protocol. At the same time there was a ritual about his dinners. At each lady's plate there would be a spray of orchids that he would expect her to pin upon her dress. Fruit in a great bowl would be set in front of him. He would munch grapes between mouthfuls as a Frenchman munches bread, and he would personally select the fruit for each guest in turn.

After dinner the party would move into the billiard room. Sometimes Lipton would play a little. Though he held the reputation of being the world's best loser, he preferred to win when he played billiards. A man now in his late sixties recalls an occasion before World War I when he was staying in the same hotel as Lipton in the South of France. For three or four evenings he had watched Lipton playing with one of his secretaries and had noticed that Lipton always won by a few points. On the fourth night Lipton had been invited out and his secretary suggested to his fellow guest that they play a 250 up. The man in question was a very reasonable club player, who was accustomed to making breaks of 30; he was surprised to find himself beaten by 100 points. That had been before the war. Now in his seventies Lipton was content to play a single 100 up, watch for an hour or so, and then go back to his study for two or three hours' work. His guests had retired before he left his desk.

Usually one of his guests was a business colleague. When there was business to be discussed he lost all sense of time. H. A. Snelling, who lived at Brighton, invariably had to remind him that his last train left at midnight. "So it does, so it does," Lipton would say. "Now be sure and ring me up when you are safe back home." The chief was always there to take the call. Snelling never knew whether Lipton was concerned over an employee's welfare or was merely making sure that he really had gone home and not to a West End night club. He did not spare himself and he did not spare his staff.

Upon his guests, however, he made few demands. There was only one period of a visit that he regarded as a parade, and that was on Sunday after lunch, when he assembled all his guests to drive out and distribute chocolate among the children of North Mimms. It had begun, this custom, fifteen years before when his car had broken down at Cooper's Green and the children had shown such friendliness and concern that he had promised to return there on the following Sunday.

He kept his promise; he continued to keep his promise.

Sunday after Sunday he would motor out, his car stacked with chocolates. As many as five cars have been known to make the expedition. Louis would appear with a great stack of fur coats over his arm, and every guest would find one to fit him. Lipton led the way, perched high in a 1910 Mercedes, in his fur coat and goggles, driving at a pace that many of his guests found terrifying.

The chocolates were stored in hampers, and he would distribute them himself, deploying all his old skill of showmanship, opening the top box, taking out a chocolate, examining it critically with cocked head, then biting it in half, closing his eyes thoughtfully, and nodding his head approvingly as he handed the other half to the nearest child. Then he would form them in a queue; there would be as many as three hundred sometimes, and the guests would observe how the parents of the first children would try to smuggle their charges into the back of the queue so as to get a second box. So much a feature of the neighbourhood were these expeditions that a local minister complained that he could no longer get a congregation for Sunday school and urged that Lipton complete his tour well before three.

Right up to his death he maintained the tradition of a Sunday expedition. It was the only demand he made upon his guests. Osidge was an easy house in which to visit. As long as you were punctual for dinner you could keep what hours you chose. Though Lipton himself was a teetotaller, wine was served at meals. You had only to ask a servant to bring you anything you wanted. A heavy drinker might have missed the presence of a decanter that he could visit whenever he had the impulse, a clumsy person might have felt in danger of destroying every ·time he moved some valuable piece of china, and the extrovert might have felt himself embarrassed by an atmosphere in which the limelight was always directed upon the host; but those were not the people whom Lipton liked to have about him. He chose for his friends those who liked being with him and who respected his idiosyncrasies. He had no lack of friends, of real friends. There were a number of hangers-on, but Westwood kept a diligent watch for them. No one was allowed to be a nuisance.

Lipton was one of those who have to do everything in just the way they want; then he could be genial and expansive, full of good humour and good stories, ready to do anything for anyone. Everyone who got to know him well knew that he was at heart a very kind and very simple man. On the surface his life appeared to be closing in a warm sunset glow, but beneath the surface a situation was in process of creation whose full development was to spoil many of his last days—at least in England.

§ 16

To THE average well-informed London clubman there can scarcely have been a public figure whose general prosperity seemed more firmly based than Lipton's in the spring of 1925. Nothing could have been less expected than the announcement later in the year that his firm was being forced to pass a dividend. It came without any warning. In 1924 there had been a slight drop in profits, from £337,056 to £292,244, and a dividend of 10 per cent was declared in place of the usual dividend of 12 per cent, but the chairman had accounted for this by the universal lowering of prices and of the general cost of living. The prospects, he said, were encouraging, and he was following the old policy of expansion by opening a number of new branches. There seemed no cause for alarm. And when the interim dividend was passed six months later, A. Emil Davies appears to have been the only economist to be at all disturbed, with the *Wood Green Sentinel*, of all unlikely papers, printing his criticisms, which appeared in the *New Statesman*, with the surprising editorial comment, "Shall we sometime see an amalgamation of Lipton's with Maypole and Home and Colonial?" Six months later, however, the true nature of the situation was apparent. The profits were down again and the dividend was passed. The reasons given for this sudden fall were the fall in commodity values and the poor localities where the branches operated. *The Times*, commenting on this explanation, said:

"These have doubtless been important handicaps, though as an explanation of the bad report they would sound more convincing had the very unfavourable trading results obtained by this company not been accompanied by the enjoyment of continued prosperity on the part of other concerns of a similar character."

The shareholders were no more easily satisfied than *The Times*, and a good many criticisms were directed against the chairman. So strong was the public's faith in Lipton, however, and so loyal was the press to him as a whole that the incident actually provided favourable publicity. One of the shareholders had complained that Lipton was overtaxing his strength, that instead of knocking off work at 5 P.M. he went on to 3 A.M., the shareholder's point being that Lipton should delegate his work to younger men. The press, however, concentrated on the first part of the speech, and a number of papers carried stories of the peculiar complaint of the Lipton shareholders that their chairman overworked, while one paper carried a cartoon of Lipton in sailor's dress overtaxing his strength by dancing horn-pipes.

There were no such pleasantries twelve months later. By 1926 it had become very clear that the failure of the previous year was not due to a temporary setback but to a basic fault; the presence as deputy chairman of Sir John Ferguson, who had been Minister of Munitions during the war, was ample proof that Lipton was aware of this.

The shareholders' meeting was a dark day for Lipton. Its telling can be best left to *The Times*:

"Dissatisfaction with the poor report of Lipton, Ltd. was made very apparent yesterday by the crowded and critical meeting assembled at Winchester House. Sir John Ferguson, the new deputy chairman, who was given a good reception, was unable to give the shareholders much comfort. He said the ramifications of the company were so widely spread and of such a huge and interdependent character that it would take a much longer time than he had yet at his disposal to submit well-considered proposals to his colleagues.

"Some of the speakers at the meeting met with con-siderable interruption and many of those present made no attempt to conceal their desire for the resignation of the old members of the board. Protests of the kind when companies are doing badly are not always justified, though in this case it is to be hoped that the very natural restive-ness shown by the spectators will enable a most searching investigation to be made and thoroughgoing reforms introduced. Industrial depression scarcely affords an explanation of the company's misfortunes, for in spite of the same depression the company's competitors continue to flourish."

Yes, it was a dark day for Lipton. The shareholders were placing their confidence very obviously in his deputy. Lipton's opening speech was indeed little more than an introduction of Sir John, and though he himself rose afterwards, to move the adoption of the report, his statement that the business was sound at core was listened to impatiently. Lipton was never good with shareholders, or rather he was never good in the face of criticism. He made a bad impression. It is sad to recall that this was his last appearance before a body of English shareholders.

The next year cannot have been easy for him. A committee of management was busily investigating his activities, calling for explanations, trying to clear up the widespread problem. The men who comprised the committee were his friends. They were doing their best to help him. But he could hardly have been expected to realise that. William Blackwood has said that "he was like a child from whom a beloved toy had been taken roughly and cruelly. He did not realise that what had been done was in his own best interests. He was full of pathetic regrets and rather stupid resentments."

Next year when the shareholders met, Lipton was no longer in the chair; his place was taken by Sir John Ferguson, whose name now appeared as executive chairman in the prospectus. In his speech he said: "Sir Thomas Lipton, the founder of the business, whose whole life has been spent in the service of the business, expressed a desire to be relieved of all active management of the business, but he accepted the office of life president and chairman, a position which we hope he will fill for many years. The duties of this office will only entail his attendance at City Road for board meetings."

The post was clearly not one which Lipton could be happy holding. He could never work in a subservient position. It would have broken his heart to go down to City Road and not go into his old room and sit at his old roll-top desk. It was a situation that obviously could not last, and within two months a rumour that a strong syndicate headed by the Van den Bergh interests and Meadow Dairy Company had virtually acquired control by purchase of Lipton's holdings was sending up the value of the £1 shares to 18/9d, a rise of 5/– in a week. On the ninth of September the rumour was confirmed, with Lipton holding the title of honorary life chairman, "which is obviously," *The Times* remarked, "a tribute to his work as creator of the business." The sum paid to Lipton by the new syndicate is reported to have been three quarters of a million pounds. It is reported that he signed his abdication in the stateroom of the *Shamrock*.

That is the story as the press carried it during thirty months. As to the story behind the story, one must rely to some extent on guesswork. Why was it that this business, built up so carefully over so many years on so sound a base, following natural laws of development, that had through nearly thirty years, including one major and one minor war, maintained a steady flow of dividends, why should this business suddenly collapse at a time when its competitors were doing well?

In his speech of explanation to the shareholders in 1927,

P

Sir John Ferguson offered a number of secondary causes. "Under the old regime," he said, "no attempt had been made even in prosperous years to strengthen the financial position of the company by writing down the goodwill." In 1923 a revaluation upwards of certain of the company's freehold and leasehold properties, plants, machinery, etc., had increased, and would continue to keep high for several years, the annual charges of depreciation. It was, moreover, clear that the business had been milked in order to pay the dividends of 1923 and 1924.

It has been suggested in certain quarters that where finance was concerned Lipton was affected by the trait that is to be found in so many men who pass quickly from poverty to wealth, of taking large sums of money negligently and small sums of money seriously. Even at the end of his life Arnold Bennett found it required an effort of will to take a two shilling taxi for a journey that threepence could have accomplished in a bus. And Lipton, who would spend a hundred thousand on a yacht, would shake his head ruminatively over the purchase of a hundred pound desk for his New York office. A hundred pound is a lot of money," he would say. It was a sum that he had treated once with the greatest reverence, whereas a hundred thousand was beyond the imagination of the young man who had slept under the counter of the store in Stobcross Street. A hundred thousand, fifty thousand —they were sums distant beyond computation. A bird is not supposed to be able to count beyond two, so that if you leave three eggs in her nest she is as happy as if five were there. All she can tell is that her unit of computation has been passed. Sums like a million dollars belonged to the later Lipton. The younger Lipton had been confused beyond a certain point by the row of noughts. And the younger Lipton was always working in the subconscious of the later Lipton, so that to the end of his days the multi-millionaire who cheerfully signed five-figure cheques for Lipton, Ltd. thought twice before spending ten pounds on himself. It has been suggested that this double vision, this double standard in regard to money, was responsible for his difficulties: and it may very well have been a contributory cause. But it can scarcely have been more.

The real cause of the trouble was, according to Sir John Ferguson, the falling off of the trading at the branches, and that was a question of Lipton's personal management. Lipton's was essentially a one-man business. And a business of such vast ramifications was too much for a man of over seventy, who was no longer devoting all his energies to his business, who was absorbed by another passion, yacht racing. He never asked advice; he could never co-operate in management. He was impatient, quick-tempered, ruthless where business was concerned. He could not tolerate inefficiency. Though he had the greatest sympathy for the poor and though this sympathy provided the core of his success—for he anticipated the taste and needs of the poor customer—he had no sympathy for the individual who had failed to carry out his orders. He fired the incompetent without compunction. He did not ask himself what would happen to the man's dependents. The man would manage, as he himself had managed. He had a quick eye for anything he disliked and a good memory for anything he disliked. He would walk quickly round a store or depot, make mental notes, then as he left issue his instructions. "Fire so-and-so," and on his return he would make sure that that so-and-so had been fired. Members of his New York staff, after he had sailed for England, would await with dread the flow of cables which would start arriving when the *Leviathan* was two days out. "Fire the advertising staff. Fire Jacobson." Sometimes it was possible in New York to conceal and retain the victims of disapproval. But in England it was not possible. The branches were too close to City Road; when a man went, he went. As early as July 1925 A. Emil Davies was calling attention in the *New Statesman* to the fact that since the war only one person besides the chairman had stayed on the board throughout the entire period, seven gentlemen having left after, in many cases, a very brief tenure of office; Mr. Davies went on to state that "heads of departments and managers of tea-rooms were changed with the same frequency."

In early days this ruthlessness was one of the causes of his strength. He could not afford, in a business of his kind, to be indulgent towards an inefficient manager out of consideration for his wife and children. But the very characteristic that was his strength when he was young and middle-aged was the rope that tripped him in the end. He was let down by his branch managers and by his staff in City Road because he had lost his sense of the right man for the right job. His eye was out. He looked for men like himself, self-sufficient, hard-working, direct, with an effective manner. He had always disliked dressiness. A man who appeared for an interview in spats and gloves was very unlikely to be appointed. He distrusted anyone who drank, and he preferred the man who did not smoke. He knew what he was looking for, men who were like what he had been fifty years before.

That was one of his mistakes. The world had changed.

The man of the people, the self-made or rather self-making man—for he wanted to choose not so much men who had arrived as men who had their way to make—no longer looked like the men he had picked in the eighties and the nineties. Thirty years of popular education had made a difference; the ideas that were in the air had made a difference. The officer who had served in World War I found himself, when he was recalled to the colours in World War II, dealing with quite a different type of private soldier: a man who was neater, better-educated, quieter, more independent, more self-reliant, but self-reliant in a different way, in a much less self-assertive way. It was a point that Lipton at the end of his life did not recognise. He looked for the same characteristics in his branch managers in the 1920s that he had demanded in the 1890s. But the men who possessed those characteristics—and there were plenty of them—were not the best examples of the modern type. He was taken in by the noisy, aggressive, brash type who talked big, promised a lot, but beneath his bluster was lazy and often dishonest. At the end of his life he made a number of unfortunate appointments.

He had, moreover, begun to distrust his staff. He had studied to some purpose the methods of the secret service. His house was not only wired against burglars. When a couple of buyers came out to discuss a project he liked to listen to their conversation for a few moments without being seen. Some of his sofas contained microphones. He learned quite a lot that way, but he also overheard much that would have been better unheard. He grew suspicious.

It was his rule that every employee home on leave should call on him before he returned to duty, and it was no uncommon thing to have Lipton say, "I'm not too happy about that chap of mine in Karachi. You might have a look at him as you pass through and send me a note marked 'Private' as to how he strikes you."

Stories like that got round. The managers felt that they were being spied upon. The best work is not got out of the best men under those conditions. The staff had ceased to work together in the way it had. Sir John Ferguson, in his first speech as executive chairman, endorsed the report of the advisory committee as justifying the board in making changes in the organisation and personnel. At the same time Lipton had said in his last speech to the shareholders, "The business is sound at core," and Sir John pointed out that there was no lack of actual funds to meet expenses. It was a question of reorganisation and retrenchment.

Sir John did not hold out any promises of immediate results, and The Times commented:

"Obviously it is a very uphill task to check the decline of a business and to bring about an upward trend, and we venture to think that for some time to come the share-holders will have to be patient."

But both The Times and Sir John were over-pessimistic. There was a great deal to be done, certainly; at the meeting in July 1928 the shareholders were informed that the general administration of the new board had necessitated the drastic cutting down of an overgrown head office and rearrangement of duties. In May 1929 they learned that the capital would have to be reduced by a quarter of a million pounds, since years would have to elapse before the heavy arrears of preference dividends were paid off. They were assured, however, that if this sum were written off and ordinary shares were issued to the preference holders, there would be a benefit to them of nearly 80 per cent of the profits available for ordinary shares.

There were constant interruptions at the meeting in 1928; the recommendations were greeted with a sullen acceptance of the inevitable. But in point of fact the work of recovery was carried out far more quickly than had been expected, and by 1930 Lipton shareholders were again beginning to receive dividends.

One who now stands high in the directorate of Lipton's, who was then a very junior clerk, can remember well the anxieties and the rumours that ran round the office. He remembers the first day when Lipton's car did not drive up as usual to the City Road. The chief was ill, so the office was informed. But there were no paragraphs about his illness in the papers, neither that day nor the next. Then one afternoon a secretary was observed clearing up books and papers. Strange faces were seen about the office. Familiar figures disappeared. There were interviews from which high-up executives emerged with anxious looks. Soon it was not only the secretariat but every clerk in the office who had to face investigation; who had to answer questions as to the nature of his duties. No one knew when his turn would come. The man who supplied this information was as anxious as anyone else about his fate. Anxious though he felt, however, on his own account, he had sympathy to spare for his old chief.

He had never been brought into official contact with his chief, but once, during his first year on the staff, he had happened to be in the office lift at the same time as Lipton. He had felt terrified at being alone with the great man. He had wanted to huddle away inconspicuously into a corner, but Lipton had turned towards him, had smiled as an uncle might, and laid his hand upon his shoulder. "Well, my lad," he said, "and how long will it be before you'll be one of the directors of this business? There's plenty of room up at the top, you know." That office boy, whose name Lipton never knew, was one of the men who helped to restore the business in the course of a few years' time to a position as strong as it had held in the 1900s. Lipton had been perfectly justified when he said in that last speech to his angry shareholders that the business was sound at core. It was; it always had been. Only it had needed reshaping and redressing.

If he could return to-day to London and see the new premises that have been built exactly opposite the old ones, if he could travel through the country and see the four hundred prosperous shops that bear his name and where his name is honoured, he would be proud to think how much of his work has survived. But it was a sad day for him when he signed away his holdings in the company he had built up, from nothing, on the pattern his mother had laid down. For thirty-five years every weekday he had spent in London had started with a drive from Osidge, first behind his Kentucky trotters, later in his Daimler, to the side-door entrance in City Road, to the roll-top desk and the fireplace with the carved elephants and the outlook through the window on to the low stretch of houses that have been replaced by the new Lipton offices. His London life was over, and it is symptomatic that in the year 1926 his vast eighty-four-album collection of press cuttings closes. He had lost interest in the person he had become.

Or rather he had lost interest in the person he had become, in London; in New York, on the contrary, his stock stood as high as it had ever done. He had retained control of his New York business, and that business was in a highly flourishing condition, in which connection it is worth pointing out that the time and money he spent on yachting had a much greater publicity value in America than they did in England. Much greater interest was taken in the races in America than in England, in large part because they provided a spectacle in which many thousands could take part; in lesser part because the challenger, as visitor, has always a news value that the resident cannot have. It was in fact discovered after Lipton's death that very considerable advertising campaigns had to be undertaken to make good the loss of publicity that had attended his visits to New York. It was estimated that half a million dollars spent upon the challenge for the America's Cup was worth three quarters of a million on an advertising programme. His English business may possibly have suffered by the amount of time and capital that he had expended on his yacht racing, but his American business was the gainer. His American business was, moreover, more compact and easier to handle. It is also possible that he gave it more attention, that he was more interested in it, that the American side of his life had become more important to him than his English side. He had always been happy in America; he had always been happy with Americans. Since Edward VII's death he had come to feel himself more at home there, and among them. In the later years of his life it may well be that there was a swing of concentration away from England and towards New York.

Certainly during his last five years all the drama, the colour, the glow of living were concentrated in America.

His life in London was that of a retired business man. Osidge had become his office now, and one room was devoted to his work. He lived quietly, unadventurously. Motoring was his chief interest apart from yachting. He took long daily drives into the country. On Sundays after his visit to Cooper's Green he would go round to his friend and neighbour, Lord Inverforth, for an hour or so of hymn singing. That was how he had spent Sunday evenings as a boy in Crown Street and as a young man at Cambuslang in Johnstone Villa. On weekday evenings he would have his doctor, Mr. Fairweather, round for dinner, and afterwards they would play billiards. Sometimes he would go to the theatre with Tom Dewar. The Ivy was his favourite restaurant. Occasionally he would attend a public dinner. It was a tranquil life. The days of the long business conferences, with Snelling ringing up from Brighton to say that he had got home safely—they were over.

In New York, however, it was a very different matter. There he was as much in the limelight as he had been in London in the 1900s. The brave pageant of the jazz age was in full display, and though nothing could have been farther from Lipton's tastes and temperament than all that went with it—the speak-easies and the hip flasks, the John Held, Jr., cartoons, the cars parked outside country clubs on Saturday night dances, the gangsters and the Charleston—yet nonetheless he had his place in the parade.

Jimmy Walker, as far as New York went, was the showman, the compère of the piece, and Lipton's presence there was one of the mayor's many turns. Grover Whalen was the commissioner of police, and between them they did their stuff. Never had the town been gayer than it was then. Good times were in the air, and the years fell away from the old campaigner when he saw the skyscrapers of downtown Manhattan.

He was feted from the hour of his arrival. There was nothing he loved better than driving behind a police escort in an open car. He would tell the chauffeur to drive slowly, and when they were reaching Fifth Avenue he would take off the fedora hat he had been wearing and pull out from under the seat his yachting cap. "They'd hate to see me without this," he'd say, and he'd tell the chauffeur to drive more slowly still.

Children on the sidewalk would wave their hands at him. Their fathers would call out, "When are you going to take that cup home, Tommy?" It was a Roman triumph. When he drove down to the river to take the Lackawanna Ferry to Hoboken, his escort always drove him straight to the head of the queue. It was his boast that he was the only man in New York who could drive straight from his hotel to his office floor. Had he bet, he would never have lost a bet on that. The elevator in the Hoboken offices was so large that he could drive his car right into it and be taken to the twelfth storey, to his office door. When he left, there would be a ten-pound cannister of tea for every member of his escort, and for special persons there would be a gold and green enamel pin with the *Shamrock* on it.

He was playing hard there, but he worked hard as well. And his secretary, John Westwood, was very firm in his protection of him. Hard things have been said about John Westwood: "the head mogul of an invisible government" was John L. Hickey's description of him. But such things were said by self-seekers who had ends of their own to further. Without Westwood, Lipton could never have done all he did. He travelled with a staff of two secretaries and a valet; his plans were further complicated by such idiosyncrasies as refusing to drink local aerated water and bringing his own with him. There were also his own capricious last-minute decisions. He would, for instance, take his chauffeur out for a short drive, then suddenly decide to drive on to Toronto and see a local manager. He rarely carried money on him. Westwood had always to be ready for such emergencies. Lipton was not easy in those last years. It was out of loyalty that Westwood stayed with him.

In his New York office he was as autocratic as he had been in City Road. Things had to be done in his own way. He refused to have the office modernised. To-day his old study is panelled in oak, with red leather chairs, a green carpet, and a green leather sofa; it has bookshelves and it has pictures—one of them a portrait of himself. Modern New York has made a speciality of elegance in offices, but there are few as attractive as those on the twelfth floor of the Lipton offices in Hoboken, looking down on the repair yards, looking across the Hudson to Manhattan.

In Lipton's day there was none of that. His attorney, Willard Taylor, nearly got fired for suggesting that it was time he had the place done over. Here as in City Road he liked glass partitions so that he could see what everyone was doing.

His own room was cut off from the rest of the office by an oak partition, on which were hung a painting of Osidge and pictures of his yachts. He had a private dining room where he would invite members of his staff to lunches that were in fact business conferences. They were not cosy meals. Ginger ale was the only alternative beverage to water, and heavy piles of rice garnished with mango chutney were an uncomfortable diet for men accustomed to lunching on a sandwich and a cup of coffee. His New York visits were, in fact, by no means comfortable occasions for his staff. Everyone knew his position to be precarious. "The old man" was on the alert. He had realised that the trouble in England had been his choice of managers. All his troubles —the canteen scandal pre-eminently—had come to him through the insufficiency of his subordinates. He was not going to have any trouble of that kind here. He knew the dangers that beset an absentee owner. He was wary and he was watchful. He was afraid that things were being plotted against him behind his back, that on this side of the Atlantic some equivalent of that advisory committee might be planning a *coup d'état*. He would resort now and again to the device of playing one man against another. Sometimes he would pose as being naïve, and short shrift befell the employee who fell for that one.

Yes, they were uncomfortable times. There were sighs of relief, not when the *Leviathan* sailed—for who knew what the streams of cables might contain—but when the *Leviathan* was safely docked. Yet at the same time right through the office there was a deep sense of loyalty, of affection for him. "He was all right if you took him in the right way." That is what all his old employees say of him. They will say it almost grudgingly. Then the expression on their faces will change; they will smile reminiscently, almost fondly. "After all," they will say, "there was no one like him." And then they will produce some endearing incident like that of the office boy in the elevator to whom he had said, "How long will it be before you'll be one of the directors of this business?" Some casual little word or action that bound that person to his memory all his life.

He was quick-tempered, he was irascible, he was incalculable, impatient of criticism and of opposition: but at the same time there was nothing trivial about him, nothing petty. He was on a big scale. He had that immense gusto, that zest for living. There was about him the glamour of the past. He had done so much and he had come so far. He had crowded seven lives into the space of one. You had the sense when you were in his company of looking upon innumerable other worlds and ways of living that time had integrated into his career and person. He was all that. And yet at heart he was a very simple person. Everyone who knew him has said that same thing of him.

There was nothing devious about him. You met the whole man, straightaway, face to face. And finally there was his charm, the twinkle in his eye, the brogue in the voice, the sense you got in his company of the sun coming from behind a cloud, wrapping you about with warmth and light. It was not a conscious quality. It was not a card he played. It was not water turned on from a faucet. It was spontaneous geniality, a sudden outpouring of good feeling towards the world in general and you in particular. It was irresistible. There was no one like him. That was what it all came back to in the end.

§ 17

His collection of press cuttings closed in the year 1926; he kept no diary. His correspondence was dictated and of a business nature. What we know of his life during his last five years comes from references in the press and from the reminiscences of his friends. A great deal of the time he was in America. In the autumn of 1927, within a few days of the resignation of his chairmanship, he was on his way back to the United States, announcing on the *Leviathan* that he was soon going to issue a challenge for the cup. He made the biggest American trip that he had undertaken since the war. He went to the Coast and assured the Breakfast Club of Los Angeles that though he had the largest and costliest collection of silver cups in the world he would trade them all for "that mug." He cracked jokes with reporters with his old-time liveliness. "My only blood relatives," he told them, "are some New Jersey mosquitoes who welcomed me sixty years ago."

In February the Atlantic Yacht Club, presided over by Fleet Captain A. V. Guidet, was entertaining him with a dinner at the Ritz, in the course of which he offered, in the hope of encouraging small-boat racing in Gravesend Bay, a cup to be held by the club and raced for there by yachts of international class. In his speech of acceptance Guidet presented him with a silk burgee for his next *Shamrock*. When he left in March he was seen off by the president of the New York Athletic Club, William Kennelly.

In September he was back again. Kellogg also was travelling on the *Leviathan* with the treaty to renounce war in the ship's strongbox. In tribute to this important piece of cargo Lipton gave up his special suite to the Ambassador. "First time I crossed I travelled steerage. I'm used to discomfort," he remarked. Kellogg was exhausted after his negotiations. He must relax over some detective stories. He asked Lipton if he had any.

That October, with the stock market rattling daily to

new high levels, a small group of millionaires gave themselves a dinner at the Astor. Lipton was the oldest, the tallest, and most erect. By May he was back again, offering a six-thousand-dollar silver trophy for the annual regatta of the Philadelphia Outboard Motor Boat Association, to be held in late June in the Schuylkill River. In June he learned that the New York Yacht Club had at last accepted his fifth challenge for the cup.

It was, he said, one of the happiest moments of his life. Not only had his challenge been accepted, but on his own terms. There were to be no time allowances and no handicaps. All boats would be similar in design, all would start together, and the yacht that came home first would win. It was what he had been negotiating for for thirty years.

In October, when the New York Athletic Club feted him in their gymnasium with a dinner attended by a thousand guests, he said in accepting a bronze plaque from Major Kennelly, "At last I have a boat built entirely to my specifications." But for time allowances and handicaps he might have won in 1901; he almost certainly would have won in 1920. This was his best chance. Never had he felt more confident, more jubilant. It looked as though at the very end of his life he were to be granted the prize that for thirty years had occupied his dreams and hopes.

His thoughts were concentrated now upon the race. He could think of nothing else; he could talk of nothing else. In September, when he was invited to speak at the Sixth Annual Radio World's Fair at Madison Square Garden, he kept to his subject to begin with. Radio was, he said, one of the wonders of the world; it brought practically all the civilised world into close contact. But when he began to tell his listeners that the *Erin* was the first vessel to have a private installation, nothing could prevent his passing from the *Erin* to the *Shamrock*. "If any of my listeners," he said, "have been away from their native land for over seventy years, they will well understand how eager that cup must be to get back home even for a week." His eyes lit and twinkled when he spoke. He sounded like a young man on the brink of a high adventure, and his audience loved him for it. There was scarcely a person in America who did not hope that at last he was going to pull it off.

In England, too, there was a recrudescence of interest in the race. Although the glamour and colour of his life had now become centred in America, he was no less an honoured and respected personality in England. There was no sense of his being under a cloud. Lipton himself was touchy about his enforced retirement, but the average Englishman was scarcely aware that a crisis had taken place. Lipton's failure to pay a dividend had not made front-page headlines. The average Englishman does not bother to do more than run his eye, if that, over the financial columns of *The Times*, and he quickly forgets what he has read there. If he had been asked in a questionnaire in 1929 as to the present status of Sir Thomas Lipton, the most he could have said was that he thought he had read something somewhere about Sir Thomas's having decided to retire from active business so as to devote all his energies to yacht racing, which he would have considered a very sensible thing for a man of nearer eighty than seventy to have decided. Though Lipton himself may have nurtured harsh feelings at the treatment which he had received in City Road, the position which he held in the heart of the average Englishman was not impaired. He was an institution. Everyone was delighted that the old boy was going to have another shot.

§ 18

O N THE fourteenth of April 1930, *Shamrock V* was launched by Lady Shaftesbury. Never had Lipton appeared more confident. He spent his eightieth birthday on the *Erin* watching *Shamrock V* at work. "I am out to do it," he said. "I mean to do it."

There was the old vigour in his voice. He had issued his first challenge light-heartedly enough, but the caprice had become a passion now. He had cracked his jokes. He had said that he got better publicity when he lost than when he won. There was nothing people liked better, he said, than a good loser. But he was no more sincere when he said that than is the novelist who, when he has at last written *the* novel of his life, will not allow himself to be congratulated on his reviews but pretends that what really pleases him is the sum that he has snared from Hollywood. Whatever he may have thought in 1899, there can be no doubt now that he wanted desperately to win. He was an old man of fourscore years. If he could pull it off at last, it would be indeed a chance that would redeem all disappointment, that would settle every score, cancel every grievance.

During the early summer of 1930 tributes as warm as any he had been ever paid were profusely proffered. On July 8 in the Fishmongers' Hall he was lunched by the Honourable Company of Master Mariners. Both the Prince of Wales and Ambassador Dawes were present.

The Prince expressed the belief that even in the United States a victory for *Shamrock* would be popular. The Ambassador said, "Britain has shown us that she possesses the fastest airplane and the fastest car. If she produces the fastest yacht, American disappointment will be assuaged by her appreciation of the fine sportsmanship of this veteran now making his fifth attempt." Rudyard Kipling, who was wearing a soft collar that the representative of the *New York Times* described as being both American and of ample dimensions, nodded his head approvingly. As Lipton rose to speak the cheering could be heard right across the thousand-year-old Billingsgate Fish market that lay below the windows of the dining hall. He stood for a moment straight and tall, looking down at the crowded tables.

How often in the past over the last thirty years had he not risen at this and the other table to reply to this same toast, his health. Already across the Atlantic committees were discussing details, secretaries were preparing invitation lists of banquets in his honour. The familiar scene would be re-enacted, the familiar speeches made. There was nothing all that special, for Lipton, about this particular occasion. Was he, though, as he stood there for a moment silent, warned by some premonitory voice that this was the last time he would stand in London at such a table? Did he guess that this luncheon in his honour was in fact London's good-bye to him? "Your Royal Highness, Your Excellencies, my lords, and gentlemen." For a sentence or two his voice boomed with its rich brogue through the familiar opening, then gradually it began to falter; he hesitated, checked, began a sentence, then stopped altogether. He had intended to speak extempore, but he could not manage it. He picked up the manuscript of his speech, put on his spectacles. He looked very old as he stood there, peering through his glasses, reading out the same expressions of goodwill that he had been making for thirty years, the familiar peroration about there being no sportsmen like Americans, that whenever he was dealing with Americans, in business as in sport, he could be certain that he would get fair play.

He had looked old on that July afternoon in London, but he had fully recovered his vitality ten weeks later when the *Leviathan* sailed up from quarantine on a foggy September morning. Never had he had such a welcome. New York was in the mood to honour him. Last autumn the stock market collapse had broken many minor bank balances. But the buoyant optimism of the city refused to believe that anything serious had happened. It was just a settling of the ground. The summer had been long and warm. There was a keen bite in the September air. It was impossible to feel depressed upon such days.

New York was in the mood to put on a show. And Jimmy Walker and Grover Whalen were the men to do it. The fog did not help them any, and the heavy wind interfered with the nation-wide broadcast they had prepared, but thousands lined the Battery, excursion boats paddled alongside to cheer. A special tug with a police escort came bustling out. "Even when I came here as an emigrant I was never received by the police," he said. "I'm certainly getting to be the devil of a fellow."

He had his sallies ready. To Mary Curley, daughter of the mayor of Boston, he wisecracked that he had always known that Boston had the most intelligent citizens in the country, since they had thrown the tea overboard when they had discovered it was not Lipton's. It was a triumphal progress, with the ferries saluting him and fireworks being shot up through the fog, with the police escort leading him to the Biltmore and a man shouting from the sidewalk, "You've got to win the cup—I've put so much money on you that I'll be in the workhouse if you don't." "Reserve a bed for me too," Lipton shouted back. Even at the turn of the century it had not been better.

This time it had been decided to hold the races at Newport instead of Sandy Hook. The weather was likely to be better. The crowd would be easier to control. Never had the fashionable resort known more excitement. Special cars were running from Chicago, the bar was filled with yachts, the narrow streets were blocked with automobiles, blimps purred noisily in the sky above, Ocean Drive was made a one-way street, the Saunderstown and Jamestown ferries were put back on summer schedule, the hotels were crowded; everything was set for the biggest match in the history of yachting.

And then . . .

But it is difficult to explain, difficult to record dramatically what happened then. A yacht race is very difficult to describe. It is too technical; it is too long-drawn. There is all that tacking, that manoeuvring for position. Only the expert can tell what is being attempted and what is being threatened. You can describe the setting, Newport with its long stretch of sand, its low line of dunes, its naval base, its old town section along the water front. You can describe the fleet of three hundred craft following the race. You can describe the city of Lowell furnishing an orchestral concert. You can describe how back in England, in

Gosport, the shipyard was lit with electric signs and the streets were thronged with crowds impatiently waiting for the bulletin. You can describe what happened on the *Erin*, but the race itself, the drama of the actual race, that eludes description. A yachtsman could describe it for other yachtsmen in terms of technicalities, but to the layman it would be incomprehensible. The recorder of that week at Newport can only report the facts.

The first race was won by *Enterprise*. It was a straight there-and-back race. Owing to a shift of wind, there was no windward leg, and in the opinion of that sound judge, Herbert L. Stone, there was no reason why good sailing should not have won the race for *Shamrock*. It was a race that in point of fact told little. Harold Vanderbilt said afterwards that it was a good race and the *Shamrock* was a fast yacht. Lipton's comment was, "If I were not disappointed I should be in a mental home. I'd be more optimistic of getting first prize if the last boat over the finish were the victor." Even so, it was an open issue still.

It was the second race that was decisive. It was a foggy day, with the yellow lightship off the reef standing out in contrast against a grey-blue background. The racers faded away like dream ships in the mist, and the guests on the *Erin* had to listen to the race by wireless. Probably very few of them realised what was happening out there in the fog. The first leg of the race was the first trial to windward, and the superiority of the *Enterprise* at every point showed that the outcome of the series was not in any doubt. As Stone says, "The crew of the *Enterprise* knew it and the crew of the *Shamrock* must have sensed it."

Lipton must have known it, too, but he did not allow his knowledge to interfere with his duties as a host. He was resolved that the atmosphere of the party should not be overcast. He did not discourage Miss Evelyn Law, the show girl, when she offered to dance a hornpipe if the *Shamrock* won. When the result came through he turned laughingly towards his guests. "There'll be a big change after tonight; I'm going to put the ladies in full charge," he said. He then turned to one of the prettiest of his party. "How would you like to be the captain?" The answer came back pat: "I'd like to be your captain any time, Sir Thomas." But when the party dispersed "a gloom thick as the fog that had blotted out the end of the race pervaded the *Erin*." "It's a great disappointment," Lipton told the press. "Something apparently is wrong."

He knew that he was beaten, as surely as the skipper of the *Enterprise* knew that he had won. "I make no comment on the race," said Vanderbilt.

In England the press was trying to provide an alibi by explaining the *Enterprise's* victory in terms of the duralumin mast and the new drum winches, the general tone of their reports being that "gadgets had beaten man power." Which was, of course, to a certain extent true: *Enterprise,* owing to the mast designed by W. Starling Burgess, whose father had beaten the British challengers of the eighties, needed less ballast than *Shamrock* did, while an innovation in the boom enabled the mainsail to slide from one side to another and take in more breeze. Captain Nicholson described the Burgess mast as the greatest engineering feat in the development of racing yachts. Stephens was less enthusiastic. He was a conservative and remarked that a boat like *Enterprise* didn't need yachtsmen but hurdy-gurdy grinders from the Bronx. It was just an affair of turning handles. "How much," he wrote, "mechanical contrivances contributed to *Enterprise's* snappy work with sheets and halyards it is hard to say. Certainly the trimming was accelerated by the drum winches below. Also the backstays were better tended mechanically than by hand. The duralumin mast contributed. It weighed fifteen hundred to two thousand pounds less than *Shamrock's*."

There were many technical explanations of the *Enterprise's* better showing, but it must at the same time be pointed out that all these gadgets were available for Captain Nicholson. And Lipton was too good a sportsman to put up that kind of alibi. He knew the answer. He was up against something stronger than he had met before. During the last ten years yachting in America had advanced far faster than it had in England. Possibly there were more rich men in America who could give their time and money to it. But that again is another alibi. The fact remains and is incontrovertible that yachting in America touched in 1930 a high peak, and that among many great yachtsmen Vanderbilt was first. He loved the sea; he knew the sea. He stood at his own helm and beat the best that a syndicate of millionaires could put against him. The victory of *Enterprise* was not the victory of gadgets but of personality. Her skipper was a great sportsman in a great day of sportsmen. And when memory lists the figures of that decade, as it recalls them in their youth and vigour, Lenglen and Borotra; Red Grange and Babe Ruth; Dempsey, Carpentier, and Tunney; Jack Hobbs and Bobby Jones, there in the forefront of that proud gallery must stand the picture of Harold Vanderbilt, tall, thin, determined, in white flannels and blue yachting coat, bent over his wheel under a slouch canvas hat.

Never in his long career was Lipton's sportsmanship put to sterner test than in the last two races. Always up to now, even though he had been beaten, he had put up a good fight, even in 1903. But this time it was only the generosity of the press that prevented the match from being written off as a walkover after the second race. Lipton displayed high courage. How tested his temper was can be shown by an incident on the day of the third race, when the British warship, the *Heliotrope,* sent over ten sailors as the *Erin's* guests. The sailors were embarrassed and stood rigidly at attention when he greeted them. Their lack of response annoyed him. "What's the matter with you? Don't you speak English?" he snapped. A second later he was apologising, was putting them at their ease, leading them over to the buffet, assuring himself that they were having a good time. It was a momentary flash of temper, but it showed the strain he was living under.

It was the only sign he was to show. To his guests aboard the *Erin* he remained a genial host. He had little hope that the third race could end any differently from the other two as he seated himself on the main deck of the *Erin* in an easy cane-backed chair. Only a miracle could win the race. For a moment it half looked as though that miracle might have happened. *Shamrock* outmanoeuvred *Enterprise* at the start. If she could hold her own to the windward mark there was just a chance that she might win on the run home. He watched her eagerly through his glasses. A quarter of an hour passed. Half an hour. *Shamrock* still held her own. Was there, after all, a chance? Was fate to play into his hands at last? His excitement mounted. His natural optimism was reasserted. And then suddenly, in a second, it was all over. Another accident. The mast had snapped. Lipton jumped to his feet and ran over to the rail. The bright and buoyant creature, a gleam of green and white that a moment earlier had been battling foot by foot and yard by yard in the desperate struggle of the windward thrash, was now a helpless wreck, wallowing in a shroud of canvas.

The last race was sailed two days later. By now public interest had begun to wane. The result was beyond question. Nevertheless, there was a large crowd upon the *Erin*. It was a long, slow-passing day for Lipton. He breakfasted late and without hurry, not joining his guests till the yachts were jockeying for a start. At the start there was some excitement when *Shamrock* shot into the weather berth at the line, but soon she fell off to leeward, and when it was realised that she could not point with Enterprise on the crucial windward leg; hope failed. With the race a third over, *Enterprise* was a mile and a quarter ahead, with *Shamrock* following "on wearying wings." Most of the morning until lunch Lipton spent upon the bridge. He was alone and glad to be. This was the end, not of a race, not of a series, but of something more, of all that had symbolised for him during thirty years the romance and glow of living. Never again would he watch a small green cutter spread its immense wings of sail on this side of the Atlantic. It was the end and his heart knew it. It was over, his life's grand passion—the challenge, renewed and re-renewed, and all that went with it. Never again. He was acquainted in that hour with the common lot. He was old who had once been young, and the tale was told now.

On the windward leg *Enterprise* eased up a little to guard against any unforeseen weather freak or breaking-point pull. But towards the end she was canvas-covered and driven out again, with every thread of hemp and wire holding, to break the record for the course by three minutes and five seconds. As she approached the finishing line Lipton left his guests to chatter on the sun deck and gathered the reporters round him at the after rail. "It's no good," he said. "I can't win. I can't win." He shook hands with them one by one. They remarked that he had lost his buoyancy of manner. He looked tired and worn, with the twinkle gone from his eye. He moved dispiritedly among his guests, seemingly glad to be able to throw off at last the mask of gaiety with which he had covered his defeats. At the same time he was loath to have his friends depart. He wanted to prolong to the last moment this "last time."

Next day the *New York Times* in its leader said, "If sentiment could have gained the victory, the America's Cup would be in the hands of Sir Thomas Lipton," and its tribute to Harold Vanderbilt was commiseratory. "It was not an easy, it was almost a thankless task to defend the America's Cup when thousands of his fellow countrymen were almost clamouring for failure." Throughout the country there was a general feeling of anticlimax, of disappointment, of everybody wishing that it could have turned out differently: an unsatisfactory feeling and by no means a generous one to Vanderbilt, who had put up one of the finest performances in the record of the New York Yacht Club; a feeling, however, that was fortunately to be dissipated within a few hours of *Enterprise's* victory by a letter that appeared on the front page of the *New York Times* over the signature of Will Rogers.

"What do you say to this?" the letter ran. "Let everyone send a dollar apiece for a fund to buy a loving cup for Sir Thomas Lipton bigger than the one he would have got if he had won, contributed to by everybody that really admires a fine sportsman. Send it to, I would suggest, a Lipton Cup Fund in care of Mayor Walker in New York. Let Jimmy buy it and present it on behalf of everybody with an inscription along this line: 'To possibly the world's worst yacht builder but absolutely the world's most cheerful loser.' You have been a benefit to mankind, Sir Thomas, you have made losing worth while."

It has been said that the idea came from the head and heart of that excellent one-time Scotsman, Colonel William Rankin, whose father, Hector Rankin, fought as a Highlander in the Crimean War, and who had since 1924 acted as Lipton's publicity advisor in New York. Whosever idea it was, it was a happy one. It was the only way in which Sir Thomas could return to England a contented instead of a disappointed man. Which was the one thing everyone had feared, that at the end of his life he would go back to England sad and broken-hearted.

The idea caught on at once. Jimmy Walker welcomed it. "There might be some doubt about his ability to win the cup, but no doubt about his ability to capture our hearts." Letters approving the scheme flowed in. Edward E. Spafford wrote: "Mr. Lipton has come to this country on several occasions for the purpose of lifting the cup. He has lifted the hearts of the people of the country, who are anxious for him to lift a cup filled with the admiration of the people," while Patrick Quinlan of the Associated Silk Manufacturers suggested a peerage because of his efforts in cementing international goodwill—"Earl Lipton of Tyrone." Within ten days sixteen thousand dollars had come in, and Lipton himself had so recovered his good spirits and good humour that by the time he sailed on the twenty-seventh of September he was promising to make yet another challenge for the cup.

§ 19

WITHIN two months Lipton was back and the cup was ready. Designed by Tiffany, it was eighteen-carat gold. It stood eighteen inches high, with two handles and a cover. Its base of sterling silver had been sent by a group of Utah mine owners. It was finished in a dull burnished colour and darkly oxidised. Surmounting the cover was a design of shamrock leaves. There was a model in bold relief of the America's Cup, an enamelled shield of the United States seal, an enamelled insignia of the Royal Ulster Yacht Club, and an enamelled device of Lipton's private signal. The inscription on it read: "In the name of the hundreds and thousands of Americans and well-wishers of Sir Thomas Johnstone Lipton, Bart., K.C.V.O." The cup can be seen to-day in the Old Glasgow Museum at the People's Palace.

The gift of this loving cup was, in almost every way, the proudest event in Lipton's life. There must have been times, many times in the last five years, when he had wished that he could have been spared the day when he sold his holdings in his London business; when he must have pictured as his proudest moment the day in Glasgow when he received the freedom of the city. He must have often wished that it could have ended there. But for all that heart searching this day made full amends. He could have found no more fitting climax.

In a sense it was a rather sad occasion, or at least it seems so to us now in retrospect. It was the climax not only to a career but to the whole way of living that that career had symbolised. The world of Thomas Lipton, the world of free enterprise, of boundless unfettered opportunity, all the parade and the extravagance that had gone with it, they were over now. The period of controlled economy was about to start. On every side portents of that new world were visible. When Lipton had sailed for London in late September the sky was blue, the sun was shining, and the air was keen. Hope was in the air. Now, two months later, that hopefulness was gone. Not only did winter lie upon the city's roofs, it lay upon the city's heart. The stock market crash of the preceding autumn was, it was abundantly clear now, no mere reorganisation into truer values, no inevitable and necessary subsidence of soil. It was the prelude to depression.

The unemployed were selling apples on Fifth Avenue at five cents apiece. Hoover was asking for $150,000,000 to aid the workless. New York State faced a deficit. Clergy were working without pay. Thousands of homeless cats had become a civic problem. These were the headlines that greeted Lipton. Depression was under way. Everyone knew it now. Everyone was talking of it. No one knew where it would end. But no one even yet would have dared to prophesy the weeks and months of deepening and widening gloom that would have to be endured before the streets were placarded with the blue eagles of the NRA; eagles that heralded a very different world from that in which Lipton had grown up. In a certain sense the giving of this loving cup was the last gesture of that world.

In retrospect it is hard not to look back to the occasion without a certain nostalgic melancholy. But the ceremony was fully festive. Jimmy Walker and Grover Whalen saw to that.

The aldermanic chamber of City Hall was hung with flags and every chair was occupied. The dais and balcony were festooned with streamers. The police band played martial music. A chorus of radio announcers broadcast the ceremonies. The mayor was in his gayest mood. Dark days lay ahead of him, and he must have known it. The Seabury investigations had begun. Roosevelt, as governor of New York State, had warned him only a few days before that public servants had no right to claim immunity before a special grand jury. Public and private problems lay ahead of him. New York could afford no longer a casual wisecracking administration. Dark days lay ahead for Jimmy Walker between this hour of celebration and the hours, sixteen years distant, when he was to lie in state in the chapel on Eighty-first Street with a queue stretching right into Madison waiting to pay him final honours. He must have foreknown that such days lay ahead. But no sense of that foreknowledge was allowed to damp his spirits.

First he called upon Hector Fuller, a monocled and very English figure, to read out Will Rogers's cable:

"I am sorry I can't be with you, Sir Thomas, but if you ever tried earning a living under a Republican administration you would know you haven't got any time to go gadding around. You think this is a fine cup. Say, this is nothing to the one we are going to give you when you lose next time. I am already starting in on it. I love you, Sir Thomas, but I won't drink that damned tea. Come West, young man." For some obscure reason of his own Fuller omitted the reference to tea and thereby lost a laugh, but that was the cable as the papers printed it. Then the mayor turned to Lipton.

"You are," he said, "the gamest loser in the world of sport. It is not simply a goodwill cup from America. It could not have carried a more widespread affection and admiration if it had come to you from the League of Nations. Take it to your native land where there will be no constitutional impediment to your full enjoyment of it."

With one hand upon the cup, Lipton rose to face the cheering hall. "Although I have lost, you make me feel that I have won. But I will try again. Yes, I will try again." He paused, hesitated, then suddenly sat down. There was an awkward pause, but only for a second. Jimmy Walker was ready for emergencies of that kind. "I'm not surprised," he said, "that Sir Thomas finds it hard to speak. I sometimes do myself, though for other reasons. I think his speech will sound very well, read in Mr. Fuller's very English accent." And he handed the manuscript to Hector Fuller.

By the time the speech had been read out Sir Thomas had more or less recovered. He began to rise to his feet when the band played "The Star-Spangled Banner," but Jimmy Walker put his hand upon his arm, restraining him. He insisted, however, on rising for the last bars of "God Save the King." Outside City Hall there was a huge crowd waiting there to cheer him. It was a great, a very great occasion.

He left New York a few days later, full of plans for returning in the spring. He had to live in the present and the future. He would challenge, he said, next autumn. He would race again in 1932. He could not allow himself to face the possibility of this being a farewell visit to New York.

At the same time a premonition may well have warned him that it might prove to be, as he went round the factory at Hoboken; as he stood in the windows of his office looking down on the repair yards, looking across the river to Manhattan; as he walked through the packing and the blending rooms; as he lifted up a handful of tea out of a bin, holding it under his face so as to get through the warmth of his breath the full aroma of the tea. He had done this so often in the past; did he realise that he was doing it now for the last time?

In the tasting room, standing beside one of the big brass cuspidors, was a tall, lean, good-looking, well-dressed young man. Lipton checked at the sight of him. "You are Slater, aren't you?"

"Yes, sir."

He was answered in an English accent. Though he always had American salesmen on the road, he often brought out Englishmen as tasters.

"Weren't you to have gone out to Colombo at one time?"

"To Calcutta, sir, and then the man I was going to replace changed his mind."

"Yes, I remember. You were very disappointed. You wanted to see the world. When this opening came a few weeks later I thought of you."

"Yes, that was it, sir."

"Well, and has it turned out happily?"

"I'm being married, sir, next month."

"Then I guess it has. Good luck, my boy, good luck." He

R

paused reflectively. How much of life depended upon chance. A man in Calcutta suddenly changes his mind about coming home, and a girl in Brooklyn of whose existence for the whole of his life he will remain unaware has her whole way of living realigned. How little a thing would have been needed sixty years ago to realign his own life in just that way? It he had met a girl on that first visit whose hold had been stronger than his mother's . . .

Who knows but that next day as the *Leviathan* drew out of dock his thoughts were with the Englishman from whose destiny his own had been so different, yet might have been the same. So little a thing had been needed sixty years ago. If the equivalent of that someone in Calcutta had changed his mind . . . Was that how his thoughts were working? Maybe it was. But if it was, we may be very sure that ultimately he shook his head. High over Hoboken was the sky sign he had set there. In the storeroom was the gold loving cup and the bound volume containing the many hundred letters that had accompanied the subscriptions. No, he would not have changed it.

§ 20

WITHIN a week of his return to England his Christmas cards were in the mail. He set great store by them. The design each year was similar; they were green with the Union Jack and the Stars and Stripes crossed upon the cover. Inside was a coloured reproduction: in 1929 he had sent a picture of his estate house in Ceylon, in 1928 of Osidge; it was the *Leviathan's* turn this year. Inside certain of the cards he wrote in his own hand: "Very soon this dear old ship will bring me back among you."

He refused to admit that he was over eighty. He refused to be relegated to the past. He had said that he was going to challenge for the cup again, and he began that inevitable preliminary to such a challenge, the discussion with the New York Yacht Club as to the conditions under which the next race should be sailed. He talked as confidently about 1932 as in 1902 he had talked about 1903, and he fitted a new steel mast on *Shamrock V* in readiness for the summer regattas.

For the most part he lived quietly at Osidge. Tom Dewar had died a few months before, and he was lonely now. Dr. Fairweather dined with him most evenings, and they played billiards afterwards. Duncan Neill was a constant visitor to discuss *Shamrock VI*. William Blackwood came out to discuss the autobiography. On Sunday evenings he would go round to Lord Inverforth's for hymn singing after supper, choosing the hymns that had been his mother's favourites. Resolutely though he refused to live in anything but the present and the future, his thoughts were turning more and more to Glasgow. In January, in memory of his mother, "his guiding star," as he called her in the deed of gift, he donated ten thousand pounds to the poor of Glasgow. And when in April Lord Provost Kelly and Sir John Samuel reported how they had used the money, he was so delighted with the way in which they had portioned it out in tickets entitling the poor to food and coal that he gave them another ten thousand. In that same month he read the news that Spain had become a republic, that the King and Queen of Spain were exiled. Alfonso, whom he had driven down to Southampton in his Daimler, Alfonso and his beloved Princess Ena!

In May he would be eighty-one, and to celebrate the occasion his friends in England, in particular Lord Shaftesbury and Sir Philip Hunloke, had planned a surprise present for him. On the thirteenth of May a letter bearing the red letter heading of the Royal Yacht Club informed him that he had been elected to the squadron. That letter, even more than the five-cent apples on Fifth Avenue, even more than the proclamation in Spain of a republic, was a portent of a changing world. In the world to which Thomas Lipton had been born and flourished in a millionaire, even if he was the friend of royalty, could not be admitted to the Royal Yacht Club if his fortune had been made in trade. The world of privilege in which the property that was not inherited was suspect, the world in which an English judge could assert that it was better for a peer to starve than to cadge orders for the sale of beer, that world had had its day. The letter upon Lipton's desk was proof of it.

How much this belated compliment meant to Lipton it is hard to say. Though he loved publicity, he was very uncommunicative about himself. He had never said that he resented not having been elected. But when in 1917 Shane Leslie, in *The End of a Chapter,* referred to his having been blackballed, he threatened a libel action and insisted on the passage's removal. Now when the press asked him for his comment he merely said that it was "very gratifying. I am sure it will interest my many friends in the U.S.A."

That August he went to Cowes, flying the white ensign. *Shamrock V* with her new steel mast was entered for the King's Cup. It was the first time that a *Shamrock* had been entered for this race. Until this year it had been restricted to members of the Royal Yacht Club, a condition which for the last twenty years had robbed the race of much of its significance. It had been little satisfaction to the owner of *White Heather* to win a cup that did not involve his beating *Shamrock*. This year, however, the first occasion that Lipton was eligible to enter, the race was thrown open to any British yacht with a 60-foot load water line. It was a runaway win for *Shamrock*. Lipton accepted his congratulations with a flattered smile, but he did not attend the Royal Yacht Squadron's dinner afterwards.

That week and the weeks that followed were triumphant ones for Lipton. *Shamrock* won the big race on the Friday for yachts of the J class, leading all the way; then, going down to Weymouth, she proved her superiority over *Britannia*, which had not been entered in the King's Cup race owing to an accident on the first day of the regatta, the second mate having been swept overboard and drowned. Although *Shamrock* had been no match for *Enterprise* at Newport, she was very clearly in home waters the best yacht afloat.

And all the time negotiations were continuing with the New York Yacht Club. In August the *New York Times* was headlining the probability of Lipton's challenge arriving in September and pointing out that this time the challenge would come not from Ulster but from the Royal Yacht Club, also that the *Erin* would be flying the white ensign instead of the "red duster" of the merchant fleet. Then it was announced that Sir Thomas and the New York Yacht Club had agreed that below-deck winches and duralumin masts were banned and cabin accommodation was required. It was further added that George V had had his old cutter, the *Britannia*, altered and berigged to fit these standards. As regards the other clauses on which agreement had been reached, the *New York Times* commented, "To the non-mathematically versed, the new rule is worse than a Chinese puzzle or Professor Einstein's theory of relativity."

A challenge was confidently expected, yet at the same time it was no real surprise when it was announced late in August that the challenge was to be postponed. Indeed, the news was received with some relief. Many felt that in a time of depression yacht racing on such a scale was an unjustifiable extravagance. There was the fear, too, of an anticlimax. It was better, everyone was agreed, to wait a little. By mid-September the sense of relief was greater. The economic depression that had been slowly gathering in Europe broke in full force on England. First a National Government was formed in order to save the pound, then within three weeks of its being formed England abandoned the gold standard and hoteliers in the South of France were refusing to cash English cheques. The world of Thomas Lipton was crumbling fast.

That was in the third week of September. Ten days later, when sterling currency was bending before its first major blizzard, Lipton caught a chill during a motor drive. He took it lightly. On Wednesday, the thirtieth, though he stayed indoors, he worked throughout the morning, and in the evening he had some friends to dinner. He was cheerful, animated, and played a game of billiards. But later that night he was found in his room, collapsed and losing consciousness. Two days later he was dead. He had known little sickness in his life, and his end was easy.

He would have been happy if he could have read the obituaries that appeared next day. Every paper carried his photograph in the familiar yachting cap and the familiar loose-knotted polka-dot blue tie. Perhaps the tribute that would have appealed to him the most was the one that appeared in the *New York Times:* "Men will speak of him in superlatives."

Every obituary referred to the part he had played in maintaining amicable relations between Britain and America, and indeed few Britons have better served as an ambassador of goodwill. Before he crossed for his first races in 1899, Joseph Chamberlain begged him to keep uppermost in his mind the maintenance of good relations. It was better to lose a race than generate ill will. It was good advice, but in Lipton's case it was unecessary.He had an intuitive sense that never failed him. In thirty years he never did or said a thing that was misunderstood or misinterpreted. It was an astounding feat. Anyone who has the good fortune to have roots in the two countries knows to his cost how easy, how inevitable, it is to make mistakes, to say, with the best intention in the world, a tactless thing. Lipton never did. He had an extra sense, a power of divination, where those he cared for were concerned.

As a storekeeper in Glasgow his appreciation for and sympathy with the people whose needs he served were the secrets of his success. He talked their language and he guessed their thoughts. In the same way in America and with Americans, a sixth sense told him what was at every crisis the wise thing to do or say. His instinct never failed. He loved the country and he loved its people. He saw things through their eyes. That was the key to his popularity in America. He loved the country, and the country knew it.

One incident will show the extent to which that loyalty

was returned. When he left America in 1928 the trans-atlantic telephone was a recent toy and telephones from ship to shore the newest thing; so new that a telephone call to Lipton on the *Leviathan* made headline news. No one knew, however, what the message was: or rather no one knew that the message of casual well-wishing contained the word "Goodrich," which was a code meaning "No need to worry." If on the other hand the word "Goodyear" had been included in the message, Lipton would have been warned that "the cat was out of the bag."

The cat in question was a Russian lady with a royal title with whom Lipton had corresponded indiscreetly. The Princess had threatened that, unless she received adequate compensation, financial or matrimonial, she would issue an injunction to prevent Lipton's sailing. He had avoided this injunction by being smuggled onto the *Leviathan* a day before passengers were allowed aboard, so that while the Princess's representatives were lying in wait for him outside the Biltmore, he was snug in his suite with an armed police escort guarding the approaches. The code word "Goodrich" assured him that no story had broken after he had sailed. Later the lady's feelings were soothed with a cheque for ten thousand pounds. All seemed to have ended well.

Two years later, however, in the second winter of the depression, the bank through which the cheque had passed went into liquidation. The account was subjected to a public audit, and during the audit the *Mirror* got onto the story of the cheque. It planned to make a front-page splash with it. Lipton's friends were warned. They did their best. They entreated, they cajoled, they threatened. All to no effect. Editor after editor shook his head. The story was too good to waste.   Finally in desperation they took it to the very top.   The great man listened to what they had to say, thought for a moment, then raised the telephone. "Kill that Lipton story" was the order.

Two months later the story reached the *News*. Once again Lipton's friends went from editor to editor, to be met each time with cynically shaken heads. Once again they went to the highest court, to Patterson. "Listen," they said, "Lipton's eighty. There's a chance at last of his getting elected to the Royal Yacht Club. If you print this story you may ruin it." Patterson took no longer to decide than his rival had. "The old boy's too good a sport to have that done to him by an American," and he raised the telephone.

The fact that two proprietors of sensational newspapers should have been ready to kill a good story, to break their own rules out of a personal regard for him, is really a greater proof than the gold loving cup of the regard in which Lipton stood in America's esteem.

The obituary notices did not exaggerate.

The funeral was arranged to take place in Glasgow on the Wednesday.

Thousands that morning filed past his coffin as it lay before the altar in St. George's Church. Long before the ceremony began, not only the church but the streets outside were crowded. All traffic was held up. When the service was finished it was a full quarter of an hour before the congregation could follow the coffin from the church.

The Southern Necropolis is a poor people's cemetery on the south side of the river. It was through streets familiar to Lipton's boyhood that the cortege proceeded slowly, down Trongate, past the dark slim steeple of the old City Hall, down Saltmarket, across the river, and into Crown Street. The pavements were lined three-deep, and heads were craning from every window. It was a dull, damp day; it had not actually rained for several hours, but there was a surface of slime upon the paving stones and the far end of the street was blurred in a kind of twilight. Just before they reached Dixon's "Blazes" they turned to the left into Caledonia Street, a wide, straight street of dark, rectangular, three-storeyed houses that is not without its dignity, the dignity of things that are built solidly and unpretentiously, that are meant to last. At the end a tapering church spire gives it a pictorial balance. To the right is the six-foot wall of the necropolis, with the leafless boughs of a few stunted trees scarcely surmounting the monoliths that stand about.

It was here that ninety years ago Lipton's father had bought a lair for thirty shillings on the death in infancy of his first son Christopher. Through the next twelve years the Lipton parents were to stand there three more times in mourning for a child died young. How little they can have thought when they stood there then that one day that grave would be covered with many hundred wreaths.

In London at St. Columbia's a memorial service was attended by a congregation of five hundred. Here, as in Glasgow, the organ played "Flowers of the Forest." Dr. Fleming spoke of "his filial love, his desire to save his mother from all want, his zest in living, his human largeness of heart."

Many mourned him. He had many friends, but in the

truest sense his life had been solitary since his mother's death. He had no living relative. He had no close ties. His will contained only one or two small personal bequests.

With the exception of Osidge, which he directed to be used as a nursing home, he bequeathed his entire estate to Glasgow, to be applied to "the endowment and/or enfranchisement from existing debt of infirmaries and/or hospitals for the relief of the sick and poor and/or individually or collectively to the endowment or relief of the poor and destitute within the city of Glasgow and/or Cambuslang." The trustees were Lord Inverforth, H. A. Snelling, Duncan Neill, Colonel Spens, and James Brooks. By the time his various interests had been resolved and a very large sum of money paid in death duties, almost a million pounds was available for Glasgow.

To Glasgow he also left his collection of yachting trophies, with the exception of the loving cup presented to him by American friends in 1899, which he deeded back to the New York Yacht Club. The collection is stored to-day in the old Art Museum, now known as the People's Palace, that stands in Glasgow Green, very near the spot where the Crown Street Clan sailed the small wooden boats they cut out of the lids of boxes with their pocket clasp knives.

The collection is stored in a special Lipton room. It contains more than sixty trophies. It also contains a number of framed addresses from such dissimilar organisations as the Citizens of Nish, the employees of Lipton, Ltd., the Empire State Society of the Sons of the American Revolution, and the Mutual Welfare League of Sing Sing Prison. There are autographed photographs from Queen Victoria, Edward VII, Queen Alexandra, George V, Queen Mary,

and the King of Italy. There are a number of original cartoons; there are photographs of the various *Shamrocks*.
There are also a number of personal presents, the cigar
and cigarette case, the matchbox and Jubilee scarfpin, and
a gold scarfpin with enamel shamrock bearing the figure
of a yacht set with diamonds that Edward VII gave him.
There are a number of presents from Queen Alexandra,
paper knives and ash trays and a set of waistcoat buttons,
and the cigarette case and lighter that had been once the
personal property of King Edward. There is a cigarette
box from the ex-Empress Eugénie, a trinket box from the
King of Italy, a gold-and-enamel yacht-club badge from
the King of Spain.

He also bequeathed to Glasgow his photograph albums
and the collection of his press cuttings. These press cuttings fill more than eighty volumes and are stored in the
Mitchell Library.

His story is in those volumes. In a sense it is a very
simple story; certainly it is a straightforward story: the
story of a man of immense vitality, of immense ambition,
honest and single-minded, who accepted his day uncriti-
cally. That is indeed the salient, the determining fact about
him. Most men who achieve anything significant in life
are rebels at the start. Rebellion is their springboard.
Scientists, soldiers, pioneers, industrialists, they have all in
their different ways held the telescope to their blind eye
in disobedience of foolish orders; they have reacted against
old-fashioned methods and ideas, against obstructionism
and narrow-mindedness. They were in conflict with their
world. Lipton never was. He accepted from the beginning
not only his world but his own place in it. He took the

parable of the talents literally. His duty as he saw it was
to improve his station.

It is astonishing, indeed, how little he introduced, how
little new he brought into commerce; he initiated hardly
anything. Each new Lipton's market had as its model that
first shop in Stobcross Street, and that first shop had in its
turn been modelled on his parents'. What his parents had
done on a minute scale he did on an immense scale. That
is the Lipton story in a line. He had no impulse to alter
the existing fabric. He accepted Crown Street. Let Crown
Street stay the way it was. He would root himself in a
thousand Crown Streets.

He never planned his career strategically. He never
needed to. His mother had done that for him. She was
the commander-in-chief; he was the chief of staff. It was
not for him to question or work out first principles; it was
for him to exploit each tactical situation as it came. He
"saw big," but only within those limits. As each new problem came he acted shrewdly, promptly, and decisively.

His mother had bought upon the spot, and so did he,
carrying to its ultimate and logical conclusion the principle of cutting out the middleman, with his own stockyards
in Omaha, his own tea gardens in Ceylon, his own or-
chards in Kent. One thing led automatically to the next.
A man of intense ambition, of immense power of concentration, of great personal charm, with a genius for showmanship, he accepted the standards of his day, he let himself be modelled by his day. We understand his day the
better for seeing what his day made of him.

"Timeliness," H. G. Wells has said, "is an essential factor in the make-up of a successful novelist," and Lipton,

who was so completely of his time, was lucky in the hour of his birth. At no matter what time he had been born, a man of his character and gifts would have achieved success of a marked order. That success, however, would have been conditioned by the social and sociological framework of his day. He would never have rebelled against the existing order. And at no other period of history could such a man have achieved honourably so spectacular a career. Had he been born in 1800, before the days of steam, he could not have travelled fast enough to create and then control a commercial empire. Had he been born half a century later, his boyhood and his early manhood would have been cut across by wars. His opportunities to expand would have been hampered by currency controls and curtailed by taxes. He was born to a period of unfettered private enterprise. No inspector of schools complained when he became a shop boy at the age of ten. He did not have to get a passport or a quota number when he crossed the Atlantic steerage. Income tax stood at 2 per cent when he went back to Chicago to open negotiations for his stockyard. Theodore Roosevelt had not yet opened his attacks upon the trusts.

Had Lipton been born in 1900, he would no doubt be now, at fifty, living comfortably, entertaining amply, travelling widely. But he would be doing that, not on the interest on his investments or on the legitimate profits of his business, but on an expense account which would not be taxed. He would be "doing well," but he would be doing well without the old panache. How he would resent having to justify his expenditures, having to justify his friendships to the inspectorate of inland revenue!

He was lucky in the hour of his birth. All through his

life the time factor was on his side. He could not have arrived in America more opportunely, with the Civil War just ended but with the labour market crowded in New York so that he was forced to seek employment in the South: those three years of wandering between the Atlantic seaboard and the Mississippi were more valuable than any diploma. He saw America as a poor man sees it, which the European who is not an emigrant rarely does. The average European does not go to America until he is established; then he meets his opposite numbers. However many months he spends, however much he may feel at home there, he can never have roots there as he has in the country of his birth, in the city where he has struggled for self-establishment. Lipton knew America as Americans themselves know it, by having struggled there. Nor was he ever to mistake Manhattan for America.

He was equally lucky in the hour of his return to Scotland, at a time when the lessons he had learned in America were likeliest to bear fruit. As an advertiser he had a five- to ten-year start. Later, when tea became a popular beverage—it was a luxury in the fifties and beer was the usual drink in the servants' hall—he had his chain of stores ready to sell good tea at a lower price than his competitors. Had his mother died ten years earlier, he might well have married Catherine McLeod or some equivalent of her; if he had, he would not have made so effective, so concentrated an entrance into London life; he would have been occupied with family obligations, while again had his mother lived ten or even five years longer, he would have stayed on in Glasgow. He would have come too late to London. He moved south at the right time; and the seven or eight years of loneliness, when he worked unspar-

ingly to forget his loneliness, coincided with the period
when work of just that concentration was required to turn
him from a millionaire into a multi-millionaire.

Nor again could he have chosen a better time to turn
his business into a public company. Britain was at a level
of prosperity that she had not reached before and has not
known since. National confidence stood high. The South
African war—the first troubler of that confidence—was
some months distant. Lipton was the new man and the
coming man, the magician who turned everything to gold.
At no time could he have sold out at higher profit. Nor
could he have found a better time to relieve himself of the
full responsibilities of a one-man business. The Edwardian
decade was starting, and he was the right man for it. At
no other time in history has there existed a court society
of such varied cosmopolitan brilliance that was both accessible to a man of Lipton's background and so congenial
to a man of his tastes and temperament. His friendship
with Edward VII was the most important relationship in
his life, and he met Edward when each had to give what
the other needed, when Edward was in the mood for a
bluff, good-natured man, a good talker, unsycophantic,
unencumbered, who was just too rich to have an axe to
grind.

The rewards of success came to him when he could
enjoy them most. He could not have chosen ten better
years to play in. The *Erin* was the focus of that playing.
And Lord Dunraven's quarrel with the New York Yacht
Club had provided exactly the right background for the
spirit in which he made his challenge for the cup.

Later, when the tide turned, when the inevitable swing
of favour that accompanies a change of regime was threat-

ening to push him into an antagonistic mood, the first war intervened. When the war was over he had reached the immunity of age. He had become a grand old man. Finally fate gave him an effective exit. He was a great showman. He would have loathed an anticlimax, and that almost certainly is what a sixth attempt upon the cup would have proved to be. His last hours in his long-loved New York were among his proudest there; it was all as he would have wanted it.

He accepted his day, he served his day, and his day worked for him. He trusted his day, and his day rewarded him.

S

POSTSCRIPT

THE eighty-four volumes of press cuttings that he bequeathed to Glasgow have provided the framework
for this biography. Little has been written about Lipton.
The name appears in the indices of most Edwardian biog-
raphies, but the references are brief and factual. There is
no one alive who knew him when he was young; those few
who were his friends in the Edwardian Era are now old
men who even then were his juniors by at least half a
generation; many have memories of him during his last
decade, but they were in their twenties and thirties when
he was over seventy. Yet even so, if the subject of this
biography has acquired for the reader during its course
a human flesh-and-blood personality, it is in the main to
personal reminiscences that I, as its author, stand indebted.

Lipton was one of those who retained right to the end a
zest for the next item on the programme. He never grew
old in heart. He never lost an essential boyishness. When
he recounted his early struggles he seemed, even when he
was close on eighty, to be talking of something that had
happened yesterday; so that conversations with his associates and employees and the recollections of men such as
Grover Whalen and Colonel Rankin in New York, in London of H. A. Snelling, in Glasgow of John Glaister, and
in Ceylon of Simon Perera, once his servant and now chief
steward at the Negombo resthouse, who still wears on his
tunic the buttons of the Royal Ulster Yacht Club—such
conversations and recollections have built up for me, touch

by touch, feature by feature, a composite picture of the man he was.

In the same way have the sights that were familiar, the places that he frequented—the dark closes of the Gorbals, the masts of the Broomielaw, the fireplace in the City Road with its carved elephants, the high hills of Dambatene with the neat rows of tea shrubs, the Hoboken factory —re-created the background against which he lived. Osidge, in particular, did this.

I went there on a September morning, the day after I had come down from Glasgow after a week in the Mitchell Library. In 1934 the Piccadilly tube was extended into Hertfordshire, and Southgate, with a change at King's Cross, is now forty minutes away from Paddington. A station or so before you get there, between Wood Green and Arnos Grove, the line comes out into the open and runs between a succession of two-storeyed suburban villas interspersed with trees, oaks and poplars for the most part, with an occasional rough yard or two of hedge to suggest that open country has been only recently built over.

Southgate itself is like a hundred other stations lying on the fringe of London. It is all very neat and tidy, with a fruit store and a bookstall and a tobacconist's; a rounded entrance and a sheltered courtyard where you can queue for buses. A broad and curving street runs at right angles to it, a street like a hundred others, with its three or four public houses, its shops and offices, its Woolworth's, its Littlewood's, and Barclay's branch. Only a Londoner could tell that a quarter of a century ago this had been a village; only a Londoner would detect a 1920 air about the red brick façade above the shops, would recognise as survivals the trees that line the pavements.

Osidge is a five-minute walk from Southgate Station. Once it was the fifth in a succession of largish houses, isolated by extensive properties. Now it stands alone, faced by a short row of comfortable, detached early Victorian villas. Its gardens are screened from the road by a high wooden fence. Over the entrance in a curved iron frame is the lettering: "Thomas Lipton Memorial Hostel."

I was accompanied by Tom Mason, the historian of Southgate, whose wife was for many years the local secretary of the Queen's Nursing Association, which now owns the property. When Lipton died, so Mr. Mason told me, the house was in such bad repair that for three years no hospital would accept the gift of it. Finally, by selling more than fifty out of the sixty or so acres in which it stood, sufficient funds were obtained to renovate and restore it as a nurses' hostel. In consequence of that sale the surrounding neighbourhood is covered with bijou residences, but the house and garden of Osidge are very much as they were.

In its way it is a rather surprising place: the house you see from the drive is altogether different from the house you look at from the garden. In the early twenties Beverley Nichols described it in *Twenty-Five* as "one of those roomy squarely built mansions that stand in respectable gardens on the outskirts of North London." And that is how you see it from the short curving drive, as a square central block of recently repointed yellow-brown brick with a number of lower additions on either side of it. From the garden, however, it not only looks a considerably older house but a house that has been built upon a different pattern. It is faced with stucco, and a wooden verandah running along its entire length under a low protecting cover and joining the additions to the central block gives it at the same time a colonial air and an effect of having been planned and built all at one time and in one piece. From the drive Osidge is essentially English, the kind of house you would find nowhere else; looking at it from the garden, with its immense dark cedar in the foreground, you feel that you might be anywhere.

Inside the house has been changed considerably. The billiard room is now an office; the orangery, a massage room. The vivid wallpapers, the aspidistras in their glazed yellow pots, the black china Negresses, the heads of animals—all these have gone. The rooms have been repapered and the floors recarpeted; most of the old furniture has been sold, but enough remains to give an indication of Lipton's tastes: to give a sense of his personality. In the hallway, on each side of a clock constructed in the centre of a wooden half-life-size statuette of an alpine climber, are large glazed oleographs of Mr. and Mrs. Lipton. A ponderous mahogany sideboard with stands for cups or trophies that only a golf club could accommodate today stands opposite. There is also a small chair with a musical apparatus in its seat that plays a tune when you get up from it—"Dolly Gray," "Rule Britannia," or "Blue Bells of Scotland."

On the mantelpiece of the small sitting room where the matron receives her visitors is a photograph, dated 1888, of a very beautiful girl in her later teens. It is signed "Victoria Mary." On the mantelpiece, beside an inlaid enamel clock in blue and gold decorated with nymphs and cupids, is a silver-framed photograph of that same girl taken in 1931; it is signed "Mary R.I."

In the corridor leading into the dining room is a black

marble table with three plaques set into it. The plaques are supposed to contain specimens of every variety of marble. At the foot of the stairs is a five-foot Burmese gong with a black ebony elephant beside it. In the dining room opposite, another immense sideboard, this one of burr walnut, faces a clock face set into a large wooden replica of the three round-towered fortresses of Gibraltar that the Dorsets wear upon their cap badge.

I would give a lot to have seen the house as it was in Lipton's day. In the 1920s, when Beverley Nichols paid his visit, its decorative scheme must have seemed overpoweringly close to a period against which contemporary taste was in reaction. Today, in the early 1950s, it might well provide a companion picture to *Lady Windermere's Fan*.

In the upper part of the house considerable alterations have been made. The large guest rooms have been partitioned off to accommodate the nursing sisters. Lipton's fifteen-foot Empire wardrobe has been split up into three sections. Only one thing is still evocative of Lipton—the green shamrock pattern that is set into the white tiling round his bathroom; that and the view remain.

From the ground-floor windows the valley is cut off by a row of roofs running outside the fence, but from the bedrooms you can get today, over the trees and villas, the same view that Lipton had from the verandah, or rather you can re-create the view.

Looking southwest, with London itself cut off from you, with the domed roof of Alexandra Palace to the left and the spire of Whetstone Church on the far hills opposite, with the low September sunlight in your eyes blurring the streets and factories, the roofs and chimney stacks that have flooded up the valley since, you can imagine how it must have looked to Lipton fifty years ago, morning after morning, before he set out to work behind his Kentucky trotters. How often, I thought, he must have seen this valley spread before his eyes as so much conquered territory, as the rich spoil of conquest. Standing where he had so often stood, I thought of all that he must have planned with this panorama before his eyes. I thought of all that he had done; I thought, too, of all that he had not done, of all that he had refrained from doing. For in a sense Lipton is one of those men whose bigness can better be measured negatively. There were so many things he did not do that he could have done so easily, that so many in his place would have done.

Many times during the last years Lord Acton's dictum has been quoted: "Power corrupts: absolute power corrupts absolutely." And Lipton's power, the power of wealth, in the nineties and up to World War I, was near enough to being absolute to have satisfied most men. He never abused that power. When he held the Chicago pork market at his mercy he made his reasonable profit and then let the barrels go. That incident is symptomatic. No one during his lifetime or after his death was to say that he had suffered an injustice at Lipton's hands. Nothing was ever said sneeringly against him. He was laughed at— or rather he was laughed with—sometimes. But it was by his foibles, his idiosyncrasies—the silver-framed photographs of royalty, the eighty-four albums of press cuttings, the garish colour scheme at Osidge—that he was made human and made lovable. No one has ever said that he behaved meanly. No one has ever accused him of sharp practice. No one seriously believed that he was personally implicated in the canteen scandal. Once when he bought a consignment of butter he unwrapped, before weighing it, the linen it was wound in. He was buying butter, he said, not fabric. That incident, too, is symptomatic. It was by such close paring that he kept his prices low; he gave full weight and he demanded it. When the profits of his business declined in the middle twenties it was because as an ageing man he could no longer keep control of so widespread a business, not because he was taking too large a share of its profits for himself.

To the end of his life he retained the standard of straight dealing with which he started it; just as he retained, although he was the friend of royalty, his sense of kinship with the poor; just as he retained his loyalty in friendship—he never betrayed a confidence, he never publicised himself by intimate disclosures about his guests—just as he retained, right to the end, the spirit of sportsmanship with which he issued his first challenge to the America's Cup. Lightly though he issued that first challenge, at the end he wanted desperately to win. But he never once gave himself an alibi; he never blamed his luck, never imputed sharp practice to his opponent. During the thirty-two years that divided his first challenge from his last defeat, in every other branch of international sport—in polo, cricket, golf, boxing, the Olympic Games—there were acrimonious passages; think of the hysteria over "body-line" cricket. But not one word of ill feeling marred the friendliness of those five contests, even though the details of the race were the subject of considerable discussion.

It is easy enough to say that Thomas Lipton merely followed the standards of gentlemanly good sportsmanship, but how many are there, over so long a period, who go on doing just that? He kept clean to the end the things he was entrusted with.

Standing in what had been his bedroom, I thought of all the trading that he had planned here. I thought of all his stunts, the "orphans," the mammoth cheese, the Lipton notes, the parades and the processions, the "buxom ladies," the Indian sandwich men, the comic posters, the funny mirrors; I thought of that widespread commercial empire, the tea gardens in Ceylon, the fruit farms in Kent, the stockyards in Omaha, all that buying and that selling over sixty years; I thought of that, and then I thought of the obverse, the negative side of it: I thought of all the traffic that he would not touch, of all the barter and the bargaining he was too big for; I thought of all the things that in that long life he never sold.

APPENDIX I

In May 1931 the press announced that *Shamrock I,* ketch-rigged and with her once vast sail area reduced to a modest thousand-foot square, rechristened *Nutshell,* with a crew of five under Kay Elba, had started from Copenhagen on a world tour during which she was to send postcards from strange parts to forty thousand Scandinavian school children.

The after fate of the challengers and defenders of the cup would make an entertaining story. *Shamrock III* was broken up. *Shamrock II* became a rum-runner during prohibition. On University Heights the mast of *Shamrock IV* marks the spot from which on November 16, 1776, the English launched their successful attack across the river upon Fort Washington and forced the evacuation of Laurel Hill. The *America* herself had a truant fate before docking finally in honoured retirement at Annapolis. Sold to an English master, she became, first as the *Camelia,* then the *Memphis,* a cruiser and a blockade runner during the Civil War, then was laid up for twenty idle years in Boston till the Navy Department took her over. In the meantime her glittering scroll of eagles, perched upon four crossed flags, was removed to decorate the door of an inn at Ryde, Isle of Wight, until it was retrieved by the Royal Yacht Squadron and sent to the New York Yacht Club.

APPENDIX II

Soosie Spareribs, or Lipton and His Hams. The monologue sung by James Willison.

It is not suggested that this is particularly amusing now, but it is interesting both as an example of what was considered funny in Scotland in the late 1870s and of Lipton's indirect publicity. It should be remembered that the dialect pronunciation of "sow" is "soo."

It opened with a song:

> *I was once a happy country chiel*
> *Wi' a braw contented wife*
> *Until I came tae Glesca toon*
> *Where wages were mair rife*
> *The day that I first landed there*
> *I was blythesome as a lamb*
> *But noo, I'm clean heartbroken*
> *And it's a' thro' Lipton's Ham.*

Then it broke into recitation:

"Maybe ye widna believe it, but it's true. Ye see, when the wife and me came tae the toon, we got off at College Station, and as we came daunerin' doon the High Street, she spies Lipton's ham shop. 'Oh, Bauldie,' says she, 'there's the shop I hae heard sae muckle aboot. Let's awa' in an' get a bit ham.' Now I'm no a ham man myself, so I said, ' 'Deed ye'll dae nothing of the sort.' She said she wid. I said she widna. We were just gaun tae hae a gran' row at the shop door, when by came a bobby, an' tell us if we didna stop our fighting aboot ham, he'd *ham*-mer the head off us. So we slippit awa' doon the street; but we hadna gone far when my wife said, 'Ye've dune me this time, but I'll sort ye when I get ye hame.' An' she did—landed wi' the butte. Which made me say, 'Eh, Soosie Spareribs, you'll be the death of me. It's enough tae mak' me pawn my togs an' gang upon the sprae.' Fra morn tae night, and nicht tae morn, the hair free out my heed is a' torn, and a' through her an' Lipton and his hams.

> *"I get nae paece by nicht or day,*
> *My life's no worth a peen*
> *The very laddies in the street*
> *On me hae get their een.*

Twas just last nicht a wee bit kid
Cried tae his chum, 'Ha, Tam,
Take stock o' the bloke that's killing his wife
For the want o' Lipton's Ham.'

"Losh I didna ken whaur I was, 'killing his wife for the want o' Lipton's Ham.' Says I, 'My bonnie laddie, if I had the sole o' my boot near your ham I'd pit ye'd hae tae sit sideways for a fortnicht.' However, I daunered on a hame, an' there she was, ready tae make spareribs o' me. Every chance she get, she has a dig at me aboot the ham. I was swallowin' my parritch in silence when she says, 'I'm tel't they're playing a gran' piece at the theatre.' Hech me, thinks I, she's rale pleasant the nicht. So I says, 'What's the name o' the play?' Says she, 'It's *Ham*let.' That was the first go off. I said, 'Susan, I think you've got *Ham* on the brain.' 'No,' says she, 'nor *Ham* on the stomach aither. But,' says she, 'I'll no be *ham*pered with you any longer. I'll leeve yer *ham*mock tae yersel. I'll no be *ham*bugged by ye. It's a bonnie thing everybody bit me can get a bit *soo* at Lipton's. I'll let you see you've got the wrong *soo* by the lug, or I'll *soo* you for a divorce or else commit *soo*icide, an' see hoo that'll *soot* you.' A' I could say was:

"*I think for peace an' quateness*
I'll gie' in this time,
My wife she's gaun tae skin an bane
For want o' Lipton's prime.
The best thing I can dae is
Tae hae a wee bit dram,
An then, tae make things square at home,
I'll buy a Lipton's Ham."